THE ROAD
TO RUSSIA

THE ROAD TO RUSSIA

ARCTIC CONVOYS 1942

by

BERNARD EDWARDS

LEO COOPER

First published in Great Britain in 2002 by
LEO COOPER
an imprint of Pen & Sword Books
47 Church Street,
Barnsley,
South Yorkshire,
S70 2AS

Copyright © 2002 by Bernard Edwards

ISBN 0 85052 898 4

Typeset in 11/13pt Sabon by
Phoenix Typesetting, Burley-in-Wharfedale, West Yorkshire

Printed in England by CPI UK

This book is dedicated to all those who fought and died
on the road to Russia.

'Death barred the way to Russia, but you crosst.'
John Masefield, *For All Seafarers*

Contents

Acknowledgements

The author wishes to thank the following for their help in the research for this book:

George C. Bean, Thomas R. Bowerman, Mike Buckingham, C. Bernard Covington, Richard Elvin, Leo Hogan, Albert Kelder, Charles A. Lloyd, Arthur MacLaren, Ian A. Millar, Frits Noorbergen, Peter L. Price, Mike Raymond, Barbara Reher, Neil Staples, Tony Thomas, Barry L. Zerby, and Flower Class Corvette Association, Merchant Navy Association, National Archives & Records Administration, National Headquarters American Merchant Marine Veterans, Public Record Office, Registry of Shipping & Seamen, US Armed Guard WW II Veterans.

Introduction

This is the story of a very gallant company of men, who in the dark days of 1942 brought their ships through to Russia by the Arctic route. They were drawn from a dozen diverse nations, but united by a common cause; to bring aid to a beleaguered ally. If by doing so they helped to change the fortunes of a war, then being dictated by the crushing superiority of the Axis Powers, they considered their work well done.

In a single voyage, the men who sailed the convoys to North Russia faced more dangers than many others faced in six years of war. Their age-old enemy, the weather, was relentless. It fluctuated from violent storms that threatened to swamp the grossly overloaded merchantmen and crush the thin-hulled escorts, to flat calms and dense fogs. Caught in fog, the ships, unable to stand still, were forced to steam blind, under constant threat of collision with each other and ever watchful for the silent approach of icebergs and growlers, some big enough to rip their bottoms open from stem to stern.

If the weather was overcome – or at least held at bay – there was still the other enemy to contend with. He, too, was relentless, attacking from the air with high-level bombers, dive-bombers and torpedo bombers, on the surface with fast, powerful warships, and from beneath the sea with the shadowing U-boat.

For much of the year, overlaying and aggravating all these dangers, was the awful, bone-chilling cold of the Arctic; a cold so intense that it immobilized the body and numbed the brain. Death followed within two minutes for any man entering the water, and those who found themselves adrift in open boats were promised a slow death by exposure or, at the very least, the pain and indignities of frostbite and immersion foot, which so often led to the horrors of amputation.

For those who won through to Russia against such fearful odds, there was no safe haven at the end. The German bombers followed them into port, and continued to rain down death and destruction as they struggled to discharge the guns and tanks they had so diligently carried across the sea. All too often, their efforts were brought to nothing as ship and cargo were blown asunder or consumed by fire. But perhaps the most bitter blow they had to take was the rejection by the people they had endured so much to help. The ordinary Russian citizen was too cowed by authority to openly fraternize, and Soviet officialdom regarded them as agents of the hated capitalist system, and put every possible obstacle in their way.

The sea road to Russia was long and fraught with many dangers and frustrations, but these men did not hesitate to tread it, not just once, but voyage after voyage. They were true heroes.

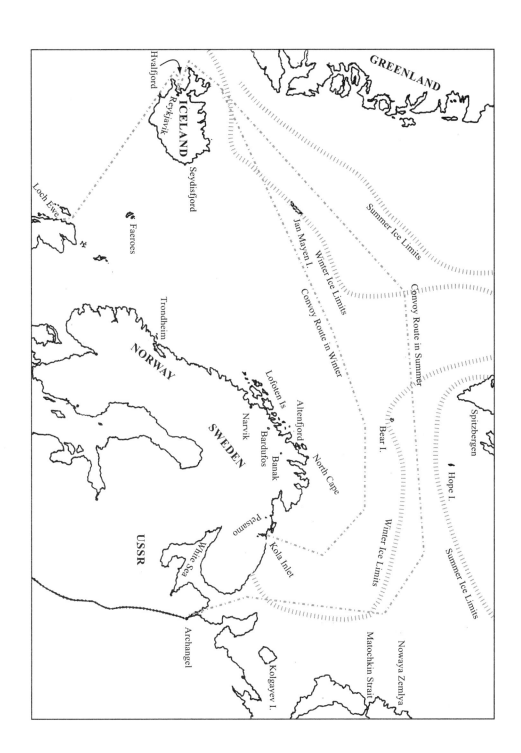

Chapter One

In 1942, when war raged unchecked over half the world, there was no supply line more bitterly contested than the 2000-mile-long sea road through Arctic waters to Russia. Sometimes likened to the road to hell itself, it was paved with good intentions, but littered with the wreckage of sunken ships and the frozen bodies of those who had fallen on the way. The British steamer *Harmatris*, commanded by Captain R.W. Brundle, was one of its first victims.

Owned by J.&C. Harrison of London, the 5395-ton *Harmatris* sailed from Glasgow on 27 November 1941, bound for Archangel, via Iceland, with a cargo of 8000 tons of military supplies. Her voyage became a test of endurance and courage for her crew from the outset. Within twenty-four hours of reaching Reykjavik, she ran into the most atrocious weather and, battered by storm-force winds and mountainous seas, was forced to heave to. This was neither a new experience, nor a serious threat to the *Harmatris*. She was a strong, Clyde-built ship, and had served her time in the North Atlantic, but she was sorely tested when, late on the night of 6 December, fire broke out in the cargo. Not unexpectedly, her cargo on this current voyage included a large quantity of small-arms ammunition – enough to blow the ship and all those who sailed in her to oblivion.

Run-of-the-mill merchant ships do not carry much in the way of firefighting equipment, nor do they, when at sea, enjoy the luxury of being able to call on the services of the local fire brigade. In a cargo ship, then, an outbreak of fire when away from the land can be a desperate business. But, led by forty-seven-year-old

1

Captain Brundle, the crew of the *Harmatris*, with one hand for the ship, and one hand for themselves as she pitched and heaved in the mountainous seas, fought a two-day battle with hoses, eventually subduing, and then extinguishing the blaze. When it was safe to do so, the hatches were opened up and it was found that, in addition to the damage caused by the fire, heavy military vehicles had broken adrift with the violent motion of the ship. They had then run amok, reducing the other cargo around them to a broken shambles. Quite clearly, the *Harmatris* was in no fit condition to continue her voyage to Russia. Brundle decided to return to Glasgow.

The old saying, 'It is an ill wind that blows nobody any good', is often challenged, but in this case the crew of the *Harmatris* were beneficiaries. The repairs to the ship and the replacement of her damaged cargo turned out to be a slow operation, with the result that Christmas 1941 was spent in Glasgow docks, an unexpected and very welcome surprise that went a long way towards compensating for the horrors of the failed attempt to reach Iceland.

The ship and her cargo made good, her crew refreshed, *Harmatris* sailed from the Clyde again on 26 December with Convoy PQ 8. The convoy consisted of only eight merchantmen, of which Captain Brundle, being the most experienced master, was appointed Commodore. His role, in addition to commanding his own ship, was to organize and lead the other ships and liaise with the Senior Officer Escort (SOE). Reykjavik was reached on New Year's Day 1942, and the convoy sailed again on 8 January, bound for Murmansk. Strong winds and rough seas were experienced for the first three days, then the ships ran into heavy field ice. It seemed that this was going to be another miserable passage for the *Harmatris*. Then, as it so often does in Arctic waters, the weather relented, giving way to light, variable winds, calm seas, and maximum visibility.

The fine weather continued, the enemy stayed away and, on 17 January, the convoy was approaching the Kola Inlet, which leads to the port of Murmansk. Captain Brundle might then have been forgiven for thinking this much maligned Russian run – admittedly as cold as charity – was really no worse than a bumpy run across the North Atlantic. The night was dark and moonless, but from the bridge of the *Harmatris* Brundle could see the reassuring bulk of the light cruiser *Trinidad* out on the starboard bow, while ahead of her, zig-zagging in broad sweeps, was the fleet minesweeper *Harrier*. On the port and starboard beams respectively, the big Tribal-class destroyers *Somali* and *Matebele* rode shotgun, and bringing up the rear of the convoy was another fleet minesweeper, HMS *Speedwell*.

The long days and nights haunting the bridge of the *Harmatris*, always on the alert for danger, were beginning to take their toll on Brundle. Now, reassured by the close proximity of the escorts, the quiet weather, and the prospect of journey's end only hours away, he decided it was safe for him to go below, even if only for a quick wash and a scrape with the razor. Leaving the ship in the capable hands of Chief Officer G.E. Masterman, he left the bridge.

As he made his way down the ladder to his accommodation below the bridge, Brundle was blissfully unaware that danger was now closer than it had ever been on the voyage so far. Hidden in the darkness to starboard, and somehow undetected by the pinging Asdics of the escorts, a German U-boat was lurking at periscope depth. *U-454*, commanded by *Kapitänleutnant* Burkhard Hackländer, had been at sea for some weeks, and had succeeded in torpedoing only one Russian anti-submarine trawler which, much to Hackländer's disgust, had stubbornly refused to sink. Now, with the appearance of PQ 8, the U-boat, which had been loitering in the approaches to the Kola Inlet for twelve hours, had a chance to redeem her fortunes.

Captain Brundle was in the act of stepping into his day room when there was a deafening explosion and the *Harmatris* lurched heavily, throwing him against the door jamb. Hackländer's torpedo had struck the steamer forward in her No.1 hold, blasting a great hole in her starboard side below the waterline. From her bridge, Chief Officer Masterman witnessed a huge column of water, containing within it smashed hatchboards, shredded tarpaulins and fragments of cargo, shooting high in the air. The ship immediately began going over to starboard.

The debris from the explosion was still showering down on the bridge when a breathless Brundle, unwashed and unshaven, reached the wheelhouse. He found that Masterman had already rung the engines to stop and the ship, as she lost way through the water, was settling by the head. Fearing the worst, Brundle ordered the boats cleared away and passed word for the crew to stand by to abandon ship. He then sent the carpenter forward to sound the bilges.

When the carpenter returned, he reported flooding in both Nos. 1 and 2 holds, and the water rising. The situation was serious but, on reflection, Brundle did not relish the thought of being adrift in open lifeboats in these icy waters and was reluctant to give the order to abandon ship. The issue was decided for him a few minutes later, when a second torpedo slammed into the *Harmatris*' port side. Fearful that more hesitation would lead to a catastrophe, Brundle signalled HMS *Speedwell*, and asked her to close his ship. When the minesweeper was in position, the crew of the crippled merchantman took to the boats and rowed across to her.

Once safe aboard the *Speedwell* with all his men, Brundle took a fresh look at the situation. Although she was so far down by the head that her propeller was out of the water, the *Harmatris* was still very much afloat, the land was nearby, and much of her 8000 tons of vital war cargo was still intact. He concluded that something must be done to try to save her. Brundle consulted with the commander of *Speedwell*, Lieutenant Commander T.E. Williams who, after some persuasion, agreed to attempt a tow. Volunteers were called for to reboard the ship, and every man of *Harmatris*' crew stepped forward. Within the hour, they were back in their ship and towing wires were being passed to *Speedwell*.

At first, there had been some confusion among the escorts as to what had happened to the *Harmatris*. Given the depth of water, and the close proximity of the land, the SOE, Captain D.K. Bain in HMS *Somali*, was at first of the opinion that the merchantman had hit a mine. Then, when it became clear that *Harmatris* had been torpedoed, Bain took *Somali*, with *Matebele* and *Harrier* in company, on an anti-submarine sweep to the north. No Asdic contacts were made, and in view of the possibility that there might be an unmarked minefield in the vicinity, Bain discontinued the search. *Somali* and *Harrier* then rejoined the convoy, while *Matebele* was ordered to stand by *Speedwell*, now with *Harmatris* in tow.

4

With order restored, the convoy reformed, with *Speedwell* and *Harmatris* bringing up the rear, and the other escorts strategically placed. The flashing light of Cape Teriberski, on the eastern shore of the Kola Inlet, was now visible at about ten miles on the port beam – a welcome sight. Unfortunately, the Russians had not dimmed the light, and each time its powerful beam swept across the surface of the sea the slow-moving ships of the convoy were shown up in sharp relief. They were sitting targets for any U-boats in the vicinity – and there was at least one. Burkhard Hackländer was still with them, having brought *U-454* to the surface and overtaken the convoy under the cover of the darkness. The friendly Russian lighthouse was giving him an advantage he had never dared to hope for. By now, Captain Bain had tightened up the convoy by bringing the merchant ships into two lines and calling the escorts in closer; a wise move, but too late.

A little after 23.00, Ordinary Seaman Ernest Higgins left the warm cocoon of HMS *Matebele*'s mess decks and resumed his post as communications number on the destroyer's 'X' gun, the after 4.7-inch. Replete and warmed inside by a hot supper, protected from the bitter chill of the night by several layers of woollen jumpers, duffel coat and balaclava, Higgins donned his headphones and settled down to wait out a watch which he was sure would be without further incident. *Matebele* was then 2000 yards to starboard of the convoy and zig-zagging, her Asdic probing underwater, all guns manned and loaded. Following in her wake was a new addition to the escort, the fleet minesweeper *Sharpshooter*, which had just joined from Murmansk. They were well into the Kola Inlet and with the visibility falling as fog patches began to form, the likelihood of any further attack seemed remote. Then, without warning, *Matebele*'s 24-inch searchlight clicked on and began to sweep to starboard. Higgins snapped alert.

The questing beam of *Matebele*'s searchlight swept around the horizon from bow to stern, swung back again, hesitating when it reached the beam, then locking on to an indistinct target. To Higgins, the target appeared to be, 'two whalers or cutters lashed together, and containing at least one man'. Then, as suddenly as it had come on, the light was doused and the inky blackness descended again. *Matebele* made no report on the sighting and it

5

has never been established what was actually seen. A possible explanation is that the 'target' was two of *Harmatris*' lifeboats, cast adrift when her crew boarded HMS *Speedwell*, but it might just as easily have been the conning tower of a submarine. However, whatever was seen, there can be little doubt that the unwise use of a searchlight betrayed *Matebele*'s presence to *U-454*, then cruising on the surface to starboard of the destroyer. Having been shown his prey, Hackländer went to periscope depth.

The diversion – and that is what it was then seen as – broke the monotony of the watch for 'X' gun's crew, but they soon settled down again to the serious business of keeping warm and staying awake. Ten minutes passed, ten minutes in which Burkhard Hackländer painstakingly manoeuvred *U-454* into position to attack. At 23.27 precisely, he fired a fan of three torpedoes.

Two of Hackländer's torpedoes missed the zig-zagging destroyer, but the third struck her squarely amidships, between her two funnels. There was a violent explosion that lifted the *Matebele* bodily out of the water, she then leaned momentarily to starboard and returned to the upright again. Fire broke out and spread at an alarming rate.

Under the direction of *Matebele*'s first lieutenant, Lieutenant Brittan, Ernest Higgins and his fellow gunners set about closing all magazine accesses on the after deck. As they were thus engaged, they heard plaintive cries for help coming from the water and saw men drifting past close alongside. They were men from the forward guns' crews who had jumped over the side when the ship was hit. Higgins and the others attempted to slip the Carley floats stowed alongside 'X' gun, but they were frozen in their chutes, and no amount of hammering would free them. The men in the water drifted away into the night and soon their cries were silenced.

Britten then ordered Higgins to take two men forward to close the magazine hatches on the foredeck, thinking it most likely that these would have been left open by the men who abandoned their ship in such a hurry. The order came too late, for as Higgins and his companions ran forward, there was a massive explosion and they were thrown back by the blast and a wall of flame. *Matebele*'s main magazine had gone up.

The destroyer was torn apart, ripped in two by her own ammunition, and she began to go down, her bow and stern, now detached from each other, rising high in the air. The prospect of jumping into dark, icy waters of the Kola Inlet filled Higgins with dread, but there was no other way of saving his life. Tightening the tapes of his lifejacket, he hurled himself over the side, closely followed by the two other men. In the water, they were joined by two more ratings, and the five men, oblivious to the grip of the freezing water, struck out, desperate to get away from the sinking ship before she dragged them down with her.

As they swam, the heavy clothing that had protected them from the cold night air at their gun stations was quickly saturated and their movements became slower and slower. It was clear to Ernest Higgins that none of them had long to live unless they were picked up within minutes – and the prospect of rescue on this black night, with visibility falling, seemed very remote. He was about to give up, to surrender to the cruel sea that was gradually numbing his body, when he saw a piece of wreckage floating nearby. This turned out to be only a coiled-up boarding net, but it offered sanctuary. Calling to the man nearest to him in the water, Ordinary Seaman William Burras, another of 'X' gun's crew, he swam towards the net. Burras followed and together they got hold of the net and pushed it back towards the others. Their efforts were wasted, for the three men had disappeared.

After a considerable struggle, as both the net and they were covered in thick fuel oil, Higgins and Burras managed to clamber astride the net. From this vantage point, they could see *Matebele*'s bow section was still afloat and standing vertically out of the water. All around them they could hear the agonized cries of drowning men, but could do nothing to help them. The slippery oil made it difficult to keep their hold on the net, but the same oil may well have been their saviour, giving them some protection from the bone-chilling cold. They were barely conscious when HMS *Harrier* snatched them from the sea.

When *Matebele*'s distress rockets soared into the night sky, *Somali*, then on the other side of the convoy, increased to twenty knots and raced ahead, coming round under full helm when she cleared the leading ship, the tanker *British Pride*. As *Somali* crossed the tanker's bows, the *Matebele*'s main magazine blew, sending a sheet of flame 500 feet in the air. With that, Captain Bain knew his race to go to the other ship's aid was likely to be in vain. Accordingly, he ordered *Harrier* to stand by *Matebele*, and took *Somali* on a high-speed sweep out as far as ten miles to starboard of the convoy, firing star shell as he went. Nothing was seen on the surface, but several Asdic contacts were made, and Bain attacked with depth charges. None of these attacks showed any positive results. Hackländer, well satisfied with his night's work, had taken *U-454* deep, and was heading out to sea as fast as his motors would take him.

Matebele, broken in two, had already disappeared beneath the waves by the time *Harrier* arrived on the scene. Of the destroyer's total complement of 219, the minesweeper found only two men alive, Ernest Higgins and William Burras. One body, believed to be that of Lieutenant Commander (E) J.T. Winn, was found later. All the others either went down with the ship, were drowned, or died of hypothermia in the freezing water. For the Allied convoys to North Russia, the honeymoon was over.

The Germans had not yet finished with the *Harmatris*. Next day, the Luftwaffe found her, limping along in the wake of the convoy at the end of *Speedwell*'s towline. The lone plane roared in at mast-top height around noon, her machine guns and cannon blazing. The guns were already manned on both ships and the reception afforded the attacker was fierce. Brundle attempted to fire *Harmatris*' PAC rockets but they were frozen in their chutes. However, the combined gunfire of the two ships was sufficient to send the aircraft on its way, pouring black smoke and losing height. It was later reported that it had crashed on shore. Another German plane approached an hour later, but sheered off when the ships opened fire, and jettisoned its bombs at least a mile away from the *Harmatris*. It then flew over high up and fired a few ineffectual bursts with its guns before making off.

At 14.30, when well into the Kola Inlet, *Speedwell* signalled that she had suffered a boiler blow-back and three men were badly scalded. A Russian tug was sent for and when she arrived the minesweeper cast off her tow and hurried into Murmansk to land her injured. The *Harmatris* reached port at 08.00 on 20 January. Captain Brundle lost no time in assessing the damage to his ship:

... I found that the iron locking bars of No.1 hatch had been blown away and the wood hatches and tarpaulins missing. The beams were strewn about the decks and parts of the cargo had become entwined with the stays and shrouds of the rigging, making the foremast look like a Xmas tree. Everywhere ice and snow covered the ship to a depth of 1 foot. No.1 hold was 3 parts full of water and we could see that the bulkhead forward had been badly fractured as was also the fore peak tank and the fore and aft bulkhead.

The Russian repair facilities being what they were, eight months would elapse before the *Harmatris* was seaworthy enough to attempt the voyage home. She sailed with Convoy QP 14 and arrived in Loch Ewe on 26 September. The delivery of one cargo to Russia had taken her ten months.

Chapter Two

It had all begun on 23 August 1939 when, with Hitler preparing to wage war on Britain and France, Germany and Soviet Russia signed a pact of non-aggression. This, in reality, was no more than an empty paper promise, for both sides knew that when the time was right they would have to fight each other. Nevertheless, this fragile pact lasted for almost two years, coming to an end on 22 June 1941 with Germany invading the USSR in force. The attack was on three fronts; Army Group North with six armoured and twenty-three infantry divisions, lunging towards Leningrad, Army Group Centre with fifteen armoured and thirty-five infantry divisions driving on Moscow and Army Group South with eight armoured and thirty-three infantry divisions advancing towards the Ukraine. Hitler planned to bring the Russians to their knees in five weeks.

Until Germany attacked them, the Russians were openly hostile to capitalist Britain, but their attitude changed abruptly when they found themselves under threat. Winston Churchill, with his usual blunt clarity, summed up the situation:

Up to the moment the Soviet Government was set upon by Hitler they seemed to care for no one but themselves. Afterwards, this mood naturally became more marked. Hitherto they had watched with stony composure the destruction of the front in France in 1940, and our vain efforts in 1941 to create a front in the Balkans. They had given important economic aid to Nazi Germany and had helped them in many minor ways. Now, having been deceived and taken by surprise, they were themselves under the flaming German sword. Their first and lasting policy was to demand all possible succour from Great Britain and her Empire, the possible partition of which between Stalin and Hitler had for the last eight months beguiled Soviet minds from the progress of German concentration in the East. They did not hesitate to appeal in urgent and strident terms to harassed and struggling Britain to send them the largest quantities of supplies on which we were counting, and, above all, even in the summer of 1941 they clamoured for British landings in Europe, regardless of risk and cost, to establish a second front.

Despite Soviet Russia's previous cosy relationship with Germany, she was now in the war and, however reluctantly, on the same side as Britain and America, who welcomed their new ally with open arms. Churchill and Roosevelt realized that with the help of this huge and powerful nation, reputed to be able to put twelve million men into the field, Hitler's ambitions might be thwarted and his eventual defeat brought about. At a conference of the three Allied powers, held in Moscow at the end of September 1941, Britain and America pledged to meet Stalin's demands for food and war materials. This was a commitment easily given by the politicians. As to delivering the goods, this was another matter altogether. America was not yet in the war and could not openly use her ships, while Britain's merchant fleet, big though it might be, was fully stretched keeping open the sea lanes across the Atlantic and to the colonies.

The only feasible way to supply Russia with the vast amounts of supplies she required was by sea through her northern ports of Murmansk and Archangel, both well inside the Arctic Circle. The word 'port' is used advisedly, for in 1941 Murmansk and Archangel were little more than glorified fishing harbours. They had deep water, but very few berths for merchant ships of any size. Cargo handling facilities were antiquated, there being no dockside cranes, no heavy-lift facilities for discharging tanks and vehicles and railway connections to the ports were poor. Murmansk was open all year round, but the Gulf of Archangel was closed by ice from the end of November to the end of May. So it was to Murmansk that most of the ships must go, even though it was only thirty miles from the front and less than half an hour's flying time from German airfields in Norway. It was accepted in London and Washington that losses in the convoys to Russia were likely to be heavy, but thought worthwhile if they helped to prevent the collapse of the Soviets. There was also a fear that if refused aid, Stalin might make a separate peace with Germany, and it was probably this fear that silenced the critics of the convoys, not least among them General Alan Brooke, Chief of the Imperial General Staff. Brooke, not unexpectedly, was of the opinion that any arms available should go to the British forces, who needed all they could get.

No one, least of all the men who were to sail in the ships, envisaged that the Russian run would be easy. Equally, no one imagined what a frightful ordeal it would become. The difficulties to be overcome were immense, the weather being not the least. The master of one British merchant ship described conditions with typical understatement:

> From February onwards it is lighting up quickly. At the end of January there are four hours daylight, end of February eight hours, end of April twenty hours, and July and August virtually twenty-four hours daylight, with sun all the time, which works along the horizon. From April to August there is really no bad weather; conditions are ideal for enemy day attack. Winter starts in September, and from October to the end of December there's a lot of fog and heavy snowstorms but not much wind. From the end of December you may get gales of hurricane strength which can last for five days, but between the gales the weather may be flat. In the winds, a big short sea is built up – seldom more than 15 feet, even in bad weather, for the seas are comparatively shallow – but in those big short seas the ship rolls like hell.

The commentator omitted to make mention of the intense cold in winter, when with temperatures dropping to minus 50°F, ships' thermometers froze solid, tons of snow and ice built up on the decks, and survival time if you went into the water was just two minutes.

The original plan was for Russian merchant ships to carry the cargoes for their own war effort, while the Royal Navy provided the escorts, but it was very soon realized that the Soviet Union, huge though it might be, had neither the ships nor the organization to handle the supplies on the scale envisaged. It would be up to the British merchant fleet initially – which was already losing up to sixty ships a month in the Atlantic – and then American ships to bear the brunt of this mammoth task.

The first convoy to Russia was code named Operation 'Dervish'. It consisted of six merchant ships, five British and one Dutch, and sailed from Liverpool on 12 August 1941, bound for Murmansk via Scapa Flow. The escort for 'Dervish' varied according to the position of the convoy, but for the most part was provided by a light cruiser, two destroyers and anti-aircraft ships, three fleet minesweepers and five anti-submarine trawlers. Distant cover was given by an aircraft carrier, two heavy cruisers and three destroyers. The weather was fine throughout and, not surprisingly in view of the strength of the escort force, the enemy made no attempt to interfere with the convoy. The ships arrived in Archangel on 31 August, delivering sixty-four fighter aircraft, thirty-two vehicles and 15,000 tons of military stores.

Thereafter, outward convoys were designated 'PQ', while those homeward, mainly ships in ballast, were prefixed 'QP'. The initials used were a tribute to Commander P.Q. Edwards, RN, who was in charge of planning the convoys. Convoy PQ 1, consisted of eleven ships, eight British, two Panamanian and one Belgian and, again heavily escorted, left Iceland on 29 September. The convoy passed through unmolested and reached Archangel on 11 October.

After the safe passage of these first convoys, it would have been easy to underestimate the dangers of attack by the enemy – and they were very real. Sheltering in the deep fjords of northern Norway were the pride of the German Navy's heavy fleet, the 42,900-ton battleship *Tirpitz*, the battlecruisers *Scharnhorst* and *Gneisenau*, the pocket-battleship *Lützow* and the heavy cruisers *Admiral Hipper* and *Prinz Eugen*. Ashore, on airfields near the North Cape, were based between 200 and 300 of *Reichsmarschall* Hermann Goering's bombers, torpedo bombers, fighters and reconnaissance aircraft. Admiral Dönitz's U-boats were mostly preoccupied with the North Atlantic, but the Ulan Group, consisting of the three boats *U-134*, *U-454* and *U-585* was based at Trondheim to cover the Barents Sea. In the early stage of the voyage, as far as Jan Mayen Island, the convoys were given some protection by long-range Catalinas flying from Iceland and the Shetlands. After that, they were on their own and dangerously exposed to attack from the air.

Seeking to put the maximum distance between them and the enemy's bases, the convoys were routed as far north as possible, right up to the Arctic ice edge, which in summer could mean reaching 75 degrees North, and within 800 miles of the North Pole. But even in this high latitude, the German airfields were only 350 miles away, less than two hours flying time for the aircraft of the Luftwaffe's *Fluggruppe* K30.

And yet the extraordinary luck of the PQ convoys continued throughout the autumn and into the winter of 1941. PQ 2 sailed with six ships on 17 October, PQ 3, with eight ships on 9 November, PQ 4, with eight ships again on 17 November and PQ 5, with seven ships on 27 November. All reached their destinations without the slightest attempt being made by the enemy to interfere with them. It was a similar story for the QP convoys, the ships returning home in ballast. This was a strange, almost unnatural experience for men accustomed to the bitter fighting of the North Atlantic convoys. Were the Germans, with all the massive firepower at their disposal on the sea and in the air, asleep? Were they afraid to come out? Or were they just biding their time?

The first indication that the enemy intended to take action against the steady flow of war materials to the USSR came early in December. PQ 6, five British, two Panamanian and one Russian merchantmen, escorted by the light cruiser *Edinburgh* and the destroyers *Echo* and *Escapade*, sailed from Iceland on 8 December, bound for Murmansk. The convoy itself was not attacked, but the fleet minesweepers *Hazard* and *Speedy*, which sailed from Murmansk to meet PQ 6, ran into four German destroyers of the Narvik Flotilla. These were new ships, large and fast, each mounting four 5-inch guns, and should have had no difficulty in dispatching the 815-ton Halcyon-class sweepers armed with two 4-inch guns. For some unknown reason – perhaps the visibility was poor – the Germans mistook *Hazard* and *Speedy* for two much larger Russian destroyers and decided not to engage. Given that the destroyers were in a majority of two to one, this was a measure of the German surface ships reluctance to stand and fight, which was to be evident throughout the campaign in Arctic waters. A few shells were thrown, four of which damaged *Speedy*, but the destroyers made a swift withdrawal when the minesweepers hit back.

PQ 6 arrived in Murmansk without loss and immediately came face to face with Soviet bureaucracy and inefficiency. Five of the merchantman languished for the whole of the winter in Murmansk discharging cargo. One of them, the Panama-flag tanker *El Oceano*, was commandeered by the Russians for their own use, but managed to escape by making a courageous dash for Iceland alone and unescorted. She reached Hvalfjord on 18 February 1942. The experience of PQ 6 did not augur well for future convoys to north Russia.

It was not until the New Year had been ushered in that the first blood was spilt on the road to Russia. Convoy PQ 7A, consisting of only two ships, the British steamer *Waziristan* and the Panama-flag *Cold Harbor*, escorted by the minesweepers *Britomart* and *Salamander*, sailed from Hvalfjord, Iceland on 27 December 1941. The 5135-ton *Waziristan*, owned by Common Brothers of Newcastle, had loaded in New York and was the first of many British ships to carry military supplies direct from America to Soviet Russia. A fierce easterly gale and thick ice resulted in the four ships becoming separated on New Year's Day, 1 January 1942, when 300 miles north-west of Jan Mayen Island. Early on the following morning, the *Waziristan*, steaming alone, was sighted by *U-134*, commanded by *Kapitänleutnant* Rudolf Schendel. One torpedo was sufficient to send the heavily-loaded British ship to the bottom. She took with her all her crew of forty-seven, the first British casualties on the road to Russia.

The *Waziristan* was a victim of circumstances rather than determined action by the enemy. If her sailing had been delayed for a few days until the other ships assigned to Convoy PQ 7 were ready, she probably would have survived. When the others, five British, two Panamanian, one Dutch and one Russian ships, had assembled in Hvalfjord, they were formed into PQ 7B, and sailed on 31 December. Although escorted by only two destroyers – the cruiser *Cumberland* failed to rendezvous with the convoy – PQ 7B had a clear passage to Murmansk, arriving on 11 January.

*

The attack on Pearl Harbour by Japanese carrier-borne aircraft on Sunday, 7 December 1941 and the subsequent destruction of the US Pacific Fleet, came as a rude shock to America. It also served to convince the isolationists and doubters in that country that the war was no longer just another European spat. And when, four days later, Germany declared war on the United States, the circle was complete. Now, at last, Roosevelt was free to send aid to the USSR in his own ships, rather than in foreign bottoms, as had been done up until then.

On that momentous day, 11 December 1941, seventeen-year-old Peter Louis Price left the Armed Guard School at Little Creek, Virginia a fully trained ship's gunner. After kicking his heels for several weeks at the Armed Guard Center in New York, on 10 January 1942, Seaman 2nd Class Price joined the US merchant ship *Dunboyne* as a member of the naval team manning her guns. The *Dunboyne* was a far cry from the sleek, grey-painted warship young Peter Price had naively imagined he would go to war in. Grey-painted she was, sleek no, and she was certainly no man-of-war. The 3515-ton *Dunboyne*, owned by the United States Maritime Commission, was a small, ugly, blunt-bowed tramp and, having been built in 1919, had seen better days.

Another month passed before the *Dunboyne* was ready for sea. Having by then loaded at several ports in the US, she had on board a cargo designed to test her seaworthiness to its utmost limits. Her holds were filled with aluminium bars topped off with coils of barbed wire, while her decks and hatch-tops were covered by 30-ton Sherman tanks, chained down, but looking vulnerable. All this the little *Dunboyne* was expected to carry on a 6000-mile voyage to north Russia at the height of winter. This was a daunting prospect for a seventeen-year-old who had never before in his life been to sea, but in his blissful ignorance, Peter Price was not in the least bit daunted.

The Atlantic crossing, in convoy from Halifax, Nova Scotia to Loch Ewe, on the west coast of Scotland, turned out to be a cruel initiation into seafaring for Price. The *Dunboyne*, visibly sagging under the weight of her cargo and dangerously top heavy, rolled her scuppers under in the long North Atlantic swell, in fog one day, battered by howling gales the next. It was thirteen days of purgatory under a dark, leaden sky, with the thermometer falling to keep pace with every mile progressed to the east and north. The ordeal came to an end when, at long last, the convoy reached the shelter of Loch Ewe, assembly point for the Russian convoys.

Loch Ewe, the 'Echo Lake' of the Gaels, lies 600 miles north of London on Scotland's rocky Atlantic coast and is as remote a stretch of water as can be found in the British Isles. It is also the only large deep-water loch on the western side of Scotland whose mouth faces north, and therefore provides shelter from the Atlantic winds. The loch is ten miles long by four miles wide, and its waters are uncluttered by rocks and shoals, giving safe anchorage for up to forty deep-sea ships at any one time. When Scapa Flow, in the Orkney Islands, became untenable due to the proximity of large German naval units, Loch Ewe was the obvious gathering place for ships loaded in British and American ports before setting off for Russia. The surrounding mountains, often hidden by low cloud, gave cover from air attack, and any enemy planes that did get through were sure of a hot reception from anti-aircraft guns strategically placed around the loch. Coastal defence batteries were sited on the cliffs, and the entrance was blocked by a boom to keep out any U-boats with evil intent. Loch Ewe also boasted, in the words of the guide books, '. . . some of the finest mountain and coastal scenery in Britain, in a region with vast stretches of roadless countryside where deer and goats roam wild and where a wide variety of birdlife, including the rare and magnificent golden eagle can be spotted . . .'. Loch Ewe was – and still is – remote, and certainly had very little to offer the seaman about to embark on a long and hazardous voyage. The only habitation on its shores, the village of Aultbea, on the east side of the loch, had only one popular attraction, the local pub, which played host to legions of thirsty seafarers, so many that the landlord eventually ran out of glasses and served beer in jam jars. To this day, the Aultbea Inn is known by the locals as the 'Jam Jar' Inn.

The *Dunboyne* was assigned to Convoy PQ 13 and lay at anchor in the shadow of the Scottish Highlands for ten days while the other ships came in, some from across the Atlantic like herself, the rest from British ports. Where required, ships topped up with bunkers, fresh water and provisions, and by 10 March

PQ 13 was at last ready to sail. The completed convoy was made up of eighteen ships, the British contingent being the *River Afton, Empire Cowper, Empire Starlight, Empire Ranger, Induna, Harpalion* and *New Westminster City*. Representing the USA were the *Dunboyne, Effingham, Eldena* and *Mormacmar*, while sailing under the flag of Panama but operated by the United States Maritime Commission, were the *Gallant Fox, Raceland, El Estero* and *Ballot*. The Honduras-flag *Mana* was also under the control of the USMC. These 'foreign-flag' ships were really American-owned and manned ships sailing under a flag of convenience, a method that had been used extensively to get supplies through to Britain before the USA came into the war. Two others made up the total complement of PQ 13, the Polish-flag *Tobruk* and the *Lars Kruse*, a Swede in exile. PQ 13's escort for the run north to Iceland was not over impressive, consisting of the Hunt-class destroyer HMS *Lamerton* and the two 1914–18 vintage destroyers *Sabre* and *Saladin*. The *Lamerton* was capable enough, but the other two, being only just over 900 tons and mounting only two 4-inch guns each, did not inspire confidence.

As might be expected at the time of the year, PQ 13 ran into the teeth of a fierce north-westerly gale as soon as it cleared the land, prompting mutterings amongst the crews of the ships – superstitious seamen all of them – about the advisability of choosing the unlucky number thirteen for the convoy. The gale was unrelenting in its ferocity throughout the whole of the miserable 700-mile passage north, and it was 17 March before the eighteen battered ships and their escorts reached the shelter of Hvalfjord, on Iceland's west coast. For many of the men, particularly in the American ships, it had been a brutal introduction to life at sea in the high latitudes.

Although Loch Ewe may have seemed to the men of PQ 13 a grim and forbidding place devoid of any attractions, when they saw Hvalfjord, they must have longed to return to that Scottish Shangri-la. Iceland, whose northern coasts touch the Arctic Circle, is said to have been first settled by the Vikings in the year 874, and has been aptly described as 'a desert of the ocean'. It is a land of icy mountains, lashed by the violent winds of the North Atlantic, where glaciers and active volcanoes live cheek by jowl, and the only vegetation is patches of scrub and the odd conifer

18

plantation. Its west coast is slashed by fjords, of which Hvalfjord offers the best – and the best is not much in these latitudes – shelter for deep-sea ships. In 1942, Hvalfjord was the last call for the convoys to north Russia, where the ships refuelled, reprovisioned and generally made ready for the demanding task ahead of them. It was not a safe anchorage where the weather was concerned, for in the long winter fierce blizzards raged through its iron-grey waters often creating havoc amongst the many ships crowded together at anchor. The holding ground was poor and ships were liable to drag, necessitating full watches being kept on bridges and in engine rooms at all times. As for the attractions on shore, there was only a single large Nissen hut where beer, when available, was sold and drunk in Spartan surroundings. Beyond this drab establishment, in the nearby capital of Reykjavik, there was no welcome for the foreign seafarer.

When Denmark was overrun in May 1940, there were real fears that German forces might seize Iceland, which lay close to the route taken by British convoys from the Americas to the North Channel. With bases in Iceland for their U-boats and aircraft, they would have been able to create havoc among the convoys, leading to a blockade and eventual starvation for Britain, which in turn would lead to surrender. This grim possibility was forestalled by the landing of British troops on Iceland within a few days of Denmark falling. The first priority was to establish facilities for the refuelling of the Royal Navy's ships, and then bases were set up for Sunderland and Catalina flying boats of RAF Coastal Command, both of which would bring about a considerable improvement in the defence of the North Atlantic convoys. On 7 July 1941, two weeks after Hitler launched his attack on Russia, the British garrison on Iceland was relieved by American forces. Although the Allied military presence brought security and prosperity to the island, which for centuries past had extracted an impoverished living from fishing and reindeer, the Icelanders bitterly resented this intrusion into their homeland – not least, it was said, through fear of German retaliation. Not surprisingly, the open-hearted Americans, who filled the shops of Reykjavik with hitherto unseen luxuries, suffered the worst abuse, but a great deal of hostility was also directed at visiting merchant

19

seamen. Those who were lucky enough to get ashore were met with undisguised resentment. They were spat at, jeered at and, should they be foolish enough to be ashore after dark, sometimes physically assaulted. It was not the welcome men, who were about to risk life and limb on the most dangerous convoy run of all, either expected or deserved.

While the ships of PQ 13 swung to their anchors in the troubled waters of Hvalfjord, news trickled in that the war beyond the Arctic Circle was turning even uglier. In winter, when the sun fails to appear above the horizon, the convoys, although having to face blizzards and pack ice, had enjoyed the protection of twenty-four hours complete or near darkness, but with the arrival of spring imminent that was changing. When PQ 12, the largest convoy yet to sail for Russia, left Hvalfjord on 1 March, it was sailing with ten hours of daylight in twenty-four, which left it dangerously exposed to the marauding U-boats and the German bombers operating out of airfields in northern Norway. At the same time, it was at the mercy of the equinoctial gales then sweeping in from the North Atlantic.

PQ 12 consisted of sixteen British, Russian and Panamanian merchant ships and two 250-ton wooden-hulled ex-Norwegian whalers, the first of a series of these ships being delivered to the Russian Navy for use as minesweepers. Close escort for the convoy was provided by a light cruiser and two destroyers. Coincident with the sailing of PQ 12, the westbound convoy QP 8, made up of fifteen ships returning in ballast or with part cargoes, left Murmansk. Heavy units of the Home Fleet were to give distant cover for both convoys in case of attack by German surface ships.

When off Jan Mayen Island on 6 March, PQ 12 was sighted by a German long-range reconnaissance aircraft, a sighting that prompted Grand Admiral Raeder to order the *Tirpitz* out of Trondheim. The 42,900-ton *Tirpitz*, with a top speed of thirty-one knots and mounting eight 15-inch, twelve 5.9-inch and sixteen 4.1-inch guns, was accompanied by three large Narvik-class destroyers. As luck would have it – and fortunately for PQ 12 – a British submarine patrolling off Trondheim saw the German ships leave and radioed a warning to the Admiralty. This brought PQ 12's distant covering force, namely the battleship

King George V, the aircraft carrier *Victorious*, the heavy cruiser, *Berwick*, and six destroyers, hurrying to the rescue.

Torpedo bombers from HMS *Victorious* located and attacked the *Tirpitz*, but were driven off by the German battleship's formidable anti-aircraft batteries. By the time *King George V* and her consorts reached the scene, the *Tirpitz* had escaped to the south. The only casualty of the action was the Russian merchantman *Ijora*, which had straggled from QP 8 and was sunk by the German destroyer *Friedrich Ihn*. The rest of the convoy arrived in Murmansk on 12 March, having lost two more ships along the way to the weather. The Russia-bound whaler *Shera* had capsized and sunk following a build-up of ice on her decks and the 4687-ton Panama-flag steamer *Bateau* turned back for Iceland after suffering heavy weather damage. The whole episode had been a fright and a lesson for both sides.

Fortunately, perhaps, for the men of PQ 13, they were not held long enough in Hvalfjord to be given the opportunity to socialize with the Icelanders. Shore-going was limited to ships' masters, chief engineers and radio officers, who were required to attend a convoy conference for briefing on routes and signals before sailing. At 06.00 on 20 March, just as a grey Arctic dawn was struggling to make itself known, steam windlasses hissed into life and Hvalfjord echoed to the clank of anchor cables being hove in. An hour later, the first ships of the convoy nosed their way out of the fjord, led by the Ayrshire Navigation Company's *River Afton*, commanded by Captain H.W. Charlton. The 5479-ton *River Afton* was designated commodore ship and carried the convoy commodore, Captain D.A. Casey, RNR and his staff of signallers. Captain Casey's role was to hold the merchant ships together and liaise with the Senior Officer Escort.

Once clear of Hvalfjord, PQ 13 was joined by the Royal Fleet Auxiliary tanker *Scottish American*, from which the escorts would refuel as necessary on the voyage. Later that day the *Bateau*, her weather damage repaired and ready to try for Murmansk again, joined the ranks. Initially, while on the west and north coasts of Iceland, waters considered to be comparatively safe from enemy attack, PQ 13 was escorted by HMS *Lamerton*, the anti-submarine trawlers *Blackfly* and *Paynter*, and another whaler on her way to Russia, HMS *Sulla*. On the

23rd, off Grimsey Island, the escort was reinforced by the light cruiser *Trinidad*, the destroyers *Fury* (Lieutenant Commander C.M. Campbell SOE) and *Eclipse*, and two more whalers, *Sumba* and *Silja*, all of which had been bunkering in Seydisfjord. For a convoy of twenty merchantmen sailing in dangerous waters this could hardly be considered as ample protection, but the Royal Navy, with commitments in so many other spheres, was over-stretched and this was all that could be spared. When the convoy approached the Russian coast, it was planned to reinforce the escort with five British minesweepers based in the Kola Inlet and the Russians had promised to send out a few destroyers, but did not seem very enthusiastic about this. For the first 150 miles east of Iceland only, air cover would be provided by 269 and 330 Squadrons of Coastal Command based in Iceland. After that, there would be only the occasional long-range aircraft patrolling out as far as the North Cape to watch over them. HMS *Trinidad*, a thirty-three knot, 8800-ton Colony-class cruiser mounting twelve 6-inch and eight 4-inch guns, although part of the close escort, was to act independently so as to be free to keep a watch on the convoy with her new radar, which had 360 degree coverage. There was one tiny cloud on *Trinidad*'s horizon, in that she had been forced to sail without sufficient anti-freeze for her guns and torpedoes. This was to have serious repercussions.

Some time before PQ 13 sailed from Hvalfjord, British Intelligence had informed the Admiralty that the *Tirpitz* had been joined in Trondheim by the *Admiral Scheer* and the *Admiral Hipper*. These ships, mounting respectively eight 15-inch, six 11-inch and eight 8-inch guns, along with their Narvik-class destroyer escorts, were within twenty-four hours fast steaming of the routes to be taken by PQ 13 and QP 9, the westbound convoy of empty ships which sailed from Murmansk on the 21st. This presented an awesome threat to the slow moving convoys, which were timed to cross halfway. To counter this threat, Rear Admiral A.T.B. Curteis was ordered to sea with a covering force made up of the new 35,000-ton battleships *Duke of York* and *King George V*, each armed with ten 14-inch guns, the battle cruiser *Renown*, Curteis' flagship, with six 15-inch guns, the aircraft carrier *Victorious*, the 8-inch County-class cruiser *Kent*, the light cruiser *Edinburgh* and the destroyers *Ashanti, Bedouin, Echo, Escapade,*

Eskimo, Faulknor, Foresight, Icarus, Inglefield, Ledbury, Marne, Middleton, Onslow, Punjabi, Tartar and *Whetland.* Submarines and long-range reconnaissance Catalinas from Reykjavik and Sullom Voe were to keep watch on the Norwegian fjords to provide early warning of the movements of the German ships. This was an unprecedented show of force by both sides, and was indicative of the importance they attached to the Allied sea lane to Russia. But of all the ships the Royal Navy was putting to sea in protection of PQ 13, the Germans feared most the *Victorious* and her torpedo bombers, which had so nearly put paid to the *Tirpitz* when she ventured out against PQ 12. The German Navy had no carriers, and following the PQ 12 incident, Admiral Raeder had demanded full air protection for his ships from the Luftwaffe. Goering, arrogant as ever, had refused Raeder's demand, and it was only after Hitler interfered and ordered the *Reichsmarschall* to cooperate that the Admiral was reassured. He then planned a combined surface, air and U-boat attack on PQ 13. With this in mind, Dönitz's Ulan Group was increased to seven boats. These were *U-435* (*Kapitänleutnant* Siegfried Stretlow), *U-436* (*Kapitänleutnant* Günter Seibecke), *U-456* (*Kapitänleutnant* Max-Martin Teichert), *U-585* (*Kapitänleutnant* Ernst-Bernward Lohse), *U-589* (*Kapitänleutnant* Hans-Joachim Horrër), *U-376* (*Kapitänleutnant* Friedrich-Karl Marks) and *U-209* (*Kapitänleutnant* Heinrich Broda). In the weeks and months to come, these Type VIIC boats were to make their mark on the convoys to Russia.

Chapter Three

Captain L.S. Saunders, in command of *Trinidad*, was fully aware of the ominous developments taking place over the horizon, as were the other escort commanders. Those in the merchant ships, although they sensed that all was not well, were largely ignorant of what awaited them. When clear of the Icelandic coast, they formed up into six columns abreast and set off to the north-east at nine knots, confident that the Royal Navy would look after them. *Trinidad* zig-zagged ahead, using her radar to scan the horizon, the trawlers and whalers formed a close escort for the merchantmen, while *Fury* and *Eclipse* hovered on the flanks like two restrained greyhounds. The weather was fine, with excellent visibility, and a fresh south-westerly breeze blew from right astern, urging them on. The temperature was falling steadily as they moved to the north, but there was a noticeable air of confidence about this multi-national assembly of ships, deep-laden, their decks covered with aircraft and tanks. They were going to deliver the goods to Russia, come what may.

The first alarm came just after noon that day in the form of a signal from the Admiralty warning of a line of U-boats believed to be forming up across PQ 13's path. The convoy, then 120 miles to the south-east of Jan Mayen Island, altered course to due east to avoid this first cast of the German net. At the same time, HMS *Lamerton* and the oiler *Scottish American* broke away for an ocean rendezvous to refuel some of the destroyers of Admiral Curteis' distant covering force.

At noon on the 24th, it being assumed that the U-boat ambush had been bypassed, course was resumed to the north-east, the convoy heading to pass south of Bear Island. At this point, PQ 13 was within 800 miles of the German airfields at Bardufoss and Banak in northern Norway, and some forty miles ahead of schedule. The weather continued to hold fine, but the barometer was falling, indicating dirty weather ahead.

When the sun went down that evening, the sky to the north was dark and threatening, and as the wind veered to the north and strengthened, the seas began to heap up. The night wore on, and the wind veered further to the north-east, bringing it right ahead, and continuing to strengthen. By midnight, it was blowing a full gale, force 9. It was straight off the polar ice cap, and had an edge to it like a whetted knife. The convoy was now in the comparatively shallow waters of the Barents Sea, and the waves were becoming steep and short. As they tumbled and broke, the wind snatched at their foaming tops, filling the air with a fine spray that froze as it hit the steel decks and superstructures of the ships. Visiblity was severely reduced, and station-keeping deteriorated into a game of blind man's buff. Soon, the lumbering merchantmen, burying their blunt bows deep as they met each advancing wave, were all but hove to. Those who were unfortunate enough to be manning the open bridges on this miserable night came to know the true meaning of 'wind chill factor', a weather man's phrase then not yet coined. They were well wrapped up against the cold with clothing issued by the Ministry of War Transport, described by one participant looking back over the years as: 'Starting from the inside, two pairs of heavy woollen ribbed long johns, then a flannel shirt and on top of this a rolled neck jersey. Then a sheepskin lined leather jerkin and on top of this all a canvas duffel coat with a hood and lined with a sort of blanket material. Heavy mitts covered the hands, and feet were protected by two pairs of woollen stockings reaching to the knee. The last thing on was a pair of seaboots which had to be two sizes too large to be able to be pulled on. You staggered about like astronauts landing on the moon.' Yet all this was as thin paper against the icy, penetrating fingers of the biting Arctic wind. It reached right into the marrow of a man's bones, dulling his senses, slowing his reactions. Conditions below decks for those attempting to rest between watches were little better. They were dry and reasonably warm, but the constant struggle to avoid being thrown about by the violent rolling and pitching of the ship left them sleepless and exhausted.

Those aboard the escort ships fared even worse. *Trinidad*, *Fury* and *Eclipse*, low on freeboard, narrow in the beam, and built for the high-speed chase, were notoriously bad sea ships, rolling their gunwales under and acquiring thick layers of ice on deck that, unless constantly chipped away, threatened them with capsize. *Trinidad* came very near to this at one point in the night, rolling over so far that it was feared she would never return to the upright again. The smaller trawlers and whalers were built with foul weather in mind and their crews were hardened in the cauldron of northern waters, but even they were finding the going hard.

Somehow, they battled on through the night maintaining a semblance of order in the convoy. But gone were the orderly ranks of ships steaming two cables apart in line astern with five cables between columns. In its place was an untidy rabble lurching along on approximately the same course and at the same pitiful speed.

By noon on the 25th, the gale had reached a shrieking crescendo, and the plunging merchantmen with their precious deck cargoes in danger of breaking adrift, were finally forced to heave to altogether, keeping the wind and sea on the bow and just sufficient engine revolutions to maintain steerage way. When darkness fell again, putting an end to any visibility there might have been, it was inevitable that the convoy began to lose its remaining cohesion, the ships drifting further and further apart, each one fighting its own lonely battle with the sea.

Only Captain Saunders in *Trinidad* was fully aware of the chaos caused by the weather. As was standard practice, the cruiser had pulled clear of the other ships at nightfall and her glowing radar screen showed clearly that as an entity the convoy had ceased to exist. Concerned at the increasing vulnerability of the merchantmen, Saunders broke radio silence to alert the Admiralty to the situation. He also radioed the other ships giving them a rendezvous to the south of Bear Island for the 27th, by which time Saunders hoped the gale would have blown itself out. For the time being however, it was every man for himself and if the enemy had been listening to *Trinidad*'s radio signals – as he surely must have been – then the dangers ahead were many and increasing by the hour.

Contrary to Saunders' expectations, when *Trinidad* arrived at the rendezvous position at dawn on the 27th, there was no let-up in the gale and, if anything, it was blowing stronger than ever. Not a single ship of PQ 13 was in sight. They were by now scattered over an area of hundreds of square miles of ocean, most of them hopelessly lost. Furthest afield was the one ship that should have been holding the others together. The Convoy Commodore's ship *River Afton*, like so many British merchant ships of her day, was woefully underpowered for her size and Captain Charlton had been unable to hold her bows up into the wind. She ended up wallowing beam-on to wind and sea and being blown relentlessly down on the rocky shores of the Lofoten Islands, on Norway's north-west coast. She was 300 miles away from the rendezvous to the south of Bear Island. PQ 13's commodore, Captain Casey, had not only lost contact with the ships supposedly under his control but was in danger of being cast up on an enemy held shore.

During the course of that chaotic morning, Lieutenant Commander Campbell, Senior Officer Escort in HMS *Fury*, received three urgent signals from the Admiralty warning that German surface ships had sailed from Trondheim and were probably intent on attacking the convoy. Up to six U-boats were also said to be in the area. Campbell ordered *Eclipse* to join him and, with the weather slowly beginning to moderate, set about rounding up the scattered merchantmen. The search was barely under the way when the whaler *Sumba* broke radio silence to report she was fifty miles east of Bear Island, making no headway against the seas and rapidly running out of fuel. Campbell had no option but to take *Fury* to her rescue, finally locating the whaler late that afternoon. *Fury* spent the next four hours steaming at slow speed while *Sumba* took on oil from a hose streamed astern from the destroyer. Given that U-boats were known to be in the vicinity, this was a highly risky operation for both ships, but there was no other way to save the *Sumba*. As his ship slow-steamed, offering a perfect target for enemy torpedoes, Campbell rued the day that these whalers with their very limited range had joined PQ 13. Far from contributing to the defence of the convoy, they were turning out to be a considerable liability – and a very dangerous one at that. *Sumba*'s call for help, though unavoidable, was the second breach of radio silence in forty-eight hours. The Germans were being given clear warning of the approach of PQ 13.

Unknown to Campbell, one ship had already met with and fallen to the enemy. She was the 4815-ton *Raceland*, a USMC ship under the Panama flag. Built in 1910 and long overdue for the breaker's yard, the *Raceland* had experienced difficulty in keeping up with the convoy right from the time of sailing from Hvalfjord. When the bad weather set in, she slowly fell astern of the other ships and out of sight, her going observed by no one. Shortly after noon on the 28th, she was alone to the south of Bear Island when German bombers found her and pounced. A few well-aimed bombs and the *Raceland* was no more. Of her crew of thirty-five, only twelve survived to take to the boats.

While HMS *Fury* was occupied in giving succour to the *Sumba*, *Trinidad* and *Eclipse* were having little success in rounding up the widely scattered merchantmen. Their search yielded only three ships, one of which was J. & C. Harrison's *Harpalion*, sister ship to the ill-fated *Harmatris*. The others were nowhere to be found.

The only good fortune to come PQ 13's way – and that turned out to be a mixed blessing – was an overnight improvement in the weather, the morning of the 28th dawning fine and sunny with a fresh breeze and good visibility. Before sunrise, Saunders took *Trinidad* on a full-speed sweep to the east, where he found the 7008-ton British ship *Empire Ranger* eighty miles to the north of the North Cape. The *Empire Ranger* had succeeded in pulling well ahead of the other ships and was in fact only a day and a half's steaming from the safety of the Kola Inlet. However, if she was to reach port, she would have to do it alone. Saunders' main concern was for the other ships and their vulnerability to attack by German surface ships. Having exchanged signals with the *Empire Ranger* and wished her good luck, he reversed course and took *Trinidad* back at full speed to join the destroyers.

The cruiser had not gone many miles to the west when a large, three-engined flying boat appeared out of the clouds and commenced to circle her. The aircraft was identified as a Blohm

& Voss 138 reconnaissance plane, which carried a crew of six and had a range of 2500 miles. *Trinidad*'s anti-aircraft guns opened up but the flying boat kept its distance. It made several more circuits, doubtlessly reporting what it had found. The Luftwaffe airfields were only 200 miles to the south and Saunders needed no crystal ball to tell him that an attack in force from the air would not be long in coming.

As she raced westward, *Trinidad* used her radar to search for *Fury* and *Eclipse*, but without success, but at 13.15 her sweeping scanner picked up another unwelcome visitor coming in fast from the south. The lone aircraft, when it came in sight, was immediately recognized as a Junkers 87B, one of the Luftwaffe's brutally efficient, gull-winged 'Stuka' dive bombers, scourge of the retreating British army in France in 1940. The attack was over before the *Trinidad*'s guns could be brought to bear. The Stuka dived hard, dropped its bombs close to the cruiser, pulled up, and then was gone, disappearing from sight as quickly as it had appeared.

This was only a warning. An hour later, the Stukas arrived in force, several flights of them flying high. This time *Trinidad*'s gunners were ready for them and put up a fierce barrage. The Stukas sheered away at first, but then climbed to about 6000 feet before peeling off one by one and hurling themselves down in a near-vertical dive, engines howling like banshees. It was a frightening experience for those on the receiving end; the Stukas were so close when they pulled up that the bombs could be seen falling away from under their wings.

Captain Saunders handled his ship magnificently, throwing her from side to side as the planes came in, and finding occasional cover in the mist patches that were now conveniently forming on the water. His actions and the lethal hail of 4-inch, 2-pounder and 20-mm shells hurled skywards by *Trinidad*'s gunners threw the Stukas off their aim and, although the cruiser was straddled several times, she suffered no major damage or casualties. Only one stick of bombs landing very close had any real effect, putting her main wireless transmitter out of action.

Air attacks on *Trinidad* continued, on and off, throughout the rest of the day, but never were the enemy bombers able to really dent the cruiser's armour. While Saunders was fighting his ship, reports were coming in of attacks on other ships. The *Harpalion* was bombed and damaged but able to carry on and, at 19.30 in the last of the daylight, the *Empire Ranger*, earlier sighted and left to her own devices by *Trinidad*, was sunk by bombers in position 72° 13' N 32° 10' E. She was only 200 miles from the Kola Inlet. The trawler *Blackfly* was dispatched to pick up survivors from the *Empire Ranger*, but on arrival found only two of her thirty-six-man crew alive. The attacks on the *Trinidad* continued sporadically throughout the day, but thanks to her gunners and Captain Saunders' skill, she was still undamaged when night fell.

In the absence of the *River Afton*, then fighting to avoid being blown ashore on the Lofoten Islands, the control of PQ 13's merchantmen should have been in the hands of the convoy vice commodore, thirty-two-year-old Captain William Collins in command of the *Induna*. But in the savagery of the storm that began on the 27th, the *Induna*, sailing as lead ship of Column 4, had also found herself alone, hammered by the seas and blinded by snow squalls.

Owned by Maclay and McIntyre, an old established Glasgow tramping company, the *Induna* had always been vulnerable, and it is hard to imagine why she was chosen as vice commodore. She was small – a shade over 5000 tons gross – and had seen seventeen years of hard tramping since leaving the slipway, which had left its marks. On the other hand, she was Clyde-built, which in an age of British shipbuilding supremacy was a mark of quality, and she was manned by a largely Scottish crew. Her total complement of fifty included ten DEMS (Defensively Equipped Merchant Ships) gunners drawn from the Royal Navy and the Maritime AA Regiment, who manned her defensive armament. This consisted of a 4-inch anti-submarine gun of somewhat ancient vintage, a quick-firing Bofors, two Lewis and two Hotchkiss light machine guns and a battery of PAC rockets. The PAC (Parachute and Cable) rocket was a device, usually mounted on the upper bridge, for use against low-flying aircraft. In theory, the rocket when fired carried 200 feet of wire cable skywards, which then floated down on a parachute to foul the propellers of attacking aircraft. In reality, the PAC was something of a liability, in that the rockets often nose-dived back onto the bridge to the great peril of its occupants.

The *Induna*, while sound and well-defended, carried a dangerous handicap on her current voyage, in that her cargo included a large consignment of gasolene in cans. Gasolene is not the best of cargoes to be living on top of under any circumstances. Of gasolene, Captain Thomas' *Stowage*, the merchant seaman's bible of cargo stowage, has to say: 'The risk of fire and explosion is ever present when this cargo is carried . . . so that the greatest care is necessary to avoid such'. In wartime, under the threat of bombs, shells and torpedoes, a cargo of gasoline is a one-way ticket to oblivion.

When, on the morning of 26 March, with no let-up in the weather, Captain Collins found himself alone in the heaving grey wastes of the Barents Sea, he was keenly aware that the danger point of the voyage had been reached. The *Induna* was within easy reach of the German airfields in Norway, the U-boats were on the prowl, and the frightening spectre of the world's most powerful battleship lurked just over the horizon. The tension on the bridge of the *Induna* mounted when, later that morning, the lookouts reported a ship looming up out of the murk astern. Collins held his course – in view of the heavy seas running, there was little else he could do – and went to action stations. A coded flag challenge was hoisted to the yardarm, the *Induna*'s 4-inch was trained around to cover the stranger – then they waited.

The other ship was gaining slowly, but she was still only a vague shape, disappearing from time to time in the passing snow squalls. It was impossible to say whether she was merchantman or warship. His flag hoist unanswered, Collins ordered the stranger to be challenged by lamp. The *Induna*'s Aldis flashed the terse message 'What ship?' There was a pause, only a matter of seconds, but long enough for the tension on the *Induna*'s bridge to become electric. Then, the other ship's lamp winked back E-M-P-I-R-E S-T-A-R-L-I-G-H-T, and there was an audible sigh of relief. She was one of their own, the 6850-ton *Empire Starlight*, a wartime acquisition of the MOWT (Ministry of War Transport) managed by the North-East Coast tramp company of Sir Robert Ropner and under the command of Captain C.H. Stein.

31

The *Empire Starlight* closed up on the *Induna*, and as the morning progressed they were joined by the *Ballot*, a 6000-ton United States Maritime Commission ship flying the Panama flag. Hard on the heels of the *Ballot* came HMS *Silja*, one of the Russia-bound whalers. The tiny *Silja* was making very heavy weather of it, sometimes disappearing from view completely as she slid into the troughs, but she was still making a credible speed. For Captain Collins, who now appeared to have gathered together the makings of a convoy, the 3-inch gun on the *Silja*'s forecastle head and the competent way in which she was being handled by her crew was reassuring. If he had then been aware of the problems this little ship would bring to his door, his welcome might not have been so warm.

The four ships continued in company, making for the rendezvous point to the south of Bear Island given by *Trinidad*. During the afternoon, there was some improvement in the weather. The wind eased and the sea was losing its force, but the snow squalls still swept in though less frequently, sometimes bringing the visibility down to a few yards. At 15.00 the alarm bells shrilled out again when a low-flying aircraft was sighted half a mile on *Induna*'s port beam. As the likelihood of meeting a friendly aircraft in these waters was extremely remote, Collins assumed the worst and told his gunners to prepare to fight.

As the plane came nearer its distinctive high wing mounting three engines and boat-like fuselage, identified it as a Blohm & Voss 138. When it was within a quarter of a mile of the *Induna* it fired a brilliant green flare, which Collins assumed must be some sort of recognition signal for which, of course, he had no answer. Now unsure of whether the plane would attack or not, and not wishing to invite retaliation, Collins ordered his gunners to hold their fire.

It seemed as if the German pilot was also undecided, for he flew straight at the *Induna*, then at the last moment banked to port and then flew parallel with the ship, so low on the water that the hull of the flying boat was almost skimming the wavetops. The plane was so close that Collins could see the two pilots in the cockpit and the front and rear gunners swinging their 20-mm cannon to cover the ship.

When it was level with the *Induna*'s bows, the aircraft suddenly sheered away and flew across the stern of the *Ballot*, which was keeping station on *Induna*'s port bow. It then banked sharply to starboard and circled around the *Empire Starlight*, to starboard of the *Induna*. Puzzled at the German aircraft's behaviour, all the ships were holding their fire, their guns tracking the plane but silent.

Crossing the *Induna*'s stern again, no more than 200 yards off, the Blohm & Voss climbed to about 200 feet and banked towards the ship. Certain that the attack was now imminent Collins passed the order to open fire. The *Induna*'s 4-inch, unable to elevate or track quickly enough, was ineffectual, but the Bofors gun, mounted on her poop had no such drawbacks. The 40-mm Swedish-built gun, with a firing rate of 120 rounds a minute and an effective range of 3500 yards, was highly manoeuvrable, its long fluted barrel easily able to lock on to a fast-moving aircraft.

The DEMS gunners manning the Bofors, led by Gunlayer T. Jackson, were experts in their own field. They held the Blohm & Voss in their sights and their first shell was seen to hit the aircraft's fuselage but glanced off without exploding. Their second round, however, went home, slamming into the plane's starboard engine. There was a bright orange flash, followed by a cloud of black, oily smoke pouring from the engine. The *Induna*'s machine guns had also opened up, spraying the now fleeing aircraft. It roared away to lose itself in the nearest snow squall and did not return. There was no means of knowing whether or not the plane made it back to its base, but its ignominious departure was a feather in the cap for the *Induna*'s gunners.

No bombs had been dropped, no damage done to any of the ships by the Blohm & Voss' guns, but the psychological effect of the visit was marked. There was not a man, above or below decks, who was not now acutely aware that, having been discovered by the Germans, an attack in force would not be long in coming. There was some consolation just before dark, when their convoy was swollen by the arrival of three more ex-members of PQ 13. They were the US-flag *Effingham*, one of Lykes Line's on passage from Boston, Massachusetts, the USMC's *Dunboyne*, and the Honduras-flag *Mana*, all three having crossed the Atlantic together. The American ships were well armed, their guns manned by US Navy Armed Guard gunners. With the presence, however small, of the Royal Navy in the *Silja*, Collins felt that he now had a convoy of substance under his wing.

Saturday, 28 March dawned cloudy, but fine. The wind had lost most of its strength, the sea was a moderate chop and, with the exception of a few passing snow squalls, the visibility was good. Morning sights showed the convoy to be 100 miles north of Norway's North Cape and just under 500 miles from the Kola Inlet. There was as yet no sign of any more PQ 13 ships; they were, in fact, still widely scattered, with *Trinidad* and the destroyers chasing them. Meanwhile, the carrier *Victorious* and the destroyer *Tartar* having suffered heavy weather damage, Admiral Curteis had concluded there was little he could now do for PQ 13, and was returning with his ships to Scapa Flow. Unaware of these developments and eighteen hours having elapsed since the Blohm & Voss was sent packing, Collins allowed himself to hope that the German plane had crashed into the sea without reporting the position of his ships. He decided to take advantage of the favourable weather and make a dash for the Kola Inlet at all possible speed, which was unlikely to be exceptional, as not one of the ships in the convoy even remotely resembled an ocean greyhound. They were functional cargo ships, their sturdy triple-expansion steam engines belonging to an era of peace, when it was necessary to deliver maximum cargo with maximum economy. Speed was not a priority.

They were at least allowed the luxury of breakfast undisturbed, the hot food chasing away the misery of the freezing night past. But the respite was short-lived. At 09.30, the enemy planes came in from the south, tiny black dots high in the sky at first and then, as they came closer, recognisable as Junkers 88 bombers, the big brothers of the Stukas. These sleek, twin-engined aircraft, with a top speed of 300 mph, bristled with machine guns and cannon and carried a two-ton bomb load slung under their wings. They belonged to *Generaloberst* Hans-Jurgen Stumpff's *Luftflotte 5*, based at Bardufoss fifty miles north of Narvik, and already blooded in the skies over the Eastern Front. What they saw now at sea were easy targets.

Induna hoisted the 'Hostile Aircraft' flag signal as a matter of course, but the signal was hardly necessary. By now there was not a gun in the convoy not fully manned, loaded and ready to fire. The Ju88s came relentlessly on, and when the range was right, the *Induna*'s Bofors opened up with its characteristic thump-thump. It was joined by every other gun in the convoy capable of being elevated high enough. As the Ju88s peeled off, they were met by such a furious hail of lead that the German pilots were forced to take evasive action and their bombs went wide, sending up tall waterspouts all around the zig-zagging ships.

The battle went on for half an hour, with the guns running hot in the ships and the bombers venting their frustration with their machine guns each time they were beaten off. Then it was all over as abruptly as it had begun. At 10.00, the bombers abandoned their attack and roared off to the south, having failed to get close enough to their targets to score even a near-miss. At the same time, in spite of the sustained barrage put up by Collins' ships, the German aircraft had also suffered no damage. However, the confidence of their crews must have been severely dented.

On board the ships, the victory was being celebrated in low key, for no one was under any illusions but that the enemy would be back. The arrival of a Blohm & Voss reconnaissance plane soon after the Ju88s had gone confirmed this. The pattern was all too familiar, the flying boat circling well out of reach of the convoy's guns, presumably reporting its movements, and homing in the next wave of bombers.

Much to Collins' surprise, the expected attack did not materialize and when, at noon, *Trinidad* and *Eclipse* were sighted to starboard, his relief was immense, if short-lived. The warships exchanged signals by lamp and kept company with the convoy for half an hour, but then moved on, Captain Saunders being satisfied that Collins had the situation firmly under control. Coincident with *Trinidad* and *Eclipse* leaving, the Blohm & Voss also gave up its constant circling and flew away. Collins now signalled his charges to increase to their absolute maximum speed, hoping to put as much distance between the convoy and the enemy by the time darkness closed in. The merchant ships responded valiantly, but the *Silja* was soon straggling.

There were now signs that the weather was again deteriorating, the sky gradually becoming heavily overcast with the cloud base down to 1000 feet and lowering. This was encouraging for now more than ever the convoy needed the cover of the weather. They pressed on for another hour and there were now hopes that the spirited defence put up by the ships and the presence of *Trinidad* and *Eclipse* might have persuaded the enemy to give up. These hopes were dashed when, at 13.30, the heavy drone of aircraft engines was heard above the cloud. The convoy went on to full alert again.

As the drone grew into an ominous roar and drew nearer, the barrel of every gun in the convoy tracked the approach of the unseen enemy. Suddenly, the roar became a high-pitched scream and a twin-engined aircraft dived out of the cloud, the black crosses on its fuselage and wings clearly visible. Gunlayer Jackson, on the *Induna*'s Bofors, immediately recognized the plane as an Me110 fighter bomber, armed with two 20-mm cannon, five 7.92-mm machine guns and a bomb load of 2200lb. This was an enemy with a very heavy punch.

The Messerschmitt roared down in a steep dive, ignoring the hail of shells and bullets thrown at it by the massed guns of the convoy. Its pilot must have been blessed with nerves of steel, and a great deal of good luck, for the plane pulled out of the dive unscathed and swept across the convoy from starboard to port, spraying the ships with its guns as it crossed overhead.

Collins, watching from the bridge of the *Induna*, saw four tiny black shapes fall away from the underside of the plane. They described a lazy parabola high above his head and neatly strad-dled the *Ballot*, which was then on the British ship's port beam. Banking sharply to port, the Messerschmitt then flew across the *Induna*'s stern and dropped another stick of four bombs close to the *Mana*. It then climbed steeply and was lost again in the clouds.

Other than a severe shaking up, the *Mana* appeared to be unharmed. The *Ballot* was not so fortunate, as was later reported by her master, Captain H. Bejer:

> One bomb fell a few yards from the starboard side at No.3 hatch. Two men, A.B. Santos and Messman da Costa were badly injured from bomb splinters and machine gun bullets.
>
> Enemy planes had earlier in the day attacked convoy and crew received strict orders to stay under deck. A.B. Santos was excused

as he was on his way up to the bridge to tell the officers on watch that he saw a plane approaching the ship.

The concussion was very violent, causing much damage on board. Several steam pipes in the engine room snapped, and the engine room was filled with steam. Electric light went out and darkened ship. Steering gear broke down. It was later discovered that one piston had been cracked.

Bilge soundings were taken but it took a long time to remove the ice over the soundings and by the time the crew left in the lifeboat, as mentioned below, we were uncertain about eventual leaks in ship's hull.

Thus with engines stopped, steering gear broken down and not knowing whether ship was leaking or not, we were left a target for the enemy, our position close to enemy territory, 100 miles from North Cape. Position N 72° 40' E 27° 35'.

About half the crew demanded to go in the boats and the other half promised to stay on board and try to bring the ship into port.

Under the circumstances – his ship was crippled and virtually defenceless – Captain Bejer had little option but to allow those of his crew who did not wish to stay with the ship to take to the boats. This they did, sixteen men in all, who were quickly picked up by the *Silja*. It was an action these men would live to regret.

The *Ballot*, now dead in the water, drifted slowly astern while her engineers worked feverishly to repair the blast damage. The ship, stopped and now undermanned, was in great danger but by no means helpless, as she was to prove when another Me110 dropped out of the clouds and charged at her head-on, guns blazing. Bejer's gunners were caught unawares, with the exception of one man manning the Lewis gun in the port wing of the bridge. He poured a long, accurate burst into the enemy plane, which banked away and flew off to the south, losing height and with white smoke pouring from its tail.

Within the hour, the *Ballot*'s engineers had patched up her steering gear and repaired all the broken steam and oil pipes on the main engine and generators and the ship was able to get under way once more. After another hour on maximum revolutions, she was beginning to overhaul the other ships, when her damaged steering suddenly failed completely and she was again forced to heave to. Then began the long, laborious process of disconnecting the steam steering engine and connecting up the emergency hand steering gear. Three hours elapsed before she was on the move again, steering from the poop, but by this time the rest of the convoy was out of sight over the horizon. Bejer now opened his Admiralty 'Stragglers Route' envelope and prepared to make for Murmansk alone. With half his crew missing, the ship in hand steering and the damaged main engine and auxiliaries requiring constant nursing, he knew that even if the enemy left him alone – and that was an unlikely possibility – this was going to be a passage to remember.

Chapter Four

As William Collins watched the *Ballot* fall further and further astern, to finally disappear in a snow squall, he feared for the American ship's safety but his main responsibility now lay with the remaining ships, the *Effingham, Dunboyne, Empire Starlight* and *Mana*, with their token escort, HMS *Silja*. It was the latter that concerned him most, for her commander had reported that her fuel was running dangerously low. Later that day, the master of the *Empire Starlight*, Captain W.H. Stein, who had considerable experience in these northern waters, suggested that rather than steer straight for the Kola Inlet and risk running into waiting U-boats, they first steam north to the ice edge, sail eastwards along the edge and then approach Murmansk from the northwest. Stein argued that the further north they went there would be less likelihood of attack by aircraft, that the U-boats would stay clear of the ice and in the end they would be able to make a quick dash for the Kola Inlet under the cover of darkness. The plan sounded workable and Collins, with not many other options open to him, agreed and set course accordingly. It was a decision he would regret making.

Second Officer Evan Rowlands took over the watch on the bridge of the *Induna* at midnight and even though he was well wrapped up with a mug of steaming hot cocoa warming his hands, he found himself shivering in the draughty wheelhouse. The night was moonless and inky black, and it was some time before Rowlands' eyes were adjusted to the dark and he was able to make out the line of the horizon and the shadowy outlines of the other ships. The convoy was still steering a northerly course,

Collins having left orders to be called when the ice edge was reached and, if the bitterly cold air was any indication, Rowlands thought this might be very soon.

His judgement proved to be right. A little before 01.00, Rowlands heard above the steady beat of the *Induna*'s engines the crackle of breaking ice as she sliced her way through the thin ice at the edge of the field. A glance over the side confirmed that they had reached the ice edge. He at once informed Captain Collins, who instructed him to hold the northerly course. This Rowlands did, but with some misgivings, for very soon they were in thickening pancake ice interspersed with growlers, the presence of which might indicate large icebergs drifting silently in the darkness ahead. The *Induna*'s speed was not affected by the ice, but Rowlands soon found he was having to make frequent alterations of course to avoid bigger growlers, not certain of how much of their bulk was below the surface. And while avoiding the growlers, Rowlands had to keep watch on the other ships all of which, only dimly visible to each other, were performing this mad and dangerous dance under the cloak of an Arctic night. It was a sight to make any shipowner's heart miss a beat as he reached for his insurance policies. The only consolation was that these ships were where no sensible U-boat commander would ever dare to venture.

Evan Rowlands ended what had been a nerve-racking watch at 04.00 on the 29th, handing over the ship to Chief Officer George Brown. Soon after Brown had taken over, the *Silja* closed the *Induna* and signalled by lamp that she was on her last few gallons of fuel and would require a tow if she was to reach Murmansk.

Captain Collins was called to the bridge and, when told of the situation, decided he could not leave the *Silja* to her fate to run out of fuel and drift helplessly in the ice. A towline was passed but it was daylight before the *Induna* set off again with the whaler in tow and the other ships following behind. Collins continued to sail deeper into the ice, which was steadily thickening, reducing the speed of the convoy to a mere handful of knots. Neither Collins nor any of the other masters had previous experience of navigating in ice and they were all uncomfortably conscious of the warning given in the *Mariner's Handbook*, which advises, 'When operating in ice, a vessel not specially designed for such

40

work runs risk of damage in the following ways: strained or broken propeller shafts, broken blades or loss of propellers, strained or broken rudder-head or rudder, damage to steering gear, damage to stern and plating, crushing of the hull and breaking of frames due to ice pressure, buckling of plating and tearing out of rivets'. It was a frightening catalogue of danger but in the opinion of Captain Collins the threat of the U-boats was even greater.

During the course of the morning, Collins altered course to the east but the ice continued to thicken, until it eventually became a solid field as far as the eye could see and the *Induna* and her tow came to a complete standstill. The words of warning in the *Mariner's Handbook* came back to haunt Collins and he signalled the other ships to alter to the south and make their own way to Murmansk. He then cast off the *Silja* and set about clearing a way for her with his bigger ship.

Fortunately, the ice had not yet taken a grip on the *Induna* and, by the careful use of helm and engines, Collins succeeded in turning her around, at the same time creating enough clear water for the whaler to come alongside. A towline was again passed and while this was being secured the sixteen men of the *Ballot*'s crew who had refused to stay with their ship were transferred to the *Induna*. The tow was recommenced – this time heading south – and by 15.00 the two ships were at last clear of the ice.

The other ships of the convoy were by this time well out of sight, and estimating his position by dead reckoning – there was no sun for sights – to be 72° N 38° E, roughly 200 miles northeast of the Kola Inlet, Collins set course to the south-west. At first they made good speed but as the night closed in, the wind freshened and it was necessary to lengthen the towline. This had the unfortunate effect of causing the *Silja* to sheer about wildly and, as the weather worsened, although the *Induna* reduced speed, the strain on the towline became too great and at 20.00 it parted.

The visibility was now poor with frequent heavy snow squalls and, as the two ships drifted apart, they soon lost sight of each other. The *Induna* turned about to search for the whaler, sounding her steam whistle and flashing lights, but the *Silja* had disappeared into the night. Collins continued to search until 04.00 on the 30th when, concerned for the safety of his own ship and the sixty-six men he now had on board, he reluctantly abandoned the search and set course for the Kola Inlet.

A powerful combination of the Luftwaffe and the unpredictable Arctic weather had succeeded in scattering the ships of PQ 13 far and wide. The *Induna*'s group had become separated off the ice edge; the *River Afton* was still to the south and straining her engines in an effort to regain contact with her charges, but to the west a semblance of order had been restored. Here the armed trawler HMS *Paynter* and the whaler *Sumba* had gathered together the British ships *Empire Cowper*, *New Westminster City* and the oiler *Scottish American*, the US ships *Eldena*, *El Estero*, *Gallant Fox* and *Mormacmar*, and the Polish *Tobruk*. The *Raceland* and *Empire Ranger* had fallen to the German bombers, while the *Harpalion*, *Lars Kruse* and *Bateau* were straggling somewhere in between. The situation, to say the least, was confused, and the odds on some of those ships getting through to Murmansk were lengthening, for yet another threat to PQ 13 was gathering to the south.

When reports of the passage of PQ 13 reached Admiral Hubert Schmundt, the German Navy's C.-in-C. North Norway, his first impulse was to order the *Tirpitz* and her consorts to mount an attack on the convoy. However, the big ships were 850 miles away in Trondheim and a chronic shortage of fuel ruled out any high-speed dash to the north by the flotilla. Schmundt was loath to miss the opportunity to inflict major damage on PQ 13, and fell back on ships of the 8th Destroyer Flotilla, the formidable *Zestorergruppe Arktis*. Stationed at Kirkenes, only sixty miles to the west of the Kola Inlet, these ships were within easy reach of the convoy. At 13.03 on 28 March, the destroyers Z-24, Z-25 and Z-26, under the overall command of the experienced *Kapitän zur See* Gottfried Pönitz who flew his flag in Z-26, commanded by *Kapitän zur See* Georg Ritter von Berger, left Kirkenes and came racing out of Varanger Fjord at full speed, heading north. Operation 'Cerebus' was under way.

To send three destroyers out to attack a convoy reported to be defended by a 6-inch gun cruiser, two destroyers and various smaller escorts might be thought to be tempting providence, but the Z-class ships were no ordinary destroyers. New ships – they

42

had left the Deschimag yard in Bremen in the spring of 1940 – they tipped the scales at 3543 tons, and were each armed with five 5.9-inch guns, four 37-mm AA guns, six 20-mm cannons and eight 12-inch torpedo tubes. Powered by two Wagner steam turbines developing 70,000 SHP, they had a top speed of thirty-seven and a half knots and a range of 2500 miles at nineteen knots. Acting together, these three powerful ships – small cruisers rather than destroyers – were more than a match for *Trinidad* and her two 1300-ton destroyers.

Reaching the open sea the German destroyers ran into indifferent weather, heavily overcast with poor visibility, with intense cold, so cold it was said, that the lookouts found their breath freezing on their binoculars. Pönitz had no up-to-date position for the convoy, so he steered due north to cross the expected route of the British ships. The German ships were not radar-equipped, so even with three of them steaming in line abreast with maximum distance between them allowed by the visibility, the search promised to be long and tedious. It just so happened that, at 19.00, in the last of the daylight, bombers of *Luftflotte 5* found the *Empire Ranger* romping well ahead of the western section of PQ 13, and sank her with a few well-placed bombs. Obligingly, the British ship broadcast an SOS, which was, of course, picked up by Pönitz's wireless operators. Pönitz headed directly for the *Empire Ranger*'s position, which was given as 72° 13' N 32° 10' E, 100 miles north-east of the North Cape. At 22.45 lookouts sighted the *Empire Ranger*'s lifeboats and the British survivors, by now cold and very miserable, were picked up. They faced the certainty of a prisoner of war camp, but it was for them the lesser of two evils. Adrift in open boats, many of them would have died.

The prisoners were questioned regarding the situation of PQ 13 but, cold and demoralized as they were, they gave nothing away, much to Pönitz's annoyance, but at least he now had a starting point. Turning to the west, he deployed his three ships in line abreast three miles apart, and steaming at fifteen knots, began to trawl for his catch.

The German commander's efforts were rewarded at 00.30 on the 29th, when an unlucky straggler from PQ 13 ran straight into his net. She was the 4687-ton Panama-flag *Bateau*, alone and lost, steaming eastwards at her best speed of nine knots. She was shown no mercy, being summarily dispatched with guns and torpedo by Z-26. Forty of her crew were killed, only six survivors being picked up. These were questioned, and unfortunately told all they knew about PQ 13 and its escort. This was unwise but, perhaps, understandable. Having survived the brutal destruction of their ship, and witnessed the death of so many of their shipmates, the six men were in a state of severe shock.

Pönitz swept the area for what remained of the night looking for other stragglers, but found nothing. At 08.30, he turned westwards again and steamed back along the estimated route of the convoy at seventeen knots. The weather was fair, the visibility excellent, and with full daylight the three German ships, deployed in line abreast, were able to cover a very wide horizon. However, they failed to sight the British ship *Harpalion*, another PQ 13 straggler which, having survived an attack by Stukas, passed twenty-five miles to the south of the destroyers on her way to the east.

During the night, Captain Saunders in *Trinidad*, had received warning of the presence of enemy surface units from the SBNO (Senior British Naval Officer) Murmansk. The signal informed Saunders that a Russian submarine had reported three German destroyers at sea and apparently heading north to intercept the convoy. This presented Saunders with a dilemma for PQ 13, stragglers and rompers excepted, was now split into two separate groups eighty miles apart. Which group should he protect? At the same time, Saunders was under orders to rendezvous in 72° 25' N 30° 00' E at 08.00 on the 29th with *Oribi* and the two Russian destroyers *Sokrushitelni* and *Gremyashchi*, the Russians being thirty-six knotters mounting 5.1-inch guns. Saunders, with the destroyer *Fury* in company, decided that the need for reinforcements was paramount and made all speed to the east.

At around 05.00, with the first pale streaks of the coming dawn showing in the sky ahead, *Trinidad*'s lookouts reported a suspicious object on the starboard bow, which had not yet been picked up by the cruiser's radar. The horizon was hazy, but at four miles the object looked suspiciously like a U-boat on the surface. *Trinidad* opened fire, but the U-boat proved to be nothing more than a shadow in the mist. The cruiser's gunfire did, however, provide a guide for *Oribi* and her Russian consorts, who joined *Trinidad* and *Fury* soon after sunrise.

With new confidence, Saunders took his reinforced flotilla to the west with the object of making contact with *Eclipse* and the westernmost group of merchantmen. Shortly after reversing course, the flotilla came across wreckage on the water and then the *Empire Ranger*'s empty lifeboats. The boats were intact, with their sails still set, but they were empty, a sure indication to Saunders that their occupants had successfully abandoned ship and had been picked up – but by whom? Having examined the boats closely, Saunders carried on to the west and at 08.30 sighted *Eclipse* who, with *Paynter* and *Sumba*, was shepherding the eight ships of PQ 13's western group towards the Kola Inlet. The two Russian destroyers were detached to assist *Eclipse*, while *Oribi* was ordered to sweep up to twenty miles astern to look for any stragglers, and then to rejoin *Eclipse*. *Trinidad* and *Fury* then turned back to the east, and increasing speed to twenty knots, set off once more to look for the missing *Induna* group. Saunders was unaware that ahead of him the weather was fast deteriorating, with dark clouds rolling in bringing with them gale force winds and blinding snow squalls. And in this deepening gloom the three ships of *Zestorergruppe Arktis* were steaming west on a reciprocal course. The two opposing forces, each as yet unaware of the other, were closing at a combined speed of nearly forty knots.

Trinidad's radar gave her the first advantage. At 08.43, its rotating scanner picked up the approaching enemy at six and a half miles. The duty operator, Able Seaman J. Anderson, identified the target blips as three large ships approaching at speed. He immediately called the bridge. Saunders sent his men to action stations and signalled to *Fury* 'ENEMY IN SIGHT'.

The German destroyers were sighted visually by *Trinidad* a few minutes later as they burst through a passing snow squall into the daylight. They were still in line abreast, with *Z-26* in the centre, and until that moment unaware of the British ships. Saunders recognized the distinctive silhouettes as big Narvik-class destroyers, fast and heavily armed, and gave them no time to recover from their surprise, opening fire even before his Yeoman of Signals had finished flashing a challenge by lamp.

45

The first encounter was brief and vicious, with *Trinidad*'s opening salvo of 6-inch shells hitting *Z-26* abaft her funnel. Smoke and flames poured from the German destroyer's superstructure. Von Berger, now fighting his own ship, replied seconds later, two shells from *Z-26*'s 5.9's exploding under *Trinidad*'s 'Y' turret, and holing her just above the waterline.

With his own ship hard hit, von Berger altered to starboard under full helm and ran for the cover of the nearest snow squall. Saunders now switched his fire to the other German destroyers, scoring hits on at least one of them before they followed *Z-26* into the squall. Fearing the enemy might retaliate with torpedoes, Saunders then broke away to starboard, and *Trinidad* heeled sharply as she swung to present her stern to the retreating destroyers. The manoeuvre, although causing the sea to pour into the hole in the cruiser's hull, was not a moment too soon. As *Trinidad* straightened up on a southerly heading, the tracks of two torpedoes were seen streaking down her port side.

The immediate danger past, Saunders brought his ship round in a 180 degree turn to go in pursuit of the enemy. As *Trinidad* steadied up again, *Z-24* and *Z-25* emerged briefly from the driving snow dead ahead, both on diverging courses and slamming into the rising seas at maximum speed, running away from the British cruiser's guns. Knowing the Germans had the advantage of him by at least four knots, Saunders let them go, preferring to seek a softer target.

It was now blowing a full gale, with the cloud almost down to sea level and driving snow obscuring the visibility. Ordering *Fury* to stay close, Saunders increased speed to thirty knots and, with the waves crashing over her bows and her damage control parties fighting to stem the inflow of water into her hull, *Trinidad* lunged after the damaged *Z-26*.

The German destroyer was still hidden from view, but showing up on *Trinidad*'s radar screen at four and a half miles. Fifteen minutes hard steaming and she was sighted two miles ahead, stern on and partially obscured by a cloud of black smoke, some of which she was making to hide her escape, the rest from fires raging amidships. *Trinidad* was overhauling her rapidly and at 2500 yards Saunders altered to starboard to cross her stern, at the same time bringing all his guns to bear. This included the port-side 4-inch guns which were very effective at this range. Von Berger was zig-zagging wildly as he attempted to escape, but he was unable to evade the combined firepower of *Trinidad*'s guns. Broadside after broadside rained down on the fleeing destroyer and her three after turrets were soon knocked out. When *Trinidad*'s guns scored another three direct hits below her bridge, Z-26 ceased to fire back.

Trinidad now came up on Z-26's starboard side, gradually overtaking the crippled destroyer. Soon the two ships were racing neck and neck, taking green water over their bows as they slammed into the waves and with no more than 1500 yards of the raging sea separating them. The British cruiser's guns were silent, but in her waist Lieutenant Commander Dent and his crew of torpedomen were standing by the port tubes. Blinded by the freezing spray lashing their faces, and fighting to keep their feet as the ship corkscrewed through the rough seas, the torpedomen struggled to train the triple tubes. Short on anti-freeze, the tubes were icing up in their mountings. Saunders was shortly to bitterly regret sailing from Seydisfjord without sufficient supplies of the essential fluid.

The order to fire as you bear had already come from the bridge and, with Z-26 square on the beam, Dent fired the first torpedo. With a dull thud, the 21-inch torpedo, its warhead packed with 750lb of amatol, hit the water with its propeller whirring and headed for the German destroyer at forty knots. The second and third torpedoes, frozen into their tubes, refused to fire.

On *Trinidad*'s bridge, Captain Saunders wiped the freezing mist from his binoculars and prepared to follow the tracks of his torpedoes as they homed in on the enemy ship. To his absolute horror, he saw Dent's lone torpedo porpoise to the surface not more than 200 yards from *Trinidad*, and then describe a complete round turn to come racing back towards the cruiser. *Trinidad* was about to earn her place in history as the only British warship ever to torpedo herself. As the torpedo raced towards them, Saunders lowered his binoculars and with amazing sangfroid was heard to remark to his First Lieutenant, 'You know, this looks remarkably like one of ours.'

Saunders put the helm hard over in an attempt to comb the track of the rogue torpedo, but even though *Trinidad*, steaming at thirty knots, responded valiantly, it was too late to save her. The torpedo hit the cruiser amidships, ironically almost directly under the very tube from which it had been launched, and narrowly missing one of her magazines, The resulting explosion blew a hole in *Trinidad*'s hull measuring forty feet by twenty feet, ruptured a wing bunker tank and wrecked the Royal Marines' mess deck.

Trinidad staggered under the force of the explosion and then took a heavy list to port as the sea poured into the open mess deck. The men on the deck probably would have escaped, had not the bulkhead of the breached fuel tank then collapsed. Thick black oil joined the water now flooding the mess deck and eighteen men lost their lives, choked by the oil and drowned as they fought to reach the upper deck. *Trinidad*'s forward boiler-room was also laid open to the sea, while the blast of the explosion fractured a number of high-pressure steam pipes. As the sea rushed in, dowsing the boiler fires, the lights went out and the space was turned into a bedlam as men, scalded by the superheated steam, screamed and clawed their way up the slippery ladder to safety.

Grievously wounded by her own hand, *Trinidad* lost way through the water, and her head fell off to starboard. All communications were down and on the bridge Saunders was receiving damage reports by messengers. The main steering had failed and a party was sent aft to man the emergency steering position, helm orders being relayed from the bridge by a chain of men stationed along the deck. Slowly, the damaged ship came back on course, but she would take no further part in the fight. As she limped along, leaning heavily to port, the torpedo mounting from which the fatal torpedo had been fired, fractured by the explosion, suddenly broke off and fell over the side into the sea. Torpedo-man Bowditch, who had fired the torpedo and was still seated at the controls, was forced to jump for his life.

Aboard *Z-26*, the carnage was even greater, but her engines and steering were unaffected and, seeing his chance to escape, von Berger called on his engineers for all possible speed and sheered away to port, making for the cover of a snowstorm some three miles away. The German destroyer had almost reached cover, when Lieutenant Commander Campbell in HMS *Fury* realized what was happening. Satisfied that *Trinidad* was in no danger of sinking, Campbell went in pursuit of Z-26 like a hound after a fox.

Unknown either to Campbell or von Berger, the two ships were heading straight for the western group of PQ 13, which was under escort by *Eclipse*, *Oribi* and the two Russian destroyers. Lieutenant Commander Mack in *Eclipse* had heard the sound of gunfire and had already altered course to investigate. This almost led to another tragedy for the British, for emerging from a snow squall, *Fury* was mistaken for the enemy by Mack. Fortunately, Mack made the challenge by lamp before opening fire, but one of the Russians, the *Sokrushitelni*, hard on the heels of *Eclipse*, opened fire, to which *Fury* replied. It was just as well for both ships that poor visibility and rough seas did not make for accurate shooting and no hits were scored by either.

When the confusion had died down, Campbell decided to return to stand by *Trinidad*, leaving *Eclipse* to go after Z-26, believed to be still in the vicinity. The German destroyer was in fact only three miles away, hidden in the snow on *Eclipse*'s port bow. The two ships sighted each other simultaneously, but Mack mistook Z-26 for *Trinidad*, while von Berger believed he had joined up with Z-24 or Z-25. Both ships flashed a challenge to the other and for a few moments, as the snow swirled around them, they hesitated. Then, the realization suddenly dawned on the British and German bridges that they were facing the enemy, and the guns crashed out.

A fierce running battle followed, in which both ships carried a severe handicap. Z-26, badly mauled by *Trinidad*'s guns, and with only her forward turrets able to fire, made smoke and zigzagged as she tried once more to escape. *Eclipse* was armed with four 4.7s, two forward and two aft, but one gun on her forecastle was frozen up, a result of spray being shipped over the bows, leaving Mack with only one forwarding firing gun. He tucked himself into Z-26's wake, safe from the German's forward 5.9s, sheering away to port or starboard when the opportunity occurred, to bring his after guns to bear.

The conditions under which *Eclipse* was fighting were appalling, sometimes bordering on the chaotic. The swirling snow and freezing spray from the bow wave which constantly drenched the destroyer's open bridge made a mockery of any organized action. It was impossible to use binoculars, and the fight became as basic as it had ever been in the far-off days of Nelson's wooden walls. It was all down to 'Mark One Eyeball' and spur of the moment strategy. Frequently, *Z-26* disappeared from view completely in the murk of snow and spray but, unfortunately for her, she was leaving in her twisting wake a clearly visible trail of oil leaking from a damaged fuel tank. In the mêlée, a breakdown of communications resulted in *Eclipse* firing a salvo of three torpedoes at a target that was no longer there. As it transpired, the torpedoes ran true, sinking harmlessly into the depths at the end of their run, and *Eclipse* avoided suffering the same fate as *Trinidad*.

The bizarre fight went on, pursuer and pursued twisting and turning as each tried to gain the advantage, yet slowly but surely *Eclipse* was gaining the upper hand. In the space of the next half hour, her 4.7s registered six hits on the fleeing German ship, one of which appeared to hit a magazine, for there was a heavy explosion followed by fire. Another of Mack's shells exploded in *Z-26*'s boiler-room and she was seen to slow down, her stern now so low in the water that the after deck was awash. She was also developing a pronounced port list. Cautiously, Mack moved up on her port side and prepared to torpedo her.

At this point, the tables were suddenly turned. Out of the snow, and only two miles to starboard of *Eclipse*, came the other two Narvik-class destroyers, racing to the aid of their flotilla leader. By this time the *Eclipse* was running low on fuel, one of her forward guns was still out of action, and she had several men injured. Faced with an overwhelming superiority of fire power, Mack wisely decided to retire before his ship was blown out of the water. His plight was not helped by a sudden clearance of the snow, giving way to good visibility. Mack rang for emergency full speed and ran for the cover of the one snow squall still lingering to the north-west. As she ran, *Eclipse* was hit four times by German shells which holed her below the waterline, brought down her wireless aerials, and caused an explosion amongst some ready-use cordite charges resulting in heavy casualties.

Luck was with *Eclipse*. The German destroyers chose not to pursue her, preferring to go to the aid of *Z-26*, which was now sinking. Under cover of the snow, Mack swung around to head to the east away from the enemy ships. Reports reaching him on the bridge indicated to Mack that *Eclipse* had not suffered any serious damage but one man had been killed and twelve injured, nine of them seriously. In addition, the hard-fought action and the extreme weather conditions were taking their toll on the rest of his crew, many of whom were near to exhaustion. To make matters worse, the *Eclipse*'s fuel tanks were nearly empty, which was beginning to affect her stability and ability to manoeuvre at speed. All this became very evident when, emerging from the snow squall, the destroyer surprised a U-boat on the surface some 400 yards on her port bow.

Before *Eclipse*'s guns' crews were able to open fire, the U-boat loosed off two torpedoes at her, the tracks of which were seen streaking towards them. At the last moment, Mack ordered full port helm and, leaning alarmingly as she momentarily gained negative stability, the destroyer slewed round to successfully comb the tracks of the torpedoes. When she lurched upright again, Mack went after the U-boat with intent to ram, but the German submarine disappeared with a loud roar of blowing ballast tanks before the destroyer's flared bows reached her. A vigorous depth charge attack was carried out, but with no positive results. *Eclipse* continued to search by Asdic, saturating the area with depth charges, but Mack was eventually forced to concede that the U-boat had got clean away.

By now, *Eclipse* was left with only forty tons of fuel in her tanks, and Mack deemed it wise to make for the Kola Inlet to refuel and land his injured. Astern of the British destroyer as she made her way to the east, *Z-26* was in her death throes. At a few minutes before noon that day, the crippled German destroyer capsized and sank. Only fifty-six of her total crew of 320 officers and men survived to be picked up by *Z-24* and *Z-25*. Among the survivors was *Kapitän zur See* Georg Ritter von Berger who, although badly wounded in the face and legs, saw his remaining crew over the side before leaving the ship himself.

HMS *Trinidad*, with *Fury* standing by her, was now also making for the Kola Inlet. The cruiser was in a sorry state, listing heavily, steering from her after steering position and limping along at speeds varying from four to six knots. Below decks, her damage control parties worked furiously to shore up strained bulkheads and pump out flooded compartments. In her sick bay lit by emergency lighting, her surgeons performed minor miracles in patching up what seemed to be an endless queue of wounded. She still had 150 miles to steam before reaching port. It would be a close run thing.

Later in the day, when the western section of PQ 13 overhauled *Trinidad* and *Fury*, *Oribi* was detached from the convoy to assist in the defence of the cruiser – and not a moment too soon. *Fury*, scouting ahead, sighted a U-boat on the surface, namely *U-585*, commanded by *Kapitänleutnant* Ernst-Bernward Lohse, one of six boats detailed to keep watch for PQ 13 as it approached Murmansk. *Fury* went straight in for the kill, but Lohse crash dived and *U-585* was going deep before the destroyer reached her. She was quickly picked up by *Fury*'s Asdics, and Campbell attacked with depth charges. Some oil came to the surface and Campbell claimed, and was credited with, a kill. German sources, however, reported that *U-585* was sunk on the 30 March to the north of the Kola Inlet when she hit a floating mine laid by her own forces. All forty-four men on board were lost.

When the furore had died down, the screen around *Trinidad* was joined by the minesweeper *Harrier*, sent out from Murmansk, and work went ahead to try to bring the damaged ship into a more seaworthy condition. By transferring fuel and ballasting empty tanks, the heavy list was reduced and the ship made more manageable. By late afternoon, she was making a respectable twelve knots. The improvement was short-lived for when darkness came, salt water in her boilers brought *Trinidad* to a complete standstill. Perversely, the night was fine and clear, with the light of a full moon augmented by brilliant displays of the aurora borealis. Stopped and drifting, despite her heavy escort, the *Trinidad* was at great risk of attack. She was then only seventy miles north of the Kola Inlet, and a signal was sent to Murmansk asking for tugs and air cover. The Russians either could not, or would not, respond for two hours later neither of these had arrived. However, the cruiser's engineers had by then succeeded in draining off the salt water from her boilers and she was soon under way again making seven knots to the southward.

But it was not all over yet. The elements now took over the attack with a strong northerly gale and *Trinidad* was soon in trouble again, steering badly in a rough following sea and in danger of broaching to. She fought on, clawing her way to the south, and at 09.30 on the 30th, entered the Kola Inlet with tugs in attendance, but under her own steam. She found *Eclipse* already in the anchorage. Bruised and battered, the big guns of PQ 13's escort force had reached Russia; the merchant ships were yet to put in an appearance.

Kapitän Georg Ritter von Berger, who had so gallantly fought Z-26 and came so near to winning the day, was snatched unconscious from the sea by a rescue boat from *Z-24*, and lived to fight another day. He was later given command of a new destroyer, *Z-32*, but met a sad and unworthy end in 1944. *Z-32* was sunk in action during the Allied invasion of Normandy and von Berger was taken prisoner by the French. While in custody near Bordeaux, he was seized by partisans and executed by a firing squad. He lies buried in a French cemetery near the mouth of the River Gironde.

Chapter Five

The *Induna*, having parted company with the other ships and abandoned the search for *Silja*, was still up off the ice edge when *Trinidad* and her escorts were approaching the safety of the Kola Inlet. Sunrise was just an hour away, but there would be little improvement in the weather with the coming of the cold, grey dawn. The wind had eased somewhat, but was still blowing force 6 from the north-north-west, and a rough sea and heavy swell were running. Above all, the blinding snow storms continued to sweep in unabated, often reducing the visibility to zero. Under the circumstances, Captain William Collins concluded that the best plan of action, for both his own ship and the lost minesweeper, was to make a run for Kola at all possible speed, and when there report the last known position of the *Silja*. After that, the Navy must look after its own.

Relieved of her tow, the *Induna* slowly worked up to ten and a half knots, the best she could do, for she was yawing awkwardly as the big following sea caught her on her quarter. For her helmsman it was a battle of wills just to hold her to her course. But the worst handicap was the lack of visibility in the snow. Radar was not an option available in the average merchant ship of 1942, and the *Induna*'s navigating officers had only their instinct and ears to guide them. Fortunately, this was a far cry from the crowded sea lanes of the English Channel, and the risk of collision with another ship was remote, but there were still sizeable icebergs about. It was a calculated risk, but Collins considered it was worth taking. By pressing on at full speed, he estimated to be in the Kola Inlet before nightfall.

Collins had not reckoned with the U-boats of the Ulan group, six of which were patrolling the area on the lookout for such as the *Induna*. It was one of these, *U-376*, commanded by *Kapitänleutnant* Friedrich-Karl Marks, that found the *Induna* as she made her bid for safety. *U-376*, a Type VIIC, had been in commission since 21 August 1941 and in all these long months she had not managed to sink a single enemy ship. Marks was on his first voyage in command, and this was not the way he had imagined it when he joined the boat in Kiel. This was at a time when U-boats in the Atlantic were sinking Allied ships at the rate of half a million tons a month. And here he was idling on the surface in this god-forsaken Arctic sea with icicles forming on his beard and not a ship in sight anywhere. When, at 07.00, the deep-laden *Induna* emerged from a snow squall heading straight towards him, Marks knew his chance had come at last. He hammered the klaxon and hurled himself down the hatch after the lookouts. *U-376* was already submerging.

Second Officer Evan Rowlands had the watch on the bridge of the *Induna* when the torpedo, unseen in its silent approach, struck the ship in way of No.5 hold on her starboard side. Murphy's Law would have it that No.5 hold was the hold packed with cans of gasoline and the effect of the torpedo was spectacular. The first explosion was muffled, but this was followed by a violent eruption and a shock wave that staggered the ship. Rowlands, who had been knocked to the deck by the force of the second blast, got to his feet and watched in horror as the whole afterpart of the ship then burst into flames. Weaving drunkenly through the curtain of flame and smoke he saw a lone figure, his clothes on fire, and probably the only survivor from the gunners' accommodation, which was in No.5 tween deck.

The *Induna* was a doomed ship and events followed swiftly. Collins gave the order to abandon ship and he and Rowlands stayed behind on the bridge, their last duty to destroy the confidential papers and code books. Having no weighted boxes for these, they burned them. This done, they knew it was time to go. The *Induna* was well down by the stern, her after deck consumed by flames that soared high in the air. It was now a question of what would sink her first, the fire or the hole in her side. Rowlands looked around for the Captain, but he was nowhere to be seen. There was no time to lose but before he left the bridge, Rowlands, giving thought to what might lie ahead, collected a sextant and binoculars from the wheelhouse.

The *Induna* carried two full-sized lifeboats, quite sufficient for her normal crew of fifty, but she now had on board sixteen extra men, survivors from the *Ballot*, some of whom should have taken their chance in the small jolly boat stowed alongside the bridge, or on rafts. When Rowlands reached the boat deck, both lifeboats were full and ready to launch. As is the usual custom in merchant ships, the Second Officer takes charge of the Captain's boat, which is the starboard side boat. In the absence of Captain Collins, Evan Rowlands was faced with a dilemma. Should he wait for Collins, who was nowhere in evidence, or take the boat away? Thirty-one men were already in the boat and the ship might go at any minute. The decision was made for him by Chief Officer George Brown who, in the absence of Collins, had taken command. It was Brown's judgement that they could delay no longer in abandoning the ship. He ordered the boats into the water, instructing Rowlands to lay off ready to pick up Captain Collins and any others that might still be on board. Brown then left the boat deck to look for Collins.

The sea was running high, and the heavily loaded boats were in danger of capsizing when they hit the water, for the men manning them – in common with most merchant seamen – were not well practised in the art of abandoning ship. But the fear of death can work miracles and both boats were lowered, cast off and cleared the ship without mishap.

When they were some 200 yards from the *Induna*, they lay back on their oars, still feeling the searing heat of the burning ship that had lent strength to their arms. As they lay there watching their ship die, there was a loud roaring close by and *U-376* surfaced, the water cascading off her rust-streaked hull. Remembering the urgings of the Admiralty to always take careful note of the enemy when he showed himself, Rowlands complied, later reporting: 'The U-boat was a large craft about 200 feet long, of about 500 tons. I noticed a jumping wire and a small gun just forward of the conning tower. It appeared to be a modern type of boat with a sharp bow. I myself did not see any markings but some of the men in our boat said they could see a number on the bows, either U-140 or U-104. There were no marks of any kind on the conning tower.' The identifying number was incorrect, but given the circumstances, Rowlands had given a fair description of a Type VIIC.

The U-boat ignored the lifeboats and motored towards the *Induna*, firing a second torpedo, which struck the ship in her No.4 hold. This time there were no more flames, just a loud explosion that threw a column of dirty water and debris high into the air. Almost at once, the *Induna* began to sink by the stern. Friedrich-Karl Marks and Evan Rowlands, enemies who would never meet, watched silently as the poor, battered and burning ship lifted her bow out of the water until it was almost vertical, and then slid under in a cloud of steam and smoke, going to her last resting place in the cold Arctic sea. After seventeen years tramping the oceans of the world she had ended her life a long way from the bustling waters of the River Clyde where she was born.

When she was gone, Rowlands looked around, seeing a sea that was suddenly very empty and uninviting. *U-376* was nowhere to be seen, Marks being anxious to put as much distance between himself and the scene of his victory before the Royal Navy arrived. The other lifeboat had also disappeared. Despite the inescapable fact that he was jammed into a small open boat certified to carry only twenty-five with thirty-one other men, Rowlands felt a momentary pang of loneliness. They were all his responsibility now. Fortunately, he had no time for self-pity. The boat had only a few inches of freeboard as it rolled in the seas; the water was pouring over the gunwales. The first priority was to bring this overloaded boat head on to the seas. They rowed and they bailed, and at last they had the boat riding well, although they were still up to their knees in icy water. To add to their misery, each time the boat dipped into a wave their backs were lashed by the freezing spray shipped over the bows.

With the boat safe for the time being, Rowlands took stock of the situation. It was not good although, spurred on by the need to survive, his crew were rowing strongly. But, not surprisingly, they were ill-prepared for the ordeal which must be ahead of them. Among them all having been on watch on the bridge when the torpedo struck, Rowlands was the only one adequately dressed, having on several layers of warm clothing, a duffel coat and fur-lined boots. Most of the others had been sleeping and, although they would have turned in fully clothed, they were not dressed for an open boat. Consequently, they were already cold, wet, becoming demoralized and, above all, frightened. Furthermore, it was the luck of the draw for Rowlands that the majority of his boat's crew were engine-room ratings from the two ships, only two of whom had more than a few months' sea service to their names. Rowlands was the only one on board with any knowledge of sailing small boats and that was limited. And, as the land lay to the south and the wind was from the north, if they were to save themselves they could not continue to head into wind and sea as they were then doing. They must turn the boat about, hoist the sails, and run before the wind.

The ship's lifeboat of the 1940s was a heavy wooden craft, very seaworthy, but not designed to do much more than get people away from a sinking ship. It was broad in the beam, blunt in the bow and manoeuvred like a disabled crab. It carried two strong canvas sails, a jib and a lug, the latter sail being secured to a boom which had to be dipped around the mast to change tack – hence the name dipping lug. This was certainly no ocean yacht, in fact, sailing a ship's lifeboat any closer than eight points to the wind was a near impossibility. A ship's boat, however, will sail tolerably well with the wind right astern, and this is what Rowlands intended to do. First stepping the mast, a not inconsiderable feat in a boat so crowded, he persuaded his inexperienced crew to turn the boat under oars, a procedure that almost ended in them capsizing. A great deal of icy water was shipped, but finally they had the wind astern. The small triangular jib was hoisted and the clumsy boat seemed to acquire a new grace, riding the waves easily, although requiring constant attention to the tiller to prevent her broaching to.

Now that they were heading towards the land, which Rowlands estimated to be only seventy miles away, and perhaps within twenty-four hours sailing, there was less despondency in the boat and there was a determined attempt to bail out the water shipped when coming about. But no one in the boat had any illusions about how serious their situation was. They were in a small and dangerously overcrowded boat and in a very hostile environment. All around them was a grey, angry sea that never gave up its efforts to overcome their boat, to throw it off course, and to fill it with icy salt water. Then to add to their discomfort, the snow came, slanting horizontal on the wind, scourging their exposed faces and coating their already sodden clothing with its white powder that turned to an icy crust in the biting wind. The *Mariner's Handbook* has a way of describing their predicament: 'The shipwrecked mariner (in the Arctic), will have to apply all his willpower and mental discipline to control overwhelming feelings of depression, concern, confusion, despair and possibly panic.'

Second Officer Rowlands later wrote in his report: 'We kept sailing all that day, the 30th March, running before the wind and towards the land. It was bitterly cold during the night and the six or seven bottles of whisky which were in the boat were passed round; I myself only had a mouthful, but unfortunately some of the men drank a great deal of spirits, several of the older men fell asleep and died during the night. In fact, most of the men who drank the whisky died in their sleep that night. We put their bodies over the side of the boat without removing their clothes.'

Providentially, Rowlands' boat was well provisioned, having on board, in addition to the usual ship's biscuits and tins of condensed milk, tins of pemmican – a high protein meat paste – Horlicks malted milk tablets, chocolate and chewing gum, all in ample supply. However, much of this turned out to be of little use. In the extremely low temperature, the milk was frozen in the tins, likewise the pemmican, and the hands of the survivors were so numb with cold that they were unable to get the food out of the tins. It was fortunate that none of them were yet really hungry, and they got by with the Horlicks tablets, chocolate and the occasional dry biscuit. What they all craved most was water to drink and this was a serious problem. The fresh water on board, carried in wooden breakers, or barrels, in the bottom of the boat, was frozen solid, and the only way to get at it was to break open the barrels with an axe and chip off pieces of ice to suck. Inevitably, the ice became contaminated by the salt water sloshing about in the bottom of the boat, and only served to increase their thirst.

They continued sailing, sometimes taking to the oars to

generate some warmth in their bodies, but this turned into a pointless exercise, their limbs being too numb to make more than a pretence at rowing. In an effort to create some shelter from the wind and waves, Rowlands cajoled the more active into rigging an improvised windbreak using the main sail, but this had little effect. The elements continued to exact a steady toll. On the first night, seven men had died, lulled by the whisky into giving up the fight, and from then on one or two slipped away each day and were tipped over the side without ceremony. Most of those who lived on were in a pitiful state, having frostbite in their hands and feet. The boat was now leaking and slowly filling, piling on them the ultimate agony of being forced to sit with their feet and lower legs immersed in icy water. Rowlands rallied those who were still able to move into baling and pumping out with the bilge pump, thereby, perhaps, helping to keep some of them alive. The battle was hard fought, but at last they managed to halt the rise of the water, but even so, four more men died that night.

Rowlands' estimate of a landfall within twenty-four hours proved to be wildly optimistic and, when the sun went down on 2 April, the seventeen men then left alive in the boat were at the end of their tether. Only their indomitable leader was still hoping for a miracle and even he began to lose heart with the long Arctic twilight closed in around them that evening. A little later, when Rowlands saw a light flash briefly in the gathering gloom ahead, he was prepared to accept that this was the first delirium preceding death. Then the light flashed again and again, and his navigation-trained subconscious began to count the interval between flashes. It gradually dawned on him that the pattern was regular. This was no figment of his tortured imagination, not even a bobbing fishing boat; it was a lighthouse. They had found the land.

Filled with a new hope of living, the survivors took up the oars again, even the badly frostbitten lending a willing hand. But although they rowed until they were exhausted, they realized they were making no progress towards the land. In Rowlands' estimation, the light was no more than four miles away but in their weakened state there seemed to be no hope of them ever reaching shore. The darkness was closing in fast and when that came it would be the end. They would not live to see another dawn.

When deliverance came – and only a few minutes later – it came not from the land or the sea, but from the air. Three aircraft, presumed to be Russian, appeared in the south, flying low. Summoning up their last reserves of strength, the survivors stood up in the boat and shouted and waved frantically. Rowlands fumbled the flares out of the locker, but they were all sodden and useless. He then resorted to waving the signal flag. To the immense relief of all in the boat, their signals were seen and the planes circled them three times before flying off towards the land. Half an hour later, at 20.00 on Thursday 2 April 1942, a date that would be forever etched in the memories of this pitiful band of survivors, a Russian minesweeper found them.

The minesweeper came alongside the drifting lifeboat and the seventeen men, too weak to climb the bulwarks, were lifted aboard. They were taken to a warm mess room, stripped of their wet clothing, wrapped in thick woollen coats and revived with coffee and vodka, the sweetest nectar they had ever tasted. Then they slept so soundly that even an attack by a German aircraft failed to disturb them.

The lighthouse Evan Rowlands had seen from the boat was on Cape Swiatoi Nos, on the eastern shore of the entrance to the Kola Inlet and in its vicinity the Russians also found the *Induna*'s other lifeboat. It contained only nine men, two DEMS gunners, one fireman, a steward's boy and five *Ballot* survivors. They had a sad tale to tell.

When the boat was launched, they had attempted to hold it alongside the ship with the intention of taking off those still on board. This proved impossible, for the rough sea running threatened to smash the boat against the ship's side and they were forced to stand off again. They then took the boat around the stern of the *Induna* to check that the other lifeboat had got away but, as they were rounding the stern, *U-376*'s second torpedo struck. They sheered away from the ship and as they did so they saw a group of men at the forward end of the boat deck, among them Captain Collins, who were attempting to launch the jolly boat. The falls of the boat appeared to be fouled or frozen and they were having great difficulty in lowering away. At that point the *Induna* started to take her last plunge and the occupants of the boat were obliged to row for their lives to avoid being sucked down with her. When the ship was gone, they searched the area for survivors, but found none.

The Russian minesweeper landed the *Induna*'s survivors in Murmansk on the morning of 3 April, where they were taken into hospital. When the final roll was called, it showed that of the *Induna*'s total complement of sixty-six, forty were dead or missing, including Captain William Collins and Chief Officer George Brown. The steward's boy, eighteen-year-old Aurele Boudreau, a Canadian and one of the *Ballot*'s crew died of exposure shortly after landing, bringing the death toll of those who had left the Panamanian ship, thinking they would be safer elsewhere, to five. Of the others, six men who were fit enough, were sent home on the next available ship while the remaining seventeen, all suffering from frostbite in varying degrees, were to endure weeks in the Russian hospital which was reminiscent of something out of the Crimean War. The Russian doctors and nurses were dedicated and professional, but their resources were totally inadequate. The front, only thirty miles from Murmansk, where the Russians were taking fearful casualties, had first demand on drugs and medicines, leaving very little for the needs of foreign seamen. Frostbitten limbs turned gangrenous and were amputated, often without the benefit of anaesthetic, for the simple reason that none was available. Twenty-two-year-old William Short, *Induna*'s Fourth Engineer, with frostbite in both legs, would never forget the agonies he endured: 'Someone said in hesitant English, "We're going to cut your legs off", and they went ahead and did it. As soon as the knife hit me, I passed out, and I was delirious for three days.'

When, six months later, the legless engineer returned to his home in Scotland, two letters awaited him; one from his employers informing him that his pay had stopped when the *Induna* went down, the other from HM Inspector of Taxes, demanding payment of tax due.

In contrast to the deplorable bad luck that dogged the *Induna* after the attack by Ju88s on the 28th, fortune smiled on the Panama-flag *Ballot*. The bombing had created havoc in her engine room, listed by Chief Engineer A.M. Lalor as:

Main condenser discharge pipe broken; the fixes of both generators broken; oil pump valve chest broken; fuel line to settler tanks
broken; starboard steam piston of steering engine broken and rod
bent; sanitary pump water cylinder box broken; low pressure
eccentric water pan broken; starboard side fan broken; electric
installations to steering engine and engine room out of order; steam
and water pipes broken and ship is leaking in fire room port side.

This was a catalogue of repairs to daunt any ship's engineer, but
Lalor and his men wasted no time on bemoaning their lot. Lives
were at stake. By 14.00, less than two hours after she was
bombed, the *Ballot* was under way again and, following instructions given in a sealed envelope on board for such an occasion,
Captain Bejer made directly for Murmansk. Steering an erratic
course with her emergency gear, but making full sea speed, she
arrived off the Kola Inlet in the early hours of the morning of the
30th. But Bejer's troubles were not all over. The dawn brought
with it a rising wind and sea and the *Ballot* became more and
more difficult to steer. Three times Bejer tried to enter the inlet,
but each time he was frustrated by the short, steep seas on the
quarter, which continually pushed the *Ballot* off course.

Bejer was short-handed and those men he had on board had
been without sleep for two days and were nearing the point of
exhaustion. His ship would not steer and there were unmarked
minefields in the area so he decided to go back out to sea. At
07.30, as Bejer was attempting to turn the ship around, she
broached to in the heavy seas and her starboard lifeboat was
smashed. This was the last straw for Bejer and, realizing it would
be folly to return to the open sea with insufficient lifeboats on
board, he determined to reach Murmansk at all costs minefields
or no minefields. Lurching from side to side as her helmsman tried
to hold her on course, the *Ballot* crabbed her way towards the
Murmansk pilot station, arriving there at 10.00 that morning.
The Russian pilot, seeing the erratic steering of the ship as she
approached, refused to take her into the buoyed channel without
the aid of tugs, and there was a further delay while they were sent
for. The *Ballot* anchored off Murmansk late that afternoon, the
first merchant ship of PQ 13 to reach her destination.

*

The *Ballot*'s fellow American, Lykes Lines' *Effingham*, did not have the same easy run. Having extracted his ship from the ice on the afternoon of the 29th, leaving the *Induna* and *Silja* still trapped, Captain Charles Hewlett decided the time had come to look after his own. The *Effingham* was carrying explosives in three of her five holds, making her the equivalent of a large floating bomb, and Hewlett was not about to take any more risks than necessary. Ringing for full speed, he set course for the Kola Inlet. In doing so, he ran straight into the arms of *Kapitänleutnant* Siegfried Stretlow who, in *U-435*, was also waiting to pick off any strays from PQ 13.

At 10.30 on the morning of the 30th, the *Effingham* was ninety miles from the Kola Inlet, and running before a howling northerly gale, when Strelow's first torpedo blew a hole in her port side in way of her No.4 hold. As luck would have it, there were no explosives stowed in No.4 and, although the ship started to go down by the stern at once, there was time for her crew to take to the boats. The *Effingham*, stopped in the water and drifting beam on to the sea and swell, was rolling heavily but, showing great seamanship, Bejer and his men lowered the boats and rowed clear. As they pulled away from the ship, they realized that in the confusion they had left two men behind, but there was no going back. The unfortunate two lost their lives when Strelow delivered the *coup de grâce* with a second torpedo, this one going home in one of the holds containing ammunition. The *Effingham* was blown apart.

As with the *Induna* survivors, the men of the *Effingham* endured a long nightmare at the mercy of the cruel Arctic weather. Cold, wet, tortured by frostbite and despairing for their lives, they sailed south before the gale, fighting to keep their tiny craft on course, but help was at hand for them. The SBNO in Murmansk, by now aware of the savaging of the eastern section of PQ 13 by the waiting U-boats, had sent out the minesweepers *Harrier*, *Speedwell* and *Hussar* to search for survivors. At 18.30 on the 31st, during a clearance in the snow squalls, *Harrier* sighted a red sail which turned out to be the *Effingham*'s No.1 lifeboat, containing Captain Hewlett, his chief officer and fifteen other survivors. For thirty-two hours these men had fought a desperate battle for survival against the most fearful odds. Six of their shipmates died along the way. Taken aboard the *Harrier*, the men were thawed out and given hot food, but for one of their number it was too late. He died on the way in to Murmansk.

The *Effingham*'s No.3 boat which had originally contained her Second Officer and eighteen crew, went through a similar long ordeal. When their boat was finally found by a Russian patrol boat on the morning of 1 April, four men had succumbed to the dreadful weather conditions.

The remaining ships of PQ 13's eastern group, the *Dunboyne*, *Empire Starlight* and *Mana*, having cleared the ice on the afternoon of the 19th, had a relatively trouble-free run into the Kola Inlet, arriving unmolested late on the 30th. They were followed in by the missing commodore's ship *River Afton*. Having become unmanageable when the gale first blew up on the 24th, and ending up off the Lofoten Islands, the *River Afton* had a remarkable, if nerve-racking passage to Murmansk, being pursued for much of the way by a U-boat on the surface.

PQ 13's western group, the *Empire Cowper*, *New Westminster City*, *Scottish American*, *Eldena*, *El Estero*, *Gallant Fox*, *Mormacmar* and *Tobruk*, joined by the bomb-damaged *Harpalion*, also entered the Kola Inlet late on the 30th. Escorted by the destroyer *Oribi*, the trawler *Paynter*, the whaler *Sumba*, and the two Russian destroyers *Sokrushitelni* and *Gremyashchi*, they had been attacked by German bombers as they approached the inlet, but the combined firepower of the ships had driven the Germans off, the *Tobruk* claiming to have shot down two of their number. This last desperate battle for the convoy had unfortunate repercussions for the New York-registered *Mormacmar* and soured her welcome to Russia. At the height of the attack, her Armed Guard gunners found themselves running out of ammunition and broke into the cargo to replenish their guns. On arrival in Murmansk, the Soviet authorities demanded that the *Mormacmar*'s gunners be court martialed for 'stealing ammunition belonging to the Soviet Union'. It required the intervention of the US Consul to halt this ludicrous farce.

Last into Murmansk was the little *Silja*, which had broken free of the ice, but again run out of fuel. She was found drifting late on the 30th by HMS *Oribi*, which had been sent out to search for her. The whaler, none the worse for wear, was towed into the Kola Inlet by HMS *Harrier*.

PQ 13 was the first of the convoys to be savaged on the road to Russia, being called upon to fight off the combined might of the German air force, surface fleet and U-boats. Five merchant-men, the *Raceland, Empire Ranger, Bateau, Induna* and *Effingham* had fallen on the way with the loss of 101 lives. The cruiser *Trinidad* and the destroyer *Eclipse* had been damaged, the *Trinidad* very seriously, and between them had lost nineteen men. The toll exacted by the enemy had been high but it was a battle well fought; however, a battle not yet over for the merchant ships that reached port. For them there were more horrors to come.

Chapter Six

In 1942, the Union of Soviet Socialist Republics, for all that it stretched from the frigid waters of the Arctic south to the Black Sea, and from the Baltic eastwards to the Pacific, had very few deep water ports of any account. When war came with Germany in the summer of 1941, the Black Sea became inaccessible, and when Japan attacked Pearl Harbour at the close of that year, Vladivostock was closed. Allied ships still had access to the Persian Gulf and the port of Khorramshar, the southern terminus of the Trans-Iranian Railway, but for military supplies coming from Britain and America this involved a 12,000-mile haul around the Cape, followed by another 2000-mile journey overland by rail. This was not a practical proposition. That left only the two ports in the north, Murmansk and Archangel in the Barents Sea. But with Archangel iced up from late November through to the end of May, Murmansk would necessarily have to handle the bulk of the cargoes. Unfortunately, apart from its ice-free status, Murmansk was the worst possible option for Allied ships to be left with.

Murmansk, which lays claim to be the world's largest city north of the Arctic Circle, lies thirty miles inland from the Barents Sea on the estuary of the Kola river. Up until the late 1920s, it was no more than a large fishing port, a collection of ramshackle wooden buildings huddled around a few even more dilapidated wharves and without land communications to the rest of the Soviet Union. Then, when the fervour of the revolution had died down, Moscow decided, with commendable insight as it turned out, that Murmansk was to be Russia's all-year-round port in the north. The railway was brought in, the town extended, largely wooden buildings again, and some new quays were built, also in wood. The cement of the day was very unstable in the Arctic conditions and, if nothing else, Russia had a vast surplus of timber.

The Second World War put an end to Moscow's plans for Murmansk to become the Liverpool of the north and in 1942 the facilities offered by the port for ocean-going cargo ships were severely limited. There were only four quays suitable for discharging cargo and they were capable of handling only five or six ships at a time between them. There were no cranes or mechanical equipment. The naval base and the commercial port, where the merchant ships discharged, were on opposite sides of the Kola Inlet and communications between the two were a major problem. The Russian telephone service was primitive and more often than not out of order, and for many months of the year the roads were made impassable by snow. Likewise, fog and gales in the inlet made contact by boat impossible. A solution of sorts was found by the Senior British Naval Officer, who kept a minesweeper permanently alongside at Murmansk as a W/T link, and in winter a trawler was used as a dispatch boat to maintain contact with ships in the anchorage. This was an expensive deployment of two naval ships needed elsewhere, but there was no alternative.

As for the organization of the port, this was a sad victim of Soviet bureaucracy. In the words of one British observer there was, 'A general lack of organisation which had to be seen to be believed, coupled with the absence of anything approaching a spirit of teamwork, which could not fail to exasperate the Allied missions which had been sent to assist with the unloading of the ships'. Imposed on top of this, and dominating all else, was the climate which was hardly conducive to fast turn-rounds. Winter in Murmansk takes up most of the year, with snow falling from September to June and, at the height of this grim season, from November to February, the sun is hardly ever seen above the horizon. The temperature then falls to around 10°F – that is 22° of frost – to which must be added an ever-present wind-chill factor.

The advantages offered by the port of Murmansk are at any

time few but in 1942 it was certainly one of the least desirable places on earth to be. The outskirts of Murmansk were then only thirty miles from the front, and only fifty miles – not more than twenty minutes flying time – from the German air bases in northern Norway, where the Luftwaffe had some 350 aircraft on the ground. There were times – all too often – when Murmansk resembled a snow fringed *Dante's Inferno*.

When the surviving ships of PQ 13 dribbled in past the bleak headlands of the Kola Inlet looking for their pilots, Murmansk was enjoying one of its rare quiet spells. This came to an abrupt end on 3 April, less than forty-eight hours after the last ship found her berth.

Reardon Smith's *New Westminster City*, commanded by Captain William Harris, both ship and master veterans of Operation 'Dervish', found a berth alongside the Fish Quay, a ramshackle wooden construction at the southern end of the port and some way from the town. The discharge of her eagerly awaited cargo had commenced within hours of her berthing and despite sporadic air raids on Murmansk, had proceeded without serious interruption. The evening of the 3rd was fine and still with no drone of approaching bombers to be heard and even the rumble of the guns at the front seemed to have subsided. With cargo work finished for the day, Chief Officer S.A. Galer, not having set foot on dry land for over a month, decided to explore Murmansk. With him went Chief Engineer C.S. A'Court and Third Officer Peter Kavanagh.

The three men were not impressed with what they saw when they walked the rubble-strewn streets of Murmansk. They found it to be a depressing place, inhabited by drab, grey people who showed no inclination to fraternize with visiting British seamen, despite the fact that these men had been through several kinds of hell to bring them the means of defending themselves. This was perhaps not surprising, in that these people were so cowed by their rulers that they were afraid to associate with these strangers who came from the capitalist world which was to communism, like daylight to Count Dracula. After an hour or so of pointless wandering in the bomb-damaged streets, and with the sun going down and the temperature plummeting, Galer suggested they return to the ship.

On their way back to the docks, the air raid sirens wailed and the three officers quickened their steps, anxious to return to their ship. They had not gone many yards when they were stopped by patrolling Russian soldiers and, on pain of being shot, were forced to take cover in a doorway. There they stayed for a while listening to the bombs coming down, but the need for Galer and A'Court, as senior officers, to be with their ship soon got the better of their patience. With the soldiers out of sight, they ventured out and set off for the docks at a brisk pace. It was now 7 o'clock in the evening, and the long twilight was setting in. As they trotted down the hill towards the Fish Quay, they had a grandstand view of the raid, which was clearly concentrated on the dock area. The twin-engined bombers – Galer identified them as Ju88s, with which he had become all too familiar with during the voyage out – were coming in in pairs, approaching from the hills to the east in a shallow dive and flattening out over the harbour for their bombing run. The defence put up by the Russian anti-aircraft batteries and the guns of the ships was spectacular, the bursting shells and curving lines of tracer turning the darkening sky into a gigantic firework display.

As they watched in awe, dazzled by the brilliant pyrotechnics, the three men heard a loud explosion which came from the direction of the Fish Quay where their ship was moored. Fearing the worst, they ran headlong down the hill. When they rounded the corner at the bottom of the hill, their worst fears were realized. The *New Westminster City* was on fire and swinging away from the quay.

Galer was first to reach the quay where he found other crew members who told him that when the ship was hit Captain Harris ordered them all ashore, leaving only himself and an injured DEMS gunner on board. When they were ashore, he had then called to them to let go the ropes to allow the ship to drift off the quay. This they had all but finished doing.

Harris' motives for attempting to get the burning ship away from the wooden quay might have been commendable but he had left himself with no men to tackle the fire. Luckily, one stern rope still remained to be let go. Galer ordered this to be left, and when the rope became taut, the ship swung back onto the quay. As she came alongside again Galer leapt aboard, calling for volunteers to follow him.

The crew of the *New Westminster City* followed their chief officer aboard to a man and they were also joined by some Russian volunteers. While fire fighting parties were being organized, Harris told of the attack on the ship. Two German bombers had acted in concert, the first one flying over the ship at about 500 feet, drawing the fire of the *Westminster*'s guns. Viewed dispassionately, this was a brave thing to do, for the British ship was armed with a 12-pounder, two 20-mm Oerlikons, two twin Marlins and PAC rockets. All of these opened up to good effect, the PACs being fired by Harris from the bridge. However, while the guns were concentrating on the first plane, the second slipped in unnoticed and dropped six bombs from low level. One hit the quay, one hit the *Empire Starlight* moored directly astern and the others scored hits on the *Westminster*. Of these, one glanced off the bridge and exploded in No.2 hold which contained, amongst other cargo, a large quantity of ammunition. The second hit the base of the funnel, the third exploded on top of the engine room and the fourth also landed in No.2 hold, probably without exploding. This hold was now well on fire. As a result of the first bomb, the gunner on the starboard bridge Oerlikon was blown out of his gunpit onto the quay. He was badly bruised but able to return on board. The gunners manning the twin Marlins, Able Seamen J. Connelly and H. Bottomley, did not have his luck, both being killed by flying bomb splinters.

By the time Harris and Galer had their firefighters in action, the bridge accommodation, Nos. 1 and 2 holds and the midships bunkers were all well ablaze. It was decided to concentrate maximum effort on No.1 hold, which also contained ammunition, and then work aft. Galer organized seven fire hoses which poured water into the hold and the fire was soon brought under control. While this was being done, Second Engineer Hughes, taking his life in his hands, went below into the engine room which was in complete darkness, and opened the valves to flood No.2 hold. Then, with the help of four Russian fire floats now alongside, the fire in the fore part of the ship was tackled from all sides.

It was not a job for the faint of heart; the ammunition in No.2

hold was now on fire and exploding, while the air was full of burning debris blown on the wind. There were times when the men on the hoses were forced to take cover, but largely showing a complete disregard for their own lives, they fought on, concentrating on the forward holds. It was a race to subdue the fires before they caused a catastrophic explosion in the ammunition and, while this was on, the bridge and its accommodation must be left to burn.

By one o'clock on the morning of the 4th, the back of the fire in the holds had been broken, but as the risk of an explosion in the cargo was still very real, Harris decided to send those crew members not actively engaged in fighting the fires along to the *Empire Starlight*, lying on the next berth astern. There, he hoped they would be at least be able to get hot food and perhaps some sleep. Captain William Stein welcomed them aboard, but he could not offer them a lot, having his own battle to fight. A stick of German bombs had started a fire in the *Empire Starlight*'s No.2 hold which contained, amongst other cargo, a consignment of irreplaceable Hurricane fighters. It was imperative that these aircraft be saved.

Meanwhile, back on board the *New Westminster City*, the fight to extinguish the fires below decks went on. Fire parties led by Captain Harris, Chief Officer Galer, Second Officer Larky and Third Officer Kavanagh were deep in No.2 hold and had reached the seat of the fire. Their hoses, combined with flooding through the bilges lines from the engine room, finally brought results and by 03.00 on the 4th the fire was out. The victory had not been won cheaply, however. There was by now so much water in the holds that the ship was sitting on the bottom forward and leaning on the quay. At this point, Harris and Galer, exhausted, their faces blackened by smoke, toured the ship to assess the damage. They were appalled by what they saw. The bridge and midships accommodation were both completely gutted and further aft the engineers' and petty officers' cabins had escaped the fire, but were so badly riddled with holes made by bomb splinters as to be uninhabitable. The only living space left intact was that occupied by the DEMS gunners under the poop. It was quite evident that apart from the damage in her holds, the *New Westminster City* was very badly knocked about but, in the opinion of Harris and Galer, she was still worth saving. That much decided, they and as many of the fire parties who could find room retired to the gunners' accommodation to snatch a few hours sleep. Tomorrow was another day.

The battle to cripple Murmansk from the air went on and the *Empire Starlight* was in the thick of it. After the raid of the night of 3 April, in which her gunners were credited with shooting down a German bomber, she remained alongside the Fish Quay and continued discharging her cargo. Throughout this work the raids went on, bombs falling day and night with very little respite. The stress on her crew, who refused to leave her, was considerable but although many bombs fell close to the ship, she escaped further damage and by the morning of the 7th all her cargo was ashore, a remarkable achievement under very difficult circumstances.

On 9 April, the *Empire Starlight* was moved to an anchorage in the Roads where, away from the main target of the bombers, she enjoyed a relatively quiet spell while her damage was repaired. Her crew had hoped they would then be able to say goodbye to this war-torn port, but they were disappointed. While most ships returned from Murmansk to the west in ballast, there were occasions when the Russians had something to offer in return for the military supplies brought in and this happened to be one of them. The *Empire Starlight* was chosen to load a cargo of ore and timber for British ports and on 13th she was given a berth in the commercial port which put her back in the heart of the war.

The incessant bombardment from the air went on, with the *Empire Starlight*'s steam winches lifting aboard slings of cargo between raids. It was slow work, a few slings in, then man the guns, and when the bombers had gone, back to the cargo. Her twelve DEMS gunners, led by Chief Officer J. Booth, who was also gunnery officer, in the words of Captain Stein, 'Behaved magnificently throughout and fought their guns with great gallantry and efficiency'. But, for all the gallant fight she put up, the enemy put another bomb into the *Empire Starlight*'s No.2 hold during a particularly heavy raid on the port. This time there was very little cargo in the bottom of the hold to absorb the blast and the damage was severe. The hull was breached and the sea poured in, flooding the hold. A suction pipe passing through

No.2 to the fore peak tank was fractured and soon the fore peak was also flooded. The bombs continued to rain down and concussion from near misses fractured more pipes and opened up cracks in the watertight bulkheads, leading to flooding in Nos.1 and 3 holds and the engine room. The *Empire Starlight* was in danger of sinking at her berth until divers were sent down to plug the leaks in her hull. Only then were the ship's pumps able to lower the level of water in her holds.

On the 16th, the *Empire Starlight* was moved to an isolated anchorage off the Mishukov shore, where it was hoped she would be left in peace to lick her wounds. This was not to be. The Ju88s soon sought her out again, using their usual tactic of sending in a decoy to draw the fire of the guns while a second plane came in with the bombs. As always, the *Empire Starlight*'s gunners fought back with great determination and skill, shooting down at least one Ju88 and forcing others to miss with their bombs. But the strain of these unrelenting attacks was beginning to tell on Captain Stein, his officers and gunners, who were sharing most of the burden. Although the *Empire Starlight* carried a total crew of seventy-six, fifty-one of these were Chinese ratings, who had gone to pieces under the bombing and were playing no part in the defence of their ship.

There were more heavy attacks on the 23rd and 24th, in which the *Empire Starlight* sustained no damage, but on the 25th she was straddled by six bombs with disastrous results. Her shell plating in way of No.4 hold was set in, resulting in the watertight bulkhead between that hold and No.5 being buckled, while the leaks in No.1 and No.3 holds were opened up again and water poured in. It was only by the superhuman efforts of Chief Engineer B. Morgan and his officers, who plugged leaks and kept the pumps running, that the ship stayed afloat. They fought a long drawn out battle, more often than not under bombardment from the air but finally, on 17 May, with the level of water in her holds rising once more, the *Empire Starlight* was moved to an anchorage above the town where the water was shallower. The port authorities no longer had any confidence in her ability to stay afloat.

Meanwhile, with the weather improving and the daylight hours extending, the frequency of the German air raids was rising to a crescendo, the bombers coming over often six or seven times a day. On the 24th, three bombs fell close astern of the *Empire Starlight* and the resulting triple explosion fractured the plating of her propeller shaft tunnel. Next day, six more bombs, again all near-misses, cracked the watertight bulkhead between the forward holds. Nos. 1 and 2 holds began to flood and no matter how hard the pumps worked, they were unable to hold the water at bay. The *Empire Starlight* was losing her fight to stay afloat.

The final blow was delivered on 26 May, a day on which the raids were so frequent that they all but merged into one long continuous attack. To Captain William Stein it seemed that his poor crippled ship had been singled out by the Germans for the severest punishment. During the twenty-four hours, a total of forty bombs rained down on the *Empire Starlight*. And yet she seemed to bear a charmed life, for she received no direct hits, but the continuous concussion of the bursting bombs opened up so many leaks in her hull that she began to settle by the head.

The ultimate indignity was heaped on this gallant ship next day, when the Sea Transport Officer, the British naval officer in charge of cargo operations, ordered the ship to be abandoned. Reluctantly, William Stein, his thirteen officers and fourteen DEMS gunners left the *Empire Starlight*. She was then moved by tugs to a lay-by berth, a berth which was to be her graveyard. There, on 1 June, the deserted ship was hit by a stick of six bombs and that evening she settled on the bottom with her decks awash. It was a sad end to a very brave ship, but even in her death throes, the *Empire Starlight* had the satisfaction of seeing another of her tormentors shot down to crash close alongside her.

The *Empire Starlight*, in addition to having survived the outward passage, had been under almost continuous attack in Murmansk for eight weeks. When the smoke of battle had cleared, Captain Stein had to say of his officers and gunners, who had fought so hard and so long to save their ship:

James, the senior gunlayer, was outstanding in his efficiency and behaviour. He remained in charge of the guns the whole time and by his cool manner and leadership inspired the guns' crews throughout the many and long attacks with never a thought for his own safety.

All the gunners behaved magnificently throughout and fought their guns with great gallantry and efficiency, damaging and probably bringing down at least two enemy aircraft. Gunner Bowdley was particularly outstanding and fought his Oerlikon gun through every attack with a coolness that was magnificent.

The fourth engineer, Walford, was also particularly outstanding and rendered valuable assistance throughout. He was particularly outstanding in fighting the fires and went into No.2 hold when that part of the ship caught fire. Chief Engineer Morgan was also outstanding; his organisation and efficiency was of the utmost value. After the second bomb hit the ship he went into the engine room, plugged up the many holes and attended to the pumps throughout the difficult pumping operations.

I would further mention the excellent and strenuous work of all my officers.

Chief Officer Booth is a very keen gunnery officer and throughout the whole period he attended to the guns and as Chief Executive Officer took a leading part in dealing with the fires caused by the bombs, etc.

Second Officer Keir was in charge of the fire parties and also assisted at the guns and displayed great courage and keenness in dealing with the fires.

Third Officer Cook was also of great assistance throughout, assisting at the guns and taking charge of fire parties.

I would also mention that the Russian authorities recommended the very gallant conduct of my gunners. During a heavy attack on the town a large air raid shelter received a direct hit and all my gunners assisted the Russian authorities to clear the wounded and to find other shelters for those who were uninjured.

For his Chinese ratings Captain Stein had no praise to offer. They had taken no part in the defence of their ship, spending most of their time ashore cowering in air raid shelters. Given consideration now, their actions were not too surprising. These men were in a very alien country, a long way from home and they must have been confused by all the horrors happening around them. It was not their war, after all. Ironically, the only fatal casualty amongst the *Empire Starlight*'s crew in her long ordeal was one of their number, killed in an air raid shelter which received a direct hit.

During the early days of her stay in Murmansk, the *Empire Starlight*, hard-pressed though she was, had also given temporary shelter to the crew of another British ship, the *Lancaster Castle*. Owned by the Lancashire Shipping Company and commanded by Captain J. Sloan, the 5172-ton *Lancaster Castle* had arrived in Murmansk on 4 February, having had a clear run through from Iceland with Convoy PQ 12. She had discharged her cargo of military stores, but she was another of those unfortunate enough to be chosen to prolong her stay by loading cargo for home. As with the *Empire Starlight*, this proved to be tempting providence too far. On 24 March, when she was alongside in the commercial port loading magnetite ore, German bombers came over in a sneak attack and before the *Lancaster Castle* was able to man her guns, she was straddled by a stick of four bombs, one of which scored a direct hit on her engine room. The main engine and most of the auxiliaries were badly damaged and ten firemen working below at the time were killed.

As the *Lancaster Castle* was now immobilized and it was not yet known whether her engines were repairable, loading was suspended and she was moved to a quiet anchorage a mile upstream from the wharves. There she lay unmolested for the next two weeks while the newly arrived ships of PQ 13 were being pounded day and night by the Ju88s. Her charmed life ended abruptly on the afternoon of 14 April when a formation of nine German bombers intent on attacking the commercial port were engaged by Russian fighters. Two of the bombers got through to the port but the other seven, frustrated in their main object, turned their wrath on the *Lancaster Castle*.

The *Lancaster Castle*'s single Oerlikon had been knocked out when she was first bombed but her gunners now manned her Marlin and Lewis machine guns, getting off a total of fifty rounds before the world around them went mad. The frustrated bombers dumped their bombs on the anchored ship, scoring five direct hits. One bomb completely wrecked her accommodation, while the other four penetrated her Nos. 1, 2 and 3 holds, exploding with such force that they blew the bottom out of the ship. She sank within minutes, fortunately settling on the bottom before her decks were completely awash. The lifeboats were lowered and her crew abandoned ship in good order. They returned on board later but there was nothing they could do to save her.

Second Officer T. Jones, of the *Lancaster Castle*, reported: 'At

Murmansk there was not sufficient hospital accommodation for the large number of casualties and survivors'. His complaint was not without justification. There was only one hospital in Murmansk, which had to deal not only with the massive number of civilian casualties caused by the heavy bombing, but also the influx of survivors from ships attacked when attempting to reach the port. Many of the latter were suffering from severe frostbite and needed surgery or amputations. The hospital was under-staffed, its equipment was primitive, drugs were in short supply and anaesthetic was at a premium. For men who had gone through hellfire at sea to bring succour to these people, to have their frostbitten limbs amputated without the benefit of anaes-thetic must have been the final indignity. And yet, for some perverse and probably political reason, the Soviet authorities steadfastly refused to allow a British hospital to be set up ashore. It was only after heavy pressure from the Admiralty that a seventy-four-bed naval hospital was finally opened at Vaenga, but it was not long before the Party bureaucrats laid their dead hands on this. In September 1942, Winston Churchill had occasion to write to Foreign Minister Vyacheslav Molotov as follows:

> The Foreign Minister tells me that he has sent you a message about the British naval Hospital at Vaenga being ordered to close and go home. I should be glad if you would look into the matter personally yourself. Terrible cases of mutilation through frostbite are now arriving back here, and I have to consider constantly the morale of the merchant seamen, who have hitherto gone so willingly to man the merchant ships to Russia. The British hospital unit was sent simply to help, and implied no reflection on Russian arrangements under the pressure of air bombardment, etc. It is hard on men in hospital not to have nurses who speak their own language. At any rate, I hope you will give me some solid reason which I can give should the matter be raised in Parliament, as it very likely will be.

Molotov, in answering Churchill's forceful but diplomatic note, was evasive, and even hinted at 'irregularities in the actions of the respective British naval authorities', but the hospital stayed and many lives were saved and the suffering of the injured made more bearable.

*

The *New Westminster City*, *Empire Starlight* and *Lancaster Castle*, along with many others, were left abandoned sitting on the bottom of Murmansk harbour, grim monuments to the brave men who had striven so hard to bring them to this foreign shore and then defend them to the end. In this common cause, twelve of their number had given their lives and an equal number suffered serious injuries.

Meanwhile, as spring turned to summer and the hours of daylight increased further, so the Luftwaffe's bombardment of Murmansk intensified. The British tanker *Hopemount*, which arrived with Convoy PQ 14, recorded 132 separate attacks during the two months she lay in the port. A report by Captain Hendrik Stuy, master of the Dutch vessel *Pieter de Hoogh*, also with PQ 14, gives an idea of the situation prevailing while his ship was loading to return to the United Kingdom:

16 April: Shifted to the jetty and started loading at 0600. Alongside the quay was the British s.s. *Dover Hill*, which had an unexploded bomb in her bunkers, probably from the same plane we gave hell on April 13. This bomb had to be dug out from under the coal, which the crew did. Up to six times the coal shifted back upon the bomb. Eventually it was disposed of.

19 April: Air raid towards noon. In the afternoon a Russian ship with quite a list was towed from the river to the port, bridge, cabins and hull were heavily damaged by a bomb explosion.

22 April: Air raid from 0145 to 0220. Several bombs down in the harbour.

23 April: Shifted from quay to anchorage near Mishikoff.

25 April: Air raid from 0300 to 0345. High level. Air raid from 1140 to 1300. Dogfights at high altitudes.

28 April: Air raids from 1820 to 1900.

29 April: Air raid from 0245 to 0340, from 1140 to 1220, from 1235 to 1320, and various raids until 1430.

30 April: Air raid from 0410 to 0450 and from 1050 to 1130.

5 May: Air raid from 0400 to 0540. This was a surprise attack and about ten bombs fell at a rather short distance from the ship in the water. More bombs were dropped.

6 May: Air raids from 1330 to 1405, from 1540 to 1630 some bombs near the ship, from 1730 to 2100.

7 May: Air raid from 0445 to 0530. Dogfights. Air raid from 1725 to 1745 and 2050 to 2100.

8 May: Air raids from 0725 to 0750, 1000 to 1015, 1210 to 1240. Received orders to sail for Archangel. Started weighing anchor at 1430. Air raid from 1430 to 1450. Another air raid while leaving Kola Inlet 1645 to 1730.

In the relative peace of Archangel, far from the front, the *Pieter de Hoogh* settled down to a more normal routine:

11 May: Anchored at 0500. In Molotovsk a very quiet time. Anchored with five American ships, the *Thomas Hartley, Beacon Hill, Israel Putnam, Frances Scott Key* and *City of Omaha*, and make life for each other as comfortable as possible. Have chess and card evenings. And once in a while on *Pieter*. Have formed a club, 'The Forgotten Convoy of North Russia', the membership of which is a 50 Rouble note with the signatures of the other members which we should always keep on us at a fine of 10 Roubles. On Monday and Thursday night to the village to see a movie, dancing afterwards with the 'local belles'. Also football, baseball and boxing games.

Such were the simple pleasures of the seamen who risked life and limb to bring succour to Russia.

Chapter Seven

Eventually, for those who had survived Murmansk, discharged their outward cargoes and, perhaps, loaded anything on offer, there came a time to go home. It would not be a journey without terrible risks, but it was infinitely preferable to being trapped within the confines of this grim, beleaguered port that reeked of fire and death. Away from the land, out on the ice-fringed waters of the Barents Sea, there were blizzards and fog and howling gales, but out there they could dodge and run, meet the enemy on their own ground.

Commander P.Q. Edwards had given his initials to the Russia-bound convoys and it was appropriate that the letters PQ were reversed for the returning ships. The QP convoys, consisting as they did mainly of ships in ballast, were always considered to stand a better chance of getting through intact. Flying light, the ships could make more speed, were more manoeuvrable, and it was a fact that the German bombers and U-boats, their priority being sinking cargoes to Russia, were unlikely to be much concerned with them. For the war-weary men manning the ships, the westward voyage was a welcome breathing space at a time when things were not going well for the Allies. The Japanese, hitherto regarded as a myopic race of little account, had swept through the East like a forest fire borne on a gale-force wind; the Pacific islands had fallen like ninepins, Hong Kong, Singapore, all of Malaya and the Dutch East Indies were all gone. The combined British, Dutch and United States fleet had been wiped out in the Java Sea; India and Ceylon were under threat and Admiral Somerville's Eastern Fleet was in complete disarray. In the Western Desert, the Eighth Army was falling back under a renewed German assault and at sea the month of March had seen 273 Allied merchant ships, totalling 834,184 tons sunk, the heaviest loss in any one month so far in the war.

Convoy QP 10, made up of sixteen merchantmen, among them four survivors of PQ 13, namely the *River Afton, Harpalion, Empire Cowper* and *Mana,* sailed from Murmansk at 17.00 on 10 April. As a result of the determined attacks on PQ 13, reports coming in that the U-boat presence in the Barents Sea had been substantially increased, and the arrival of more bombers at the Luftwaffe bases in north Norway, QP 10 was more heavily escorted than normal for a westbound convoy. The fleet minesweepers *Gossamer, Harrier* and *Hussar,* along with two Russian destroyers, saw the convoy clear of the Kola Inlet and thereafter an enlarged ocean escort took over. This was made up of the destroyers *Fury, Eclipse, Oribi, Punjabi* and *Marne,* the fleet minesweeper *Speedwell,* and the anti-submarine trawlers *Blackfly* and *Paynter,* all well-known names on the Russian run. The Southampton-class cruiser *Liverpool,* a newcomer to the area replacing the damaged *Trinidad,* was to join on the 12th, to act independently as before, keeping a watch on the convoy with her advanced-type radar. PQ 14, the next Russia-bound convoy of twenty-four ships, had sailed from Reykjavik on the 8th and units of the Home Fleet were in place to provide distant cover for both convoys.

If it had been at all possible, Reardon Smith's *New Westminster City* would have gone with QP 10, for every ship, no matter how badly knocked about, was needed at sea. Although the mass-produced American Liberty ships were now coming into service, the first of this class having been launched on 30 December 1941, the toll of British merchant ships being exacted by the U-boats was so great that their numbers were shrinking. Anyone seeing the *New Westminster City* propping up the quay in Murmansk would have been forgiven for thinking she must be a total loss. Her holds were flooded, her accommodation gutted by fire, but the SBNO was of the opinion that she could be patched up to sail again. However, given the conditions prevailing in the port of Murmansk, the shortage of materials and skilled labour and the incessant bombing, that might be some time far in the

1. The 'Jam Jar Inn' circa 1948. The building on the left was the Officers' Mess.
(Joyce Sutherland)

2. J. & C. Harrison's *Harmatris* in her peacetime livery.
(Welsh Industrial & Maritime Museum)

3. Ju88s ready for
   take-off at
   Bardufoss.
   *(Kurt Monsen
   www.nuav.net)*

4. Ju88 airborne and
   heading north to
   attack convoy.
   *(Kurt Monsen
   www.nuav.net)*

5. Ju88 scores a
   direct hit on a
   ship in Convoy
   PQ16.
   *(Kurt Monsen
   www.nuav.net)*

6. A Narvik class destroyer of the *Zestöregruppe Arktis*. *(German source unknown)*

7. The discharging berths in Murmansk in 1942. *(Russian source unknown)*

8. The Dutch ship *Pieter de Hoogh* – 7168 tons. *(US Coast Guard)*

9. Captain Hendrik Stuy, master of the Dutch ship *Pieter de Hoogh*.
(Albert Kelder)

10. US cruiser *Wichita* emerges from the Arctic mist. Photo taken from the stern of a seaplane tender. *(US Naval Historical Center)*

11. Convoy PQ17 under attack by Heinkel 115s of *Küstenfliegergruppe* 906. Torpedoed US Liberty ship blows up. *(George Young)*

12. Dutch cargo ship *Paulus Potter* – a fugitive from PQ 17 making a run for Archangel.
    (Bruno Wundshammer)

13. Near miss on the *Paulus Potter* by Ju88 of the 3rd Adler Squadron, *Fluggruppe* K30.
    (Bruno Wundshammer)

14. *U-255* alongside abandoned Dutch ship *Paulus Potter*. The first man boards. *(Hugo Deiring)*

15. *Paulus Potter* taken from *U-255* and showing wooden life raft on launch cradle. *(Hugo Deiring)*

16. The British ship *Chulmleigh*, lost off Spitzbergen in Operation 'FB'.
(Welsh Industrial & Maritime Museum)

17. Cutter from Royal Navy ship picks up survivors from life raft. *(Michael Kaufmann)*

"IN MEMORY OF OUR SHIPMATES
WHO SAILED FROM LOCH EWE
DURING WORLD WAR II
THEY LOST THEIR LIVES
IN THE BITTER ARCTIC SEA BATTLES
TO NORTH RUSSIA
AND NEVER RETURNED
TO THIS TRANQUIL ANCHORAGE.
WE WILL ALWAYS REMEMBER THEM."

18. Memorial at Rubha nan Sasan, Loch Ewe. Erected by the Russian Convoy Club in
September 1999. *(Loch Ewe Action Forum)*

future. Meanwhile, something must be done with her crew, left kicking their heels in temporary accommodation ashore. They were needed for other ships, for Britain was also running short of experienced seamen. There remained, of course, the question of the legal ownership of the *New Westminster City*. So long as her master or his deputy remained on board, then she was the property of Reardon Smith Line. Abandoned altogether, she was liable to seizure by the Russians.[1] In which case, it was decided that Captain Harris must stay with her, while his crew went home with other ships when spare berths were available. Two of the ships with QP 10, the *Harpalion* and *Empire Cowper*, both ex-PQ 13, had spare accommodation, and twenty-nine of the *New Westminster*'s crew went with them, eighteen with the *Harpalion* and eleven with the *Empire Cowper*.

Having cleared Cape Teriberski, the western headland of the Kola Inlet, QP 10 formed up into five columns abreast, and set course to the north-west, the intention being, as usual, to first make for the ice edge where the habitually foul weather and poor visibility offered some protection from the enemy. With the convoy, and sailing again as Convoy Commodore, this time in Lambert Brothers' 5138-ton *Temple Arch*, was Captain D.A. Casey, RNR, who had been frustrated in his efforts to control PQ 13 when the *River Afton* lost touch with the other ships. Casey had been forewarned of how bad things were to the north. Summer was on its way to the Arctic and heavy ice was moving south, ice floes from the ice edge and bergs from the glaciers of Spitzbergen. PQ 14, eastbound, was already experiencing difficulties in the ice. For the time being, however, QP 10 was in clear water with good visibility but there was a strong easterly wind blowing which had the mercury in the thermometer plummeting and spray freezing hard the moment it hit the deck. The nightmare of the road to Russia was beginning all over again.

---

[1] The *New Westminster City* was refloated in March 1947, patched up, and towed back to south Wales. There she was repaired and sold to Japanese shipowners, being renamed *Asakaze Maru*. She served her new owners well, finally going to the breaker's yard in 1965, twenty-three years after she had been battered into submission and sunk by German bombers in Murmansk.

Twenty-nine-year-old Chief Officer S.A. Galer, ex-*New Westminster City*, was in the *Harpalion* with seventeen others from his ship. They were sailing as 'Distressed British Seamen', a rather quaint title awarded by the civil servants to merchant seamen who, in the course of this brutal war at sea, had lost their ships. In effect they were passengers accepted on sufferance, signed on ship's articles, crammed into any accommodation that happened to be available and liable to be put to work with the rest of the crew as required. The *Harpalion*, a 5486-ton steamer owned by J. & C. Harrison of London, and under the command of Captain H. W. Williams, was carrying a nominal cargo of 600 tons of mineral ores from Murmansk. She already had a total complement on board of fifty-two, including her eight DEMS gunners, and had little room to spare. With eighteen extra mouths to feed, what limited provisions she had on board would be very thinly spread. In all respects, the voyage home promised to be a challenge. For Galer and the others, belonging and yet not belonging, it was a voyage they hoped would pass quickly.

The voyage did not have an auspicious beginning for the *Harpalion*, being allocated position number 13 in the convoy. Being ex-PQ 13, to those on board with a superstitious turn of mind this was tempting fate too far. To the more practical-minded Captain Williams this meant sailing as rear ship in the outside column, a more exposed position not to be imagined. This led him, from the time of clearing the Kola Inlet, to double up watches and keep all guns fully manned.

Williams' prudence was rewarded when, just twenty hours out of Murmansk, at 13.30 on 11 April, the *Temple Arch* hoisted a flag signal warning of the approach of enemy aircraft. The convoy was steaming at eight knots, with a following wind of near-gale force, completely overcast sky and good visibility. A few moments after the hoisting of the warning, several Ju88s appeared, racing in from astern at a height of about 400 feet. As the planes drew near, one of them peeled off, dropped down to about 200 feet above the water, and homed in on the *Empire Cowper*, rear ship of Column 4.

The *Empire Cowper*, a 7000-ton wartime replacement ship owned by the MOWT and managed by Chapman and Son of Newcastle, was commanded by Captain J.H. Wigham. She also had a cargo, albeit only 136 tons of ore and 138 tons of pit props and she also had the other eleven men from the *New Westminster City* on board. For defence against aircraft, she was armed with one Oerlikon and the usual collection of light machine guns and rockets.

Wigham was first to spot the intentions of the Ju88 and, as it lost height to begin its bombing run, he ordered his gunners to open fire. The guns spoke in unison, tracers arced up towards the incoming plane and at the same time Wigham and Chief Officer R. Morrison, one in each wing of the bridge, each launched a PAC rocket, both of which, unusually, performed faultlessly. The combined effect of the tracers and the rockets – most probably largely the fear of the latter's trailing wires that could foul his propellers – caused the pilot of the Ju88 to bank sharply to starboard as he released his bombs. They fell thirty to forty feet clear of the *Empire Cowper*, doing no more damage than deluging her bridge with icy spray and thoroughly wetting those manning it.

The *Empire Cowper* steamed on, her guns covering two more Ju88s circling at a safe distance. Wigham was on the point of congratulating himself on having got the best of the enemy, when the two bombers separated and dived on his ship, one from port and the other from starboard. The German pilots were using the proven tactic of dividing the enemy's fire and they were successful. The *Empire Cowper*'s guns opened up again, two more rockets soared skywards but she could not defend herself against an attack from two sides. The aircraft coming in from starboard appeared to stagger as if it was hit, but this did not deter its pilot from releasing three bombs, which fell in a gentle curve to land squarely amidships, right aft of the *Empire Cowper*'s No.3 hatch. The effect of three 500lb bombs bursting in the empty No.3 hold directly adjacent to the boiler-room was devastating. Deafened by the explosion, Wigham watched in horror as the whole midships section of his ship erupted. Clouds of steam escaping from the wrecked boilers mingled with smoke and flame pouring from the hold sending up a thick black pall that enveloped the bridge, shutting out the daylight, blinding and choking its occupants. The second Ju88, coming in on the port beam, flew straight through the smoke and out the other side without dropping its bombs. They were not needed.

When he recovered his wits, Wigham's first reaction was to dive for the engine room telegraph and ring the engines to stop. There was no response from below, the chains of the telegraph being broken. Wigham then fought his way down to the main deck with Chief Officer Morrison close behind. When the smoke and flame had cleared, the damage they found there was extensive. A huge hole had been blown in the port side of the hull below the waterline and on the opposite side of the ship the shell plating was bulging outwards alarmingly. It was Wigham's opinion that the ship might break her back at any time.

The engine room which was full of steam, had by this time been evacuated, with only two casualties reported, both firemen scalded by steam, one being very seriously burned. The main engine was still going ahead, but there could be no question of sending anyone back into the steam to shut the valves.

The weather was as bad as it could be under the circumstances. The wind was force 7 from the east and the ship was rolling heavily in a rough beam sea. Wigham was reluctant to risk lowering boats in such conditions. The engine was stopped by shutting the emergency valve on the boat deck and the *Empire Cowper* gradually lost way and drifted astern of the convoy. Wigham delayed making a decision as long as possible, but at 15.00, with the ship settling bodily and her broken hull creaking ominously, he gave the order to abandon ship.

The *Empire Cowper* carried two full-sized lifeboats, each certified to carry thirty men, and two jolly boats, small 15-footers really meant for harbour work and certainly not suitable for use in abandoning ship in the heavy seas running. Although he had extra men on board, a total complement of fifty-seven, Wigham decided to use only the two large boats, into which he could just about pack everyone. The conditions under which the operation was to be carried out were far from ideal, for apart from the heavy rolling, the scream of the high-pressure steam escaping from the boiler-room was deafening and the steam itself had enveloped the boat deck in a thick fog. This led to some confusion in lowering the port-side boat. Someone let slip the forward fall and the boat nose-dived into the sea, where it immediately capsized, throwing the eight men manning it into the water. Although they were wearing lifejackets, they had little chance of surviving in the rough, freezing water and were dead within minutes. One of the men lost was a member of the crew of the *New Westminster City*; a sad end for someone who had been through so much.

With one lifeboat lost, Wigham now had no other option but to make use of the two smaller boats to evacuate all forty-nine men. All three boats were lowered to the water without further trouble and Wigham and forty-one crew successfully boarded the starboard-side boats, leaving the port jolly boat for Chief Officer Morrison and eight others. However, before Morrison and his men could board their boat, it broke adrift and was swept away by a wave. The other boats were unable to get back alongside, leaving the nine men stranded on the sinking ship.

At that point, one of the Ju88s came back to finish off the *Empire Cowper*. With no other option open to him, Morrison sent his men to man the guns and the unsuspecting plane received a very hot reception. In return, the Ju88 machine-gunned the ship and then dropped two bombs, both of which scored hits on her No.2 hold. The German pilot then made an attempt to rake the *Empire Cowper*'s lifeboats with machine-gun fire but retired without scoring any hits when Morrison fired two PAC rockets.

The Royal Navy now came to the aid of the survivors, the trawler HMS *Paynter* closing the lifeboats and picking up Captain Wigham and the others. When aboard the trawler, Wigham informed her commander, Lieutenant R. Nossiter, that nine of his crew were still on the *Empire Cowper*. Without hesitation, and at great risk to his own ship, Nossiter, in an exhibition of superb ship handling, went alongside the stricken ship and took off the stranded men. When Wigham last saw his ship from the stern of HMS *Paynter* as she hastened to rejoin the convoy, the *Empire Cowper* was on fire from forward to aft and very low in the water. For her the end was very near.

In his confidential report filed on 5 May 1942, Captain Wigham wrote:

I would particularly like to pay tribute to the valuable assistance and magnificent example of R. Morrison, the Chief Officer, who was responsible for keeping together the 9 men who were left on board the ship, keeping up their spirits and morale until rescued. He acted calmly throughout, firing the two remaining PAC rockets in an endeavour to bring down the attacking aircraft. During this trying period he was greatly assisted by the Third Officer, W.N. Nicholson, who was one of the party left on board the ship. The steward, J.J. Tatlow, very courageously effected the rescue of one of the gunners, who was clinging to the bottom rung of a side ladder and freezing; he was quite unable to climb back on board. Tatlow went down the ladder, put a line around the gunner and pulled him back on board. I would also like to pay tribute to the magnificent manner in which the commanding officer of HMS *Paynter* – Lieutenant R. Nossiter, RNVR – brought his ship alongside in the heavy sea and rescued the 9 men stranded on board, and to the very fine treatment he extended to the crew while on board his ship.

There was retribution for the *Empire Cowper*. The Ju88 that had tried to finish her off escaped her anti-aircraft fire, only to fly straight into that of the *Harpalion*. The plane was still at about 200 feet, but gaining height when it roared over the Harrison ship whose gunners opened up withering fire with their Oerlikon, two twin Marlins, two single Marlins and two Lewis machine guns. The German pilot saw the danger too late to take avoiding action and ran into a concentrated hail of bullets and cannon shells. Captain Williams, ready in the wing of the bridge, hand on the pull-wire of a PAC, watched with satisfaction as the flaming tracers went home in the underbelly of the plane. It was probable that the tracers hit a fuel tank, for the Ju88 suddenly burst into flame, reared up on one wing and dived into the sea some 500 yards on the other side of the *Harpalion*. The plane sank immediately, leaving no survivors. For a fleeting instant Williams felt sympathy for the German crew, who must have died so horribly, but then put the thought from his mind. It was no time for moralizing. This was kill or be killed.

As QP 10 steamed northwards, the air attacks petered out, only to be replaced by a new and even more sinister threat. Moving out of the influence of the warm Gulf Stream, a branch of which flows eastwards past the north coast of Norway and keeps the Kola Inlet open in winter, the ships ran into heavy ice. The ice floes, flat pieces of ice fifty to 100 feet across and several feet thick, were not a great danger, but after them came icebergs.

Although the bergs did not appear to be big, no more than twenty feet high, nine-tenths of their volume was beneath the surface and they constituted a major hazard for the ships. Quite clearly, the convoy could not continue to steam in its orderly five columns abreast, and the signal was soon hoisted by the *Temple Arch* 'Speed and course as required by ice'. In other words, each master was to manoeuvre his own ships as he thought best, at the same time endeavouring to stay in company with the others. It was fortunate that the visibility was good, but with a near-gale still blowing and a heavy sea running, a certain amount of confusion ensued. Before long, the convoy's speed was down to four and a half knots, no more than a fast walking pace, and not to be recommended in these hostile waters.

The icebergs were an even greater danger to *U-435*, but everything else was in Siegfried Stretlow's favour as, late on the night of the 12th, QP 10 came crawling over the horizon into his sights. Since sinking the *Effingham* on 30 March, Stretlow had been having a lean time, motoring up and down on the surface across the convoy route, battered by heavy seas, blinded by snow squalls, his conning tower thick with ice, and the morale of his crew slipping lower and lower. QP 10, loosely scattered and slow moving, was a gift from the gods. Taking cover behind the ice floes, Stretlow began to stalk the convoy.

QP 10 was fifty-six hours out of Murmansk and 140 miles north of the North Cape when, at 01.00 on the morning of the 13th, taking advantage of the twilight, Stretlow moved in to the attack. His first torpedo hit the 5823-ton Russian ship *Kiev* steaming right in the heart of the convoy. As the First World War vintage *Kiev*, her hull blasted open and listing heavily, dropped astern, Captain Casey in the *Temple Arch* signalled a series of emergency turns, sending the convoy into complete confusion. Escorts fired star shell and searched among the ice floes for the attacker, but by this time Stretlow had gone deep and, protected by the varying layers of cold and less cold water caused by the currents which bent and deflected the Asdic beams, *U-435* made good her escape.

After the shock of the sinking of the *Kiev* wore off, the night went quiet, but now the convoy which had earlier lapsed into a degree of complacency, was on full alert. Now there were two enemies, the bergs and the U-boat, or U-boats, for there could easily be others hidden beneath the sea waiting for their chance to strike. On the bridge of the *Harpalion*, Captain Williams and his officers, heavily muffled against the bitter cold, fingered their binoculars nervously and scanned the dark horizon, where every foam-flecked wave seemed to hide a periscope.

The spell was broken when, at 03.30, with sunrise only minutes away, a dull thump was heard on the far side of the convoy and the sky was lit up by a sheet of flame. *U-435* was back, and this time her victim was the 6000-ton Panama-flag steamer *El Occidente*, lead ship of Column 5. The thirty-two-year-old ship sank almost immediately. The usual frenzy of depth charging followed as the escorting destroyers raced to and fro, but once again they were chasing their tails. *U-435*, like a vampire of the night, had slipped away before the sun came up.

Only a few men survived the sinking of the *El Occidente* and when they had been snatched from the sea QP 10 reformed and altered onto a westerly course to skirt the ice edge to the south of Bear Island. There were those in the convoy who now dared to think that the worst was over. They were wrong. Within half an hour, as a watery sun began its climb from the horizon, the enemy came back – and this time in the sky. A large four-engined aircraft, identified as a Focke-Wulf Kondor, appeared from the south and started to circle the convoy, taking care to keep well out of range of its guns. This was the now familiar prelude to an air attack. Standing to their guns, their eyes heavy with sleep, their limbs numb with cold, the crew of the *Harpalion*, along with the others, waited for the next round in the fight to reach home.

They did not have long to wait. At 05.00, Williams saw three Ju88s approaching and warned his gunners to stand to. The enemy planes did not attack immediately, perhaps deterred by the strength of QP 10's escort force, which had been reinforced during the night by the arrival of HMS *Liverpool*. The cruiser brought with her, in addition to her nine 6-inch guns, a considerable battery of anti-aircraft guns, eight 4-inch, sixteen 2-pounders, twenty-two 40-mm cannons and fifteen 20-mm Oerlikons. The Ju88s circled warily.

The attack was recorded in the *Harpalion*'s deck log as

beginning at 06.07. Being on the southern edge of the convoy, at the tail end of Column 1, she was first in line of fire for the bombers. Williams took violent evasive action and eight bombs which might have been direct hits exploded within fifty yards of the ship, sending up tall columns of water all around her. Apart from broken crockery and frayed nerves, the *Harpalion* suffered no damage and her guns continued to hammer away at the enemy.

There was a pause, a time to draw breath, to reload, and then two more Ju88s dropped out of the clouds and once again the *Harpalion* was the target. This time the aim of the German pilots was better, four bombs landing only twenty yards from the British ship's stern. They appeared to be delayed action bombs, for several minutes elapsed before they exploded, precious minutes that allowed the *Harpalion* to pull away from the danger. She was drenched with spray but again escaped damage.

Another hour and a half elapsed before the German planes came back, again a pair of Ju88s, and again the *Harpalion* was their target. One came in from ahead, the other from astern, each dropping four bombs as they sheered away to avoid the fire of the ship's guns. All eight bombs landed fifty yards off the port bow, exploding harmlessly, for the *Harpalion* was already moving away under full starboard helm.

Captain Williams now assumed the Germans had a personal vendetta against his ship and knew they would be back. And back they came, only the space of a cup of cocoa and a sandwich later. It was a single Ju88 this time and its pilot was made of sterner stuff, levelling out at 200 feet, ignoring the hail of bullets, and placing four bombs within twenty feet of the *Harpalion*'s stern.

The multiple explosion was like the crash of thunder and the combined blast of the four 500-pounders lifted the *Harpalion*'s stern clean out of the water. She rolled drunkenly as she fell back but she did not appear to have any serious damage. Then Williams noticed that her head was falling off to port and called for starboard helm. She did not answer indicating that – as Williams had feared – her steering gear was damaged. This proved to be the case.

The *Harpalion* circled to port while her engineers struggled to connect up the emergency hand gear. When this was done, the ship still did not answer and then the awful truth dawned that her rudder post was smashed, the rudder hanging useless. Williams was forced to stop his engines before the *Harpalion* became a danger to the other ships. He then signalled the nearest escort, HMS *Fury*, and requested assistance. He had, by this time, ascertained that there was no danger to the *Harpalion*'s hull and, with his engine functioning normally, all he required was help with steering the ship. He suggested to *Fury* that one of the escorting trawlers might be spared to lend a hand. The reply was not as he had hoped. The SOE, Lieutenant Commander Campbell, was of the opinion that the weather was too rough, and the danger of further attacks by enemy aircraft and submarines too great to allow reducing his force to give help to a lame duck. The *Harpalion* must look after herself.

Having brought the *Harpalion* safely through the hazardous outward voyage to Russia, survived the holocaust of Murmansk and come thus far on the return passage, Captain Williams was not about to abandon his ship now. The convoy could go its own way and he would follow, but first he must rig a jury rudder. Williams, as are all British deck officers, was familiar with page 335 of Nicholl's *Seamanship and Nautical Knowledge*, wherein is described an ingenious method of rigging a jury rudder. The method, tried and tested so the seamanship bible says, by Captain D. Forrest of the s.s. *Braddovey* when she lost her rudder in the Atlantic in 1929, involves a derrick boom with two steel doors lashed together rigged over the stern. It was an ambitious project to undertake in Arctic waters, in heavy weather and under attack by an enemy, but Williams was willing to try. He set his crew to work, but the *Harpalion*, stopped and wallowing astern of the convoy, became the target of four Ju88s, which kept up a continuous attack on the helpless ship, bombing and machine-gunning her. The bomb aiming of the Ju88s was as bad as ever and their bombs did no further damage, but their machine-gunning of the ship's decks stopped all work on the jury rudder. The *Harpalion*'s gunners did their best to beat off the German bombers, but they were now running short of ammunition. The convoy was disappearing out of sight and when HMS *Fury* came back again and advised Williams to abandon his ship, he was willing to concede defeat.

Williams sent his Chief Engineer below to open the main valve chest to scuttle the ship but he was beaten back by steam escaping from pipes fractured by the concussion of the near misses. He returned to the deck where, despite continued machine-gunning by the Ju88s, the lifeboats were being lowered. Under the steadying hand of Captain Williams, both lifeboats, containing between them seventy men, cleared the ship with the sea lapping over their gunwales. As they were pulling away, they were machine-gunned by the German planes, but someone was watching over these men and when *Fury* came along to pick them up, they were all still unharmed. When they were aboard the destroyer, *Fury* did what the enemy had failed to do, shelling the *Harpalion* with her 4.7s and setting her ablaze. Three hours later the abandoned ship was seen still on fire and with her decks awash as she settled lower and lower in the water.

Captain Williams remarked in his report:

> I should like to recommend the Naval gunners Maclean and Buckley. They manned the machine guns on the bridge whilst the remainder of the crew were abandoning ship and fought off the attacking aircraft whilst we were all safely in the boats. They were the last to leave the ship.

> During the bombing attacks the firemen left the stokehold and refused to go down again to maintain steam. I called for volunteers and the first of the crew to volunteer was Slaughter, a galley boy aged 15 years. A steward, White, then volunteered and also one of the firemen named Ulhe, and these three men went into the stoke-hold.

Unlike Captain Wigham of the *Empire Cowper*, Williams did not rate the performance of the PAC rockets highly:

> The PAC rockets which I fired were most unsatisfactory and did not appear to have any effect on the attacking aircraft. On a previous voyage I was sailing independently and was attacked by aircraft. I fired a PAC rocket, which landed on the boat deck. The second rocket fired at the same time was also unsatisfactory and its maximum height was not more than 120 feet. These rockets were kept in the chartroom and were well protected, their stands being greased and covered.

Chapter Eight

Of the twenty merchant ships that sailed from Hvalfjord with PQ 13 on 20 March, ten had been lost at sea or in the hell of Murmansk and with them had gone 180 men. PQ 13 was the first Russia-bound convoy to be put to the German sword and the mauling it received was only a curtain-raiser for things to come.

Those ships that survived returned to the west as and when the opportunity arose. Two of them, the *River Afton* and *Mana*, had made it through with QP 10. The *Tobruk*, *Lars Kruse* and *Scottish American*, were destined to lie in Murmansk until the autumn but the other five, the *Dunboyne*, *Eldena*, *Mormacmar*, *Ballot*, *El Estero* and *Gallant Fox*, all United States Maritime Commission ships, were assigned to sail with Convoy QP 11.

QP 11 left the Kola Inlet on 28 April and was made up of thirteen British and American ships, including the five PQ 13 survivors. This convoy was even more heavily escorted than its predecessor, having with it no fewer than six destroyers, HMS *Amazon*, *Beagle*, *Beverley*, *Bulldog* (SOE), *Foresight* and *Forester*, the corvettes *Campanula*, *Oxlip*, *Saxifrage* and *Snowflake*, and the armed trawler *Lord Middleton*.

The sailing of QP 11 did not go unobserved by the enemy. The convoy had been sighted by a patrolling U-boat of the Ulan Group late on the 29th. Nervous of the presence of so many destroyers and corvettes, the U-boat called for reinforcements and settled down to shadow the convoy. One of those alerted by the shadowing boat's signals was *Kapitänleutnant* Max-Martin Teichert in *U-456*, then 250 miles north-north-west of the Kola Inlet and conveniently right in the path of QP 11. Teichert, who saw action against PQ 13, albeit without success, had been at sea since the beginning of the year and was running low on fuel and stores. When news of the convoy came in Teichert was at the stage of considering a return to base with nothing to show for the patrol. He was more than willing to wait for a chance to open his score.

Two days out of Murmansk, on the 30th, QP 11's defensive screen was strengthened by the arrival of the 10,000-ton *Edinburgh*, one of the two new Town-class cruisers, formidable ships mounting twelve 6-inch and twelve 4-inch guns, with side armour designed to withstand 8-inch shells, and a top speed of thirty-two knots. The *Edinburgh* was playing a dual role, in that as well as acting as independent escort to QP 11, she was a bullion carrier for the Soviet Government, having on board $20 million in gold, a payment to America for arms received. In retrospect, it might be asked why, when carrying such a huge shipment of gold through enemy-dominated waters, the *Edinburgh* was not sailing alone and at full speed, instead of playing nursemaid to an eight-knot convoy. It can only be assumed that the Admiralty was confident that the extra destroyers would be sufficient to protect her. Subsequent events were to prove its confidence to be misplaced.

Edinburgh, commanded by Captain Faulkner and with Admiral Bonham Carter on board, took up station twenty miles ahead of the convoy, steering a zig-zag pattern and using her radar to search ahead and around. Two hours after joining the convoy, neither her radar scanner nor her lookouts saw *U-456*'s periscope break surface to starboard. Teichert's two torpedoes both found their mark, one exploding in the cruiser's forward boiler-room with devastating results, the other slamming into the cruiser's stern, destroying her rudder and two of her four propellers. This was *Trinidad* and PQ 13 all over again, only this time the damage was not self-inflicted.

Although *Edinburgh* had suffered widespread damage above and below decks, she was still seaworthy and, when the furore had died down, she was taken under tow by the destroyer *Forester*. Escorted by *Forester*'s sister ship *Foresight* and two Russian destroyers now familiar to the Allied ships, *Gremyaschi* and *Sokrushitelny*, *Edinburgh* began a slow return to Murmansk.

Teichert had not gone away but was following in the wake of

the sad procession, waiting for the opportunity to finish off the *Edinburgh*. The escorting destroyers were doubly vigilant and although Teichert made several attempts to get into position to deliver the *coup de grâce*, each time *U-456* was detected and driven off, on one occasion narrowly escaping being sunk. It is probable that the damaged cruiser would not have reached the Kola Inlet, had it not been for the arrival on the scene of three German destroyers of *Zestörergruppe* 'Arktis', the *Hermann Schoemann*, Z-24 and Z-25. The 'Z' boats, still smarting from the drubbing they received in the attack on HMS *Trinidad* a month earlier, were anxious to redeem themselves. They first fell in with QP 11 and quickly learned that there were no easy targets for their guns here. After a fierce battle with the convoys escorting destroyers, the German ships were forced to retire, having sunk only the *Tsiolkovsky*, a small Russian merchantman.

Twenty-four hours later, the German destroyers found the crippled *Edinburgh* and with a depleted escort, for the *Gremyaschi* and *Sokrushitelny* were both running short of fuel and had gone on to Murmansk. The enemy made the mistake of thinking they had found a soft target but they were forced to think again. The *Edinburgh* may have been badly damaged and had lost many men, but she still had the ability to hit back. While *Foresight* and *Forester* tackled Z-24 and Z-25, *Edinburgh* took on the *Hermann Schoemann* and punished her so hard that she eventually sank. Most of her crew were taken off by Z-24 and Z-25, but fifty-six men were left on rafts, and were later picked up by *U-88*.

There was a price to pay for the victory. *Forester* had been severely damaged in the clash with the German destroyers and had sustained heavy casualties. She now lay stopped and helpless under the guns of Z-24 and Z-25. She was saved from complete destruction by the intervention of *Foresight*, who made smoke and placed herself between the enemy and her crippled sister. In doing so, *Foresight* received two direct hits which left her with only one gun in action and her decks littered with dead and wounded. Among the dead was Captain Sloan of the *Lancaster Castle*, who had lost his ship to the German bombers in Murmansk and was returning home as a passenger in the destroyer.

With *Foresight* also in trouble, *Forester*, still lying stopped and unable to manoeuvre, was an easy target for two torpedoes fired by one of the two German destroyers – which one was not clear – but luckily, for *Forester* at least, the torpedoes were set too deep and passed underneath her. Unfortunately, one man's luck is often another's misfortune, and so it was for HMS *Edinburgh*. She then happened to be passing on the other side of *Forester* and was directly in line of fire of the enemy's torpedoes. The cruiser being of deeper draught, one of the torpedoes found a target in her hull. This was the death blow for *Edinburgh*. Already severely weakened by *U-456*'s torpedoes, she broke her back and looked to be in imminent danger of going down. At great risk to themselves, the minesweepers *Harrier* and *Gossamer*, who had been detached to help in the defence of QP 11, went alongside *Edinburgh*, one to port and the other to starboard, and took off the cruiser's crew. While the rescue was going on, much to the relief of the British force, *Z-24* and *Z-25* decided that they had had enough and withdrew.

Edinburgh was a floating wreck, but she stubbornly refused to sink on her own, and two days later *Foresight* was forced to put an end to her with a torpedo to avoid her bullion falling into German hands. The cruiser went down, taking with her the bodies of fifty-six men and the five and a half tons of gold locked in her strongroom. Her survivors, many of them injured, were taken back to Murmansk in the minesweepers.

With the exception of the burnt-out wrecks of the merchantmen, all that now remained of PQ 13 in Murmansk was HMS *Trinidad* and she had, by this time, been patched up, ironically with steel plates brought out from Britain by *Edinburgh* a month earlier. It now fell to *Trinidad* to carry home as many of *Edinburgh*'s survivors as she could cram into her mess decks. She sailed from the Kola Inlet on 13 May, accompanied by *Foresight* and *Forester*, themselves hurriedly patched up, and the two bigger and more modern destroyers *Matchless* and *Somali*. In effect, *Matchless* and *Somali* were escorting three lame ducks on what they hoped would be a high-speed dash to the nearest British ship-yard capable of carrying out more permanent repairs. However, the top speed of this all-naval convoy would be dictated by the damaged ships and was never likely to exceed twenty knots, but between them the ships mounted a very considerable array of guns and they had no slow-steaming merchantmen to look after. They also had the added reassurance that, should they get into trouble, the Home Fleet covering force, led by the battleship *Duke of York* was not too far over the horizon.

It seems certain that the Germans had advance notice of the sailing of the homeward bound British warships, for within a few hours of their sailing from the Kola Inlet two enemy aircraft were shadowing the convoy. As the days were now almost twenty-four hours long, there would be no darkness in which the ships could hide, only a brief period of twilight around midnight to mark the passing of the night. For Captain Saunders on the bridge of the *Trinidad*, the scenario was all too familiar. He was not surprised when an hour later two U-boats were sighted, lying off out of range like cruising sharks waiting for the opportunity to strike.

The first indication of a major attack in the offing came at 21.00. *Trinidad*'s radar began picking up echoes of aircraft approaching from the south-west, a few at first, then formations. The bombers were on their way and this time it was evident that they would not be attacking in ones and twos. Saunders hoisted the signal 'Prepare to repel enemy aircraft', and every gun capable of being elevated to the sky – and in the five ships that was a considerable number – was manned. In *Trinidad*, the *Edinburgh* survivors, having no action stations to go to, reluctantly sought cover below decks.

The weather could not have been more favourable for the attacking aircraft, patchy cloud and good visibility, and as the reports came through from the radar office of the increasing numbers of echoes showing up on the screen, Saunders began to have serious concern for the safety of his ship. The repairs carried out by the Russians in Murmansk were, at best, makeshift, and he had grave doubts about his ability to manoeuvre at speed to avoid the bombs about to fall from the sky. At the same time, he had no way of knowing how well his men would fight. They had been through the worst kind of ordeal in the two months past, and with seventeen of their shipmates killed in an accident that should not have happened, their morale might not be as high as it should have been.

Any doubts Saunders had about his men were swept away when the first wave of Stukas dropped out of the clouds, the roar of their engines rising to a frightening pitch as they pounced on the cruiser. *Trinidad*'s eight 4-inch guns and massed batteries of pom-poms opened up as one, throwing up a lethal curtain of steel through which the German pilots were forced to fly, but they still pressed home their attack. The Stukas were followed by the heavier, twin-engined Ju88s and *Trinidad*, twisting and turning, was bracketed by dozens of bomb bursts that filled the air with spray and flying shrapnel. Saunders, conscious all the time of the vulnerability of the welded patch on his hull, manoeuvred the 8000-ton cruiser with the light touch of an ocean yachtsman, always judging the fall of the bombs right, and always altering in time to turn a certain direct hit into a near-miss.

The destroyers with *Trinidad* also came in for their share of the bombs, for the sky over the five ships was full of diving and weaving planes. They were being kept at bay by the massed guns of the ships, upwards of fifty smoking barrels hurling shells skywards, backed by batteries of light and heavy machine guns. The sky was filled with bursts of black smoke and lines of flaming tracer. No one on either side had any illusions but that this was a fight to the death, with the advantage on the German side. There were now twenty-five Ju88s involved, each carrying up to twelve 500lb bombs, and to those on the receiving end in the ships there seemed to be an endless queue of aircraft lining up to blow them out of the water.

The attack went on for two hours without pause but, although the bombs fell from the sky like rain, the ship handling of the British captains and the thunder of their guns played havoc with the enemy's aim. There were near-misses in plenty but no direct hits. *Trinidad*, the main target of the bombers, seemed to be continually hidden by the spray thrown up by bombs bursting all around her. Saunders, by this time acting more by instinct than judgement, continued to throw his ship around, but was worried that sooner or later, probably sooner, the patch on her hull would give way, for some bombs were landing within fifty feet of her. Then a new and far more dangerous threat appeared on the horizon.

The cry of 'Torpedo bombers bearing Red 90!' sent a chill

down Saunders' spine. He swung round to see a line of ten aircraft low on the water coming in from the south. He snatched up his binoculars and as the planes came nearer he identified them as Heinkel 111s, twin-engined bombers, a type widely used in the Battle of Britain, but now adapted to carry two 1600lb torpedoes. Once again, *Trinidad* was the primary target but now her guns were split, some depressing to meet the new threat, the others continuing to ward off the bombers, who now, perhaps sensing their victim was about to meet her end, intensified their attacks.

The destroyers came to *Trinidad*'s aid, using their 4-inch guns to put a wall of fire between the cruiser and the torpedo planes. The barrage was too much for the Heinkels, who swerved away, broke up into two formations and came in from two different directions, hoping to divide the fire of the ships. The guns beat them off again, only two Heinkels getting through to launch their torpedoes at *Trinidad*. Saunders was easily able to comb the tracks of the four missiles, which sped harmlessly past on either side of the cruiser.

Captain Saunders might now have been forgiven for thinking that things were unlikely to get much worse. Then one of the destroyers reported sighting four U-boats on the surface to the north and east – jackals waiting to pounce on a wounded prey. The situation was developing into a potential disaster for the British ships and some were beginning to wonder what the Germans would throw at them next. Capital ships, perhaps? Saunders was not given the luxury of speculation, for the Heinkels were coming in again, all ten of them in line abreast on *Trinidad*'s port beam.

Watching the Heinkels skimming over the wave-tops, untouched by the shells and bullets kicking up the water ahead of them, Saunders kept a cool head, waiting for the right moment to take evasive action. This came when he saw the enemy torpedoes hit the water and a line of feathered wakes came racing towards him. He brought the *Trinidad* round to port under full helm to comb the tracks as he had done before. In doing so, he ran straight into a stick of four bombs dropped by a Ju88.

The Ju88, in its turn, ran into the combined fire of *Trinidad*'s AA guns and turned into a ball of fire, but not before its bombs had found their mark. The effect of four 500lb bombs exploding in and around the cruiser was catastrophic. One bomb landed just forward of her bridge, smashing its way through the deck to explode with terrible effect in the petty officers' mess deck. The area was completely wrecked and several fires were started. Two other 500-pounders narrowly missed the forecastle head but exploded close enough alongside to lay open the hull to the sea. The fourth bomb also landed outboard, sliding down the hull plates on the port side before exploding directly under the ill-used welded patch on *Trinidad*'s hull. The patch that had so far held firm, was torn off and the sea poured into the magazine and cordite compartments below 'B' turret.

The *Trinidad* was sorely hit, many of her complement lay dead or wounded and fires burned above and below decks, but her engines still turned, her steering still functioned, and some of her guns still fired. Damage and fire control parties were at work and Saunders decided it would be wiser to carry on at full speed, rather than slow down and become an easy target for the German planes. His ship was listing heavily, but she was brought upright again by filling ballast tanks and, although considerably lower in the water, she steamed on.

The Heinkels continued to concentrate their attacks on the *Trinidad*, intent on finishing her off, but Saunders was still weaving from side to side, frustrating their efforts. Meanwhile, the fires were out of control and water still poured into the shattered hull. Whether the sea or the fires would claim the ship first was anybody's guess.

At around midnight, when it seemed to Saunders that he and his ship could take no more, he became aware that the German planes were going away, probably having run out of bombs and torpedoes. Now, at long last, he was able to draw breath, to reduce speed and take stock of the situation. Reports reaching him on the bridge, which itself was rapidly becoming untenable as the house below was ablaze, soon confirmed the hopelessness of his ship's position. The *Trinidad* was slowly being consumed by the fires, and so many of her crew were dead, injured or trapped by the fires, that the fight to keep her afloat had been lost. Saunders decided to abandon ship before the U-boats moved in to finish the work begun by the planes.

The cruiser was stopped and all her surviving crew assembled on the quarterdeck – nothing could be done for those trapped below. *Matchless* came alongside first, taking off the wounded that could be reached, while the other destroyers circled to keep the U-boats at bay. *Foresight* and *Forester* then each took their turn, easing alongside the burning ship with hoses rigged to beat off any flames jumping across. *Trinidad* was now listing dangerously to starboard, adding to the difficulties of the evacuation. And as if things were not bad enough, a lone Heinkel had come back and seemed intent on sending the cruiser to the bottom while she lay helpless. Fortunately, in the finest tradition of the Royal Navy, two men, Commissioned Gunner Richard Bunt and Gunner Charles Norsworthy, were still manning one of *Trinidad*'s 4-inch turrets to give cover to the survivors. Training the turret manually – all the electrics were out – they waited until the Heinkel had settled on its torpedo run and fired both guns. The two shells skimmed over the water and exploded directly under the incoming aircraft. The Heinkel was lifted bodily and it banked away with smoke and flame pouring from its fuselage. Its torpedo hit the water but went off at an angle, passing astern of the cruiser.

Trinidad's guns now fell silent and the last of her survivors scrambled aboard *Somali*, which had taken her turn to come alongside. Captain Saunders was the last man to leave the ship. The destroyers then withdrew and circled slowly, silent witnesses to the death throes of a very gallant ship. *Trinidad*, however, although burning furiously and lying low in the water, stubbornly refused to sink. Eventually, it was left to *Matchless* to put a torpedo in her. Only then did HMS *Trinidad*, her battle ensigns still flying, concede defeat and slip slowly below the waves, taking with her into the icy depths of the Barents Sea the bodies of eighty men, twenty of whom were the injured from the *Edinburgh*.

The four British destroyers, *Foresight* and *Forester*, *Matchless* and *Somali*, crammed with survivors, set course to the north-west at full speed, anxious to be clear of the scene of the sinking as quickly as possible. It was certain that the German planes would be back and all four ships were running low on ammunition. As they hurried away at twenty knots – this was all *Foresight* and

Forester, both still suffering from damage received when defending *Edinburgh* could manage – a signal was sent requesting cover from ships of the Home Fleet.

The JU88s were back within an hour and the agony began all over again. The destroyers spread out and, twisting and turning, their guns hammering out defiance, they each fought their individual battle with the enemy. This time they were severely hampered, as their decks were full of *Trinidad*'s survivors and there were many injured below decks. But, yet again, the German bombers scored no hits and after a while they were driven off by the withering fire put up by the British ships.

There was a much appreciated lull, during which the destroyers pressed on to the west, but they were soon receiving somewhat vague signals reporting that unidentified German cruisers, accompanied by destroyers, had left a Norwegian fjord and were heading north towards them. It was well known that the *Tirpitz*, *Scheer*, *Hipper* and *Prinz Eugen* were holed up in the fjords and the conclusion drawn in the destroyers was that one or more of these ships, along with some big Narvik-class destroyers, was on the way to intercept them. Exhausted though they were, the men of the British ships stood to their guns. They were now dangerously short of ammunition, but the thought that the odds were stacked too heavily against them did not deter them. They would fight to the last.

A tense hour passed, then a number of unidentified ships were sighted on the horizon. It was assumed this must be the German force, and while the hampered *Foresight* and *Forester*, covered by *Matchless*, altered away to the north, *Somali*, the only one of the four with a full complement of torpedoes left, turned to engage the enemy. *Somali*, a 1870-ton Tribal-class destroyer, mounting six 4.7-inch, two 4-inch guns and four 21-inch torpedo tubes, had a top speed of thirty-six and a half knots, and might have held her own against the Narvik-class destroyers. If there was anything heavier in the German force she was likely to be blown to pieces before she was close enough to fire her torpedoes. It was only to be hoped that she would buy time for the others to escape.

As *Somali* steamed south at full speed, signal lamps winked out from the 'enemy', who identified themselves as ships of the British 10th Cruiser Squadron, much to the great relief of *Somali* and the other destroyers. They were the light cruiser *Nigeria*, flying the flag of Rear Admiral Burroughs, the heavy cruisers *Kent* and *Norfolk*, and the light cruiser *Liverpool*. The newcomers closed around the destroyers and the whole, now very formidable force set course for Iceland. The reported German ships failed to make an appearance, probably warned off by the reconnaissance plane now shadowing the British ships. This aircraft was also most certainly responsible for the reappearance of the German bombers, this time in even greater numbers. Over the five hours that followed, the Stukas and Ju88s pressed home their attack with a determination bordering on desperation, but the combined firepower of the eight British warships was such that not one bomber succeeded in scoring a hit. Finally, at around noon on 15 May, with the distance to the German airfields becoming greater and greater, the Luftwaffe accepted defeat and the bombers flew away.

The loss of two first-class cruisers within two weeks of each other was a serious blow to the Royal Navy, already heavily committed elsewhere. With summer coming on, with its twenty-four hours of daylight and clear weather on the Arctic route, Churchill was reluctant to continue with this costly supply operation. He was urged to withdraw escorts from the North Atlantic, but out there the Navy was already stretched to breaking point attempting to stem a haemorrhage running at over 100 ships a month being sunk by the U-boats.

The clamour from the Russians for more tanks, more guns, more planes was loud and unrelenting, and with good reason. By the close of 1941, the German armies had made huge inroads into Russia, being halted only by the severity of the winter. Some ground had been regained by the Soviet forces, even so, by the spring of 1942, the front lay from Leningrad in the north, south-eastwards to within 100 miles of Moscow, and then southwards to Rostov on the Don. As summer advanced, Hitler was determined to break through into the Caucasus, his goal the oilfields of Baku, and had already massed 100 divisions, eight of these armoured, supported by 1500 aircraft, all poised ready to strike when the time was right. In response, the Russians were planning a massive counter-attack, possibly before the German armies made their move, hence their demands for ever more supplies from the Allies. Stalin's plea to Churchill, sent on 6 May, was unusually restrained: 'I am fully aware of the difficulties involved and of the sacrifices made by Great Britain in this matter. I feel however incumbent upon me to approach you with the request to take all possible measures in order to ensure the arrival of all the above-mentioned materials in the U.S.S.R. in the course of May, as this is extremely important to our front.'

Stalin was referring to the ninety or more merchant ships lying in Iceland and north British ports loaded with supplies for Russia, most of which had crossed the Atlantic from America and was still awaiting delivery. The hold-up was highly embarrassing for Churchill, who replied: 'I have received your telegram of May 6, and thank you for your message and greetings. We are resolved to fight our way through to you with the maximum amount of war materials. On account of the *Tirpitz* and other enemy surface ships at Trondheim the passage of every convoy has become a serious fleet operation. We shall continue to do our utmost.'

Obviously, it was the threat of the *Tirpitz* anchored in Trondheim fjord and within easy reach of the convoys that worried Churchill most. He was not alone in this, for the thought of this 42,000-ton battleship, the most powerful warship afloat, being allowed near the thinly defended merchant ships was frightening. And backing up the *Tirpitz*'s 15-inch guns were the pocket battleships *Admiral Scheer* and *Lützow* and the heavy cruiser *Admiral Hipper*, not to mention, sheltering in fjords further north the Narvik-class destroyers, whose 5.9s had previously caused havoc amongst the convoys. British long-range bombers were flying frequent sorties against Trondheim, but these planes were operating at the extreme limit of their range and the defences of the fjord were so strong that little was being achieved. The *Tirpitz* and her consorts remained a major threat to the convoys to Russia.

The arrival in Scapa Flow of a United States task force made up of the brand new battleship *Washington*, the aircraft carrier *Wasp*, two heavy cruisers and six destroyers, helped to tip the balance. The American ships, impressive though they were, lacked experience of convoy work, but they were extra guns and the enthusiasm of their crews was unquestionable. Their avail-ability persuaded Churchill to attempt to clear the backlog of ships for Russia, which by this time had reached 107 ships now loaded, or being loaded in ports in the US and Britain. Convoy PQ 16, the largest convoy to Russia yet to be attempted, sailed from Hvalfjord on 21 May.

PQ 16 comprised thirty-six merchant ships, twenty-one American, nine British, five Russian and one Dutch. Among the British ships was a new innovation, the CAM (Catapult Aircraft Merchant) ship *Empire Lawrence*. CAM ships were selected merchant ships which carried a specially adapted Hawker Hurricane fighter mounted on a catapult on the forecastle head. Once launched, the fighter could not be brought back on board, leaving the pilot with the only alternative of bailing out or ditching alongside the nearest ship and hoping to be picked up. It was an expensive idea, but was proving successful as an answer to the Focke-Wulfs that shadowed convoys in the Atlantic. How the CAM ship would fare in the Arctic was yet to be seen.

The strength of PQ 16's escort indicated the importance attached to this convoy. As before, armed trawlers accompanied the ships until they were clear of Iceland, then the ocean escort joined from Seydisfjord. In PQ 16's case, this was made up of the British destroyers *Achates*, *Ashanti*, *Martin*, *Volunteer* and *Ledbury*, the Polish destroyer *Garland*, the corvettes *Honeysuckle*, *Hyderabad*, *Starwort* and *Roselys* (Free French), the auxiliary anti-aircraft ship *Alynbank* and the submarines *Seawolf* and *Trident*. Cruiser cover was provided by the British heavy cruisers *Kent* and *Norfolk*, the light cruisers *Liverpool* and *Nigeria*, accompanied by the destroyers *Marne*, *Onslow* and *Oribi*. The distant covering force was Anglo/American, comprising the battleships *Duke of York* and USS *Washington*, the aircraft carrier *Victorious*, the cruisers *London* and USS *Wichita*, and the destroyers *Blankney*, *Eclipse*, *Faulknor*, *Fury*, *Icarus*, *Intrepid*, *Lamerton*, *Middleton*, *Wheatland* and USS *Mayrant*, *Rhind*, *Rowan* and *Wainright*.

Against such a massive escort the German surface ships very wisely decided not to venture out of their fjords, but PQ 16 did not escape the U-boats and aircraft, some 260 of the latter mounting a series of attacks on the convoy. The U-boats claimed one merchantman, while the bombers sank six ships, including the CAM ship *Empire Lawrence*, whose Hurricane justified its existence by shooting down one attacker and damaging another before ditching. Four other merchantmen and the Polish destroyer *Garland* were damaged.

With twenty-nine out of thirty-six ships reaching their destination, PQ 16 was judged to be a success and it was the precursor of even greater efforts to clear the backlog of loaded ships for Russia. But the German capital ships hiding in Trondheim fjord would still prove a threat to be reckoned with.

Chapter Nine

As May moved into June and the wild flowers bloomed in the hedgerows of Britain, the threat of invasion had become only a distant memory, but out in the Atlantic the battle raged unchecked. Since the beginning of the year, the U-boats had already accounted for 438 Allied ships, totalling a staggering 2,375,000 tons. In the Mediterranean, the island of Malta was under siege and the necessity to force through convoys under constant air attack to supply the island was another heavy drain on the resources of the Royal Navy.

Far to the east, in Soviet Russia, the land war had entered a new and more terrible phase. The snows had at last receded, making way for the launch of Hitler's latest initiative, Operation 'Blau', and once again the German armies were sweeping south-eastwards. The River Donets had been crossed, and the oilfields of Baku and Grozny, on the shores of the Caspian Sea, seemed to be within reach of the advancing panzers. Beyond that lay Iran and her oil, and also the open back door to the Soviet Union, through which an increasing amount of Allied aid was now passing.

Russia's massive reserves of manpower would prove sufficient to absorb and halt the German advances before the oilfields were reached, but this did not still the clamour for the Allies to pour in more and more aid. In the face of Churchill's reluctance to commit more ships to the Arctic convoys, Stalin began to accuse Britain of failing to support Russia in her greatest hour of need. This was, to say the least, hypocritical, coming from a man who had, when it suited his ends, signed a pact with Hitler and, up until the time Germany turned on Russia was completely indifferent to the fate of Britain, then being bombed into submission by the Luftwaffe. Nevertheless, Churchill and Roosevelt, busy planning an invasion of occupied Europe from the west, were aware of the vital role Russia was playing in sapping the strength of the German armies. The attack on PQ 16, despite its huge escort, had been a salutary shock but the need, not only to continue the Arctic convoys but to enlarge on them, was paramount. The huge backlog of loaded ships waiting for convoy to Russia on both sides of the Atlantic had now risen to over 100. Action was needed urgently.

Convoy PQ 17, the largest convoy yet to attempt the Arctic run to Russia, began assembling in Hvalfjord in early June and by the third week of the month the fjord was sheltering forty heavily loaded merchantmen. Twenty-two United States ships dominated the fleet, and anchored with them were thirteen British, two Panamanian, two Russian and one Dutch ships. This assembly of tramps and cargo liners carried in their holds a total of 156,492 tons of cargo for Russia including 594 tanks, 297 aircraft and 4246 military vehicles, said to be enough to equip an army of 50,000 men and worth $700 million. Among the ships was a familiar name, Ayrshire Navigation's *River Afton*, about to embark on her third voyage to Russia and once again as commodore ship. Captain H.W. Charlton was still in command and with him were most of the officers who had first sailed with him in PQ 1.

It was not without much deliberation in London and Washington that such a large body of ships was to be committed to sail en masse through waters so dominated by the enemy. The presence of the German capital ships and the Narvik-class destroyers, with their potential to destroy a convoy, was enough to send shivers down the spines of the Allied naval planners. Then there were reports filtering through that *Generaloberst* Hans-Jürgen Stumpff, commanding the Luftwaffe in northern Norway, now had at least 350 Ju87s, Ju88s and Heinkel 111s massed on the two airfields at Banak and Bardufoss waiting for the opportunity to strike in force.

Unknown to London and Washington at the time – and this would really have caused a panic – the Germans were reading the British naval code and were already aware that a large convoy was preparing to run the gauntlet from Iceland to north Russia. This much had been discovered by a Soviet agent working in Germany, but with typical Soviet indifference to her allies, Moscow had omitted to pass on the information to London. The German High Command, encouraged by the recent successes of their combined air and sea operations against the convoys, had decided to mount a major attack on PQ 17. Operation 'Rosselsprung' (Knight's Move), under the command of Admiral Schniewind, who flew his flag in the *Tirpitz*, was to involve, in addition to the battleship, the pocket battleships *Lützow* and *Scheer*, the heavy cruiser *Admiral Hipper*, twelve destroyers, ten U-boats, and in excess of 300 aircraft. Guidelines for the proposed operation, issued by Admiral Raeder, were as follows:

Main task: Rapid destruction of enemy merchant ships. If necessary, these should only be crippled and the sinking left to the U-boats and Air Force. The escort force should only be attacked if this is indispensable for accomplishing the main task. An engagement with superior enemy forces is to be avoided. The operation should be executed quickly, and should be completed before an enemy covering force composed of battleships and carriers – presumably stationed in the Faeroes-Iceland area – has a chance to intervene.

The Air Force will attack only aircraft carriers and merchant vessels once our forces have engaged the enemy, unless the identity of the ships is unmistakable. It is particularly important that the Air Force fulfil the request of the Navy with regard to aerial reconnaissance, if necessary at the expense of taking part in the battle. The Navy's request is justified as it seems possible to achieve total success with the aid of our heavy forces.

Admiral Raeder was clearly reluctant to commit his surface ships against the big guns of the Home Fleet, being only too well aware of the Royal Navy's superior fighting capabilities, the threat posed by the aircraft carriers – of which Germany had none – and the might of the US Navy which was now joining the fray.

Admiral Sir Dudley Pound, the First Sea Lord, was every bit as apprehensive as Raeder. This was evident in the size of the escorting force he allocated to PQ 17. On leaving Hvalfjord, and for its passage around the west and north coasts of Iceland, the convoy would be protected by the fleet minesweepers *Britomart*, *Halcyon* and *Salamander*, the anti-submarine trawlers *Ayrshire*, *Lord Austin*, *Lord Middleton* and *Northern Gem*, the destroyer *Middleton*, and the auxilliary anti-aircraft ships *Pozarica* and *Palomares*. The AA ships, 2500-tonners requisitioned from the Macandrew Line which in peacetime had carried fruit from the Mediterranean, mounted six 4-inch, two 42-pounder and eight 20-mm guns. When off the north-east tip of Iceland, this escort would be reinforced by the destroyers *Fury*, *Keppel*, *Leamington*, *Ledbury*, *Offa* and *Wilton*, the corvettes *Dianella*, *La Malouine*, *Lotus* and *Poppy*, and a new innovation in convoy escort work, the submarines *P-614* and *P-615*. The Senior Officer Escort, Commander J.E. Broome, was to sail in HMS *Keppel*. Twenty-four hours later, an independently acting cruiser force commanded by Admiral Sir L.K.H. Hamilton would join, made up of the cruisers *London*, *Norfolk*, USS *Tuscaloosa* and USS *Wichita*[1], with the destroyers USS *Wainwright* and USS *Rowan*. Distant cover was to be provided by a combined British/American force under Admiral Sir John Tovey, C.-in-C. Home Fleet consisting of the battleships *Duke of York* and USS *Washington*, the aircraft carrier *Victorious*, the cruisers *Cumberland* and *Nigeria*, screened by the destroyers *Ashanti*, *Blankney*, *Escapade*, *Faulknor*, *Marne*, *Martin*, *Middleton*, *Onslaught*, *Onslow*, *Wheatland*, USS *Mayrant* and USS *Rhind*. Along the north coast of Norway, nine British and two Russian submarines would lie in wait to give warning of any attempt by German surface ships to sail against the convoy, and to attack those ships if possible. The whole operation was under the personal control of Dudley Pound, the First Sea Lord. Certainly, no other previous convoy in history had enjoyed such powerful protection, which indicated the importance London and Washington placed on PQ 17. This was no ordinary convoy; the credibility of Britain and America to supply arms to Russia depended on its success.

The weather was fine and clear when, at 16.00 on 27 June, the ships of PQ 17 sailed out of Hvalfjord, their destination Archangel. In the lead was the *River Afton*, aboard which were the convoy commodore, Commodore John Dowding, DSO, RNR, and his staff of five naval signallers. Dowding was an officer and seaman of great experience, having served in cruisers in the First World War and merchant ships between the wars. This, however, was Dowding's first experience of a voyage to north Russia in summer, when the daylight lasted twenty-four hours a day. Neither he nor Captain Charlton, who was on the bridge of the *River Afton* with him, anticipated accumulating much sleep on the voyage.

As soon as it had cleared Hvalfjord, the convoy formed up into two columns for the coastal passage. The *River Afton* was again in the van, with the Vice Commodore, Captain George Stephenson, in J. & C. Harrison's *Hartlebury* in the middle of the line, and the Rear Commodore, Captain John Wharton in the *Empire Byron*, a Ministry of War transport ship managed by J. & C. Harrison, bringing up the rear. Last of all came a new and very welcome addition to the convoy scene, the three rescue ships *Rathlin*, *Zaafaran* and *Zamelek*. These were three small British ships taken up from the short-sea trade. The *Rathlin*, an ex-cattle carrier had once plied the Irish Sea, while the *Zaafaran* and *Zamelek*, ex-Egyptian Mail Line, in their earlier days had shuttled passengers in the warm waters of the Mediterranean. These ships had been specially fitted out for rescue work and were carrying doctors and medical staff to deal with survivors. They were a comforting sight, although a grim reminder of what might be in store for the convoy.

PQ 17's first casualty occurred the next day, inflicted not by the enemy but by the weather. Soon after leaving Hvalfjord, the clouds had rolled in, the wind had risen, and with it came a heavy beam swell, giving the deep-laden merchantmen their first taste of the fickle Arctic weather. On the morning of the 28th, the wind had gone down, but in its place came dense fog in which were hidden large lumps of drift ice, some of them big enough to damage the hull of a merchant ship. The visibility was no more than fifty yards, which brought the convoy down to a mere snail's pace as it groped its way along with the rocky cliffs of Iceland's north coast to starboard and a British minefield to port. Not surprisingly, one ship, the US-flag *Richard Bland*, a new Liberty ship on her maiden voyage, ran ashore and was left behind. A sad end to the voyage for a ship that had crossed the Atlantic to bring aid to the Russians.

The fog persisted throughout the 28th and 29th, latterly being accompanied by showers of icy rain and sleet. Station-keeping was largely a matter of guesswork. None of the merchantmen had radar, and they were relying on following the fog buoy of the ship ahead, an ingenious device towed astern that kicked up a plume of water. PQ 17 rounded the north-west end of Iceland in an untidy straggle. Near collisions were frequent and the fog echoed to the urgent screech of steam whistles as ships loomed up on each other in the murk. Miraculously, no two ships actually ran onto each other, but there were many heart-stopping moments for those manning the bridges of PQ 17.

They were soon close to the ice edge, still in fog, and small icebergs added to the many dangers. It was one of these floating ice islands that put an end to the *Exford*'s association with the convoy. The twenty-three-year-old American ship was severely damaged when she hit an iceberg and, unfortunately, broke radio silence, not once but eight times, to call the *River Afton* asking for advice. Commodore Dowding wisely refused to answer her and the *Exford* dropped out to return to Hvalfjord, but not before she had probably given away the position of the convoy to listening German D/F stations. The fleet oiler *Grey Ranger* also suffered ice damage, but was able to continue.

On the morning of 1 July, in slightly improved visibility, PQ 17 was off the north-east corner of Iceland and was joined by its impressive ocean escort, which had been fuelling in Seydisfjord. Led by the heavy cruisers *London* and *Norfolk*, with the American heavy cruisers *Wichita* and *Tuscaloosa* they mounted between them thirty-two 8-inch, sixteen 5-inch and sixteen 4-inch guns, while their light armament totalled twenty-four 2-pounder pom-poms and seventy-five 20-mm and 40-mm cannon. They, in their turn, were screened by the two 37-knot US destroyers *Wainwright* and *Rowan*. The arrival of the salt-stained British warships and the sleek, business-like Americans put new heart into a convoy already wearied by adverse weather. Within a short time, PQ 17 had formed up into its ocean steaming order of nine columns abreast, many of the merchantmen flying their barrage balloons. With its escorts ranged around it PQ 17 was ready to challenge the enemy, a challenge that would be taken up sooner than expected. Alerted by the *Exford*'s indiscreet radio chatter, the U-boats were waiting off Jan Mayen Island, 300 miles to the north-east.

Ten boats of the 11th *Unterseebootsflotille*, commanded by *Fregattenkapitän* Hans Cohausz, were the German first line of attack on PQ 17 and one of these, scouting ahead of the line, was sighted astern of the convoy late that afternoon. The escorts immediately pounced on the shadower, which promptly crash-dived and made off. The flurry of activity again led to the breaking of radio silence, this time by several merchant ships. Any pretence of secrecy PQ 17 ever had was now lost.

The U-boats turned up in force next morning. The fog was dispersing and the sun struggling to break through the clouds, when the sinister black shapes were sighted on the fringe of the convoy slipping from fog bank to fog bank taking advantage of the disappearing cover. They made no move to attack, and whenever one of the escorts made towards them they disappeared below the waves in a flurry of foam. On the bridge of the *River Afton*, Commodore Dowding and Captain Charlton, more aware than others of the worsening situation, were feeling distinctly uneasy. The wolves were snapping at the heels of PQ 17. Their fears were not quietened when, an hour later, the first enemy aircraft appeared, a long-range Blohm & Voss 138. By noon, there were three of these flying boats circling, always staying well away from the convoy's guns.

PQ 17 was not yet within range of the German airfields in north Norway where the bombers were based, but it was in flying distance for the Luftwaffe's Heinkel 115 torpedo-carrying float planes operating from fjords near the North Cape. At 17.00, four of these slow-flying aircraft, each with a 21-inch torpedo slung between its floats, arrived and began to circle the convoy warily. The Blohm & Voss 138s, having completed their mission in homing in the torpedo planes, now flew off to the south-east.

The four Heinkels continued to circle at a safe distance for half an hour while they weighed up the odds. Then they came in, two from the port quarter of the convoy and two from the starboard quarter. They were skimming the water at a height of no more than twenty feet and, as they approached, the ships in the rear of the convoy opened fire with everything they had, including their 4-inch anti-submarine guns. The rescue ship *Zaafaran*, at the tail end of the centre column, was particularly well placed to hit back, and as one of the Heinkels lined up on the Russian tanker *Azerbaidjan*, rear ship of Column 6, she did just that. The first shell from her 4-inch was right on target, bursting on the water directly below the Heinkel. The seaplane was thrown into the air by the force of the explosion, appeared to recover, then smoke was seen coming from its starboard engine. It went into a shallow glide, dropping its torpedo harmlessly as it did and finally pancaked onto the water on the other side of the convoy. The *Zaafaran*'s gunners cheered as they watched the Heinkel's two-man crew take to their inflatable dinghy but were silent witnesses to the remarkable rescue that followed. As one of PQ 17's escorting destroyers raced towards the downed plane, another of the attacking Heinkels jettisoned its torpedo, landed on the water alongside the dinghy and took off again with the survivors before the destroyer came near. The rescue took approximately three minutes.

The shooting down of the plane and the amazing rescue of its survivors seemed to convince the other two Heinkels of the futility of their mission and they dropped their torpedoes at random before flying off after the rescue plane. The net result of this attack on the convoy was a clear victory for PQ 17's gunners and gave a huge boost to the confidence of the men in the ships. When, at 17.45, after a signal received warning of U-boats ahead, Commodore Dowding ordered an emergency turn of 90 degrees to port, this was carried out with brisk efficiency by all ships. By the time the convoy returned to its original course, the fog had closed in again, thicker than ever, ensuring that PQ 17, with regard to enemy attacks at least, could look forward to a quiet night.

The fog lifted again at 08.30 on the 3rd and the trio of Blohm & Voss scouts reappeared around mid-morning. As before, the flying boats circled out of range of the guns like watching vultures. The *Zaafaran*'s radio room reported that one of the planes was transmitting on 826 metres, sending a continuous string of 'A's, interrupted every five minutes or so by a call sign consisting of two letters and two figures, this call sign being changed every two hours. Quite clearly, the aircraft was acting as a homing beacon.

The constant circling throughout the day of the enemy planes had an unsettling effect on the convoy and whenever they ventured too near, the gunners showed their nervous frustration by opening up with a fierce barrage. And so the planes moved back out of range again to continue their remorseless watch.

At 17.00, the monotony was relieved when a Sunderland flying boat was sighted on the water. As the big, four-engined plane drifted through the ranks of the convoy in eerie silence it was seen to be entirely encased in ice. There was no point in stopping to look for survivors, but speculation on the story behind the downed British aircraft helped to while away the long night watches. Midnight came and went, marked only by the clock, for it was still full daylight, and the expected attack did not materialize. PQ 17 was by this time in latitude 74 degrees north, and only eighty miles to the south-west of Bear Island. The cold was intense, but even that was forgotten as, hour by hour, the tension mounted.

There were some in the ships, not many, who managed to sleep, fully dressed with lifejackets on, but their rest would have been sorely troubled if they had known that, as they slept, on the west coast of Norway the main strike force of Operation 'Rosselsprung' was gathering. Soon after PQ 17 was first sighted from the air on 2 July, the *Tirpitz*, flying the flag of Admiral Schniewind, accompanied by the *Hipper* and six destroyers, left Trondheim for Altenfjord, 600 miles to the north. Later in the day, the *Lützow* and *Scheer*, with a screen of three destroyers, sailed from Narvik also bound for Altenfjord. When assembled in Altenfjord, a vast, sheltered fjord only ninety-five miles from the North Cape, the attack force would be within ten hours fast steaming of PQ 17 as it passed south of Bear Island. The plan was for *Tirpitz* and *Hipper* to engage and drive off the convoy's escort, while *Lützow* and *Scheer* set about the defenceless merchant ships. With the help of the Luftwaffe and the U-boats, Admiral Schniewind expected – and not without good reason – to bring about the complete destruction of PQ 17 and as many of its escorting ships as possible. But it would have to be a fast, precise operation and finished before the heavy ships of the combined British and American distant covering force had time to intercede.

On 4 July 1942, American Independence Day, there was little

celebration in the US-flag ships of PQ 17. It was, perhaps, more a time for the men manning the ships to question what on earth they were doing 5000 odd miles from home and involved in a war that was really none of their concern. The day opened to match their mood, cold and foggy, with visibility around 1000 yards, just sufficient for the ships to keep station on each other, but poor enough, it was hoped, to deter the probing attacks of the enemy. This proved to be a false hope, for two hours after midnight the drone of a low-flying aircraft was heard and ships at the rear glimpsed a lone Blohm & Voss 138 skimming the waves astern of the convoy. The shadower was back.

After a while, the spy went away and all was quiet, but no one in this fleet of slow-moving ships was foolish enough to think the danger was over. True to form, at 03.45, the muffled drone of aircraft engines was heard again. The gun barrels moved from side to side seeking out the hated sound, then they swung to starboard as a Heinkel 115 appeared out of the fog astern, flying about thirty feet above the water. But even before the guns had a chance to fire, the plane had dropped its torpedo and disappeared back into the fog. The torpedo, its track clearly visible just below the surface, passed midway between the third and fourth ships of Column 9, the US-flag cargo ships *Carlton* and *Samuel Chase*, and found a target in the *Christopher Newport*, the lead ship of Column 8 which had fallen astern of her position. The *Christopher Newport*, another 7000-ton Liberty on her maiden voyage, took the German torpedo squarely amidships, the explosion laying open her engine room to the sea and blowing her starboard lifeboats away. She remained upright, but stopped and drifting rapidly astern into the fog.

Had a deep-sea tug then been available, the *Christopher Newport* and her precious cargo might have reached port, for she was in no real danger of sinking, but without her engines she was a lame duck PQ 17 could not afford. Her crew was ordered to abandon ship, and was picked up by the rescue ship *Zamelak*. The crippled ship was then sunk by gunfire from one of the escorting British submarines.

About 250 miles to the south of PQ 17, behind the shelter of the island of Soray, which protects the mouth of Altenfjord, the *Tirpitz* and *Hipper* had been joined by the *Scheer* in preparation

118

for the sortie against the convoy. There was, however, a cloud on Admiral Schniewind's horizon. On their way up from Narvik, the *Lützow* and her three destroyers had run into dense fog while negotiating the narrow waters between the Norwegian coast and its off-lying islands. Using outdated Norwegian charts, all four ships ran aground on a rocky shore and were so badly damaged that they were forced to put into Trondheim for repairs. Admiral Raeder, overseeing the operation from afar, was now faced with a dilemma. Earlier in the day, he had been given news of a sighting of a British fleet within 300 miles of Convoy PQ 17. This fleet, it was reported, consisted of two battleships, an aircraft carrier, five heavy cruisers and a number of destroyers. Raeder was confident that Schniewind's ships, depleted though they now were, could match the British battleships and cruisers, but it was the presence of an aircraft carrier that frightened him. The thought of *Tirpitz*, the pride and joy of the *Kriegsmarine*, being sunk by torpedo-carrying aircraft from the carrier was too awful to contemplate. He decided he could not send his ships out without Hitler's express permission and stayed his hand.

It may, or may not have been, in answer to an urgent request for Raeder, but that evening the Luftwaffe returned in force to attack PQ 17. Captain Charlton of the *River Afton* estimated that thirty aircraft took part. He reported:

They were flying in groups of five or six round the horizon and appeared to be mainly Heinkel 115s, but amongst them I spotted one JU 88. I was flying a balloon mast-high owing to the low fog and I don't know if the JU 88 spotted this, anyway he singled me out for a low level bombing attack. I heard his engines roaring but was unable to open fire as the aircraft was not visible. As the aircraft roared over a stick of bombs fell between me and an American destroyer. I was not able to open fire until the plane had passed over on account of the bad visibility. The ship suffered no damage from these bombs and meanwhile the Heinkel 115 torpedo carrying aircraft were circling low on the horizon getting into position for an attack. They flew in circles clockwise on the starboard side with a JU 88 ahead of them apparently directing operations. Having reached a position on the port beam they turned and flew towards the stern of the convoy and attacked from the starboard quarter, flying up the columns of ships. The escorting ships and rear ships of the convoy opened fire with their 4-inch guns and only four planes managed to complete their run through the convoy. The JU 88 circled the convoy watching the attack. The leader of the Heinkels flew along between Nos. 3 and 4 columns at bridge height. As he flew up the convoy all ships opened fire and several ships claimed direct hits on it. When he came abeam of me I opened fire with my Oerlikons and Hotchkiss and he crashed a little ahead of my ship. In this attack he succeeded in torpedoing the ss. *Navarino*, No.23 in the convoy. . . .

Captain A. Kelso of the *Navarino*, a 4841-ton 'London Greek' tramp owned by Goulandris Ltd., described the incident:

The convoy was sailing in nine columns at the time and the aircraft attacked between the columns. I was concerned with the aircraft leading the attack. He came up between two escorting submarines and flew up between No.4 and 5 columns and at 1800 GMT, when in position 75-57N 27-14E the sea was calm with no wind, the weather was fine and the visibility poor, we were proceeding at a speed of 8 knots on a course N45E, this aircraft flying at about 20ft above the water released a torpedo when he was about one cable away from the ship. This torpedo struck the ship amidships under the bridge on the starboard side. As the aircraft approached I put the helm hard over to port in an effort to upset his attack, and as I was doing so, someone shouted 'Torpedo!' I ran out and saw a torpedo approaching the ship 45 degrees abaft my beam. I was hoping that, as the ship was swinging, we might miss the torpedo, but unfortunately she was not quick enough in swinging and the torpedo caught us.

It was not a very loud explosion as the torpedo struck, but a great deal of water and all the bunkers were thrown into the air. The ship immediately took a list of 30–40 degrees, so that the bilge keel came right out of the water on the starboard side.

Every ship in the convoy and all the escorting vessels opened fire at the attacking aircraft; the aircraft which attacked my ship must have been riddled with machine-gun bullets and cannon fire. We opened fire when it was astern of us; there were three ships astern of me and they all opened fire as the aircraft approached. This aircraft went round my bow and landed in the water ahead of my ship in a sheet of flame. My gunnery officer claimed we brought down this aircraft, but so many guns were firing at the time that I would not like to say that any particular gunner was responsible for bringing it down.

The *Navarino* was abandoned, only one man of her total complement of sixty men, which included four passengers, was lost. The others, largely due to the calm weather, got away in two lifeboats despite the heavy list. They were picked up by the rescue ships *Rathlin* and *Zaafaran*. The *Navarino* was later sunk by gunfire from one of the escorting destroyers.

Captain Charles McGowan of the rescue ship *Zaafaran* had a somewhat different view of events:

At 1700, six Heinkel 115s, each carrying two torpedoes, were sighted on the starboard beam, but they did not come in to attack, and at 1820 twenty-five Heinkel 117s, each carrying three torpedoes, joined in with the Heinkel 115s, and pressed home a torpedo attack. The leader of the formation was flying about 1½–2 miles ahead of his formation, which came in at about 30 feet above the water. The plane was shot down by the gunners on our Oerlikon gun. The rest of the aircraft in very close 'V' formation were attacked by our Bofors gun, which was responsible for the destruction of a third plane. After the leader was shot down, the rest of the formation rose to a height of about 150–200 feet before releasing their torpedoes, which did not run very accurately. I had dropped about a mile astern of the convoy in order to have plenty of room to manoeuvre the ship. I reckon about 87 torpedoes were dropped and only three ships were hit, two of which had to be abandoned. The torpedoes were dropped on our starboard quarter and I noticed that many of them fell about half a mile away, while others were released up to a distance of 3 miles. Those dropped from a height bounced out of the water to a height of 20 feet, but they still ran, although not accurately. The tracks were straight and the torpedoes ran in the same direction as the plane was facing when released. The torpedoes were dropped three at a time, and they appeared to be about 16 inches in diameter. After releasing their torpedoes, the planes made off as quickly as they could towards the coast.

Fortunately for PQ 17 the attack, carried out by Heinkel 115s of *Küstenfliegergruppe* 906 was, at best, chaotic, and when the leader was shot down it appears to have developed into a rout, probably because the German pilots were totally unprepared for the sheer ferocity of the barrage put up by the ships' guns. Captain McGowan's estimate of eighty-seven torpedoes dropped was very near the mark and of these only three found a target. The *Navarino* was so badly damaged that she had to be sunk by the escorts and the US-flag steamer *William Hooper*, sustaining similar damage, was abandoned and later sunk by *U-334* as she drifted astern of the convoy. The Russian tanker *Azerbaidjan* was also damaged by a torpedo but managed to stay with the convoy. She reached port under her own steam, but most of her cargo of linseed oil had leaked out along the way. It was confirmed that three of *Küstenfliegergruppe* 906's aircraft were shot down and at least one other damaged.

NOTE

[1] The Hollywood actor, Douglas Fairbanks Jr., was a naval officer on board the USS *Wichita* (CA-45) on temporary additional duty when the cruiser was part of the covering force for PQ 17. As a member of Rear Admiral Robert 'Ike' Giffen's staff (Giffen flew his flag aboard the battleship USS *Washington* [BB-56]), Fairbanks was given various assignments recording US naval wartime operations for historical purposes. The following is an excerpt from his report on PQ 17:

In the midst of the slaughter, during which the cruiser force felt helpless and wanted to assist, a shocking message was received, '1911: From Admiralty to CS-1: Cruiser Force must withdraw to westward at high speed!' Admiral of the Fleet Sir A. Dudley Pound, noting that the convoy was about to come opposite the Alten Fjord and suspecting that the *Tirpitz* would sortie out and attack the Allied ships, was ordering the support force to withdraw and the merchant ships to proceed independently to Russian ports.

Abandoning the convoy made the men 'feel ashamed and resentful'. The next day Admiral Hamilton sent the following message: 'I know you will be feeling as distressed as I am at having to leave that fine collection of ships to find their own way to harbor. The enemy under cover of his shore based aircraft, has succeeded in concentrating a vastly superior force in this area. We are therefore ordered to withdraw. We are all sorry that the good work of the close escort could not be completed. I hope we shall all have a chance of settling this score with them soon.

Chapter Ten

Although two ships had been lost and one damaged, the defeat of *Küstenfliegergruppe* 906 – and it was a defeat – was a significant achievement for PQ 17. The Admiralty was notified of the outcome of the action, and it was confidently expected that a message of congratulation and approval might have been received in return, for this was a convoy that had proved it could look after itself. Commander Broome (SOE), steaming through the convoy in *Keppel* after the attack, remarked that it was, 'a tonic to see the ships all in station and looking prouder than ever. I think we all felt that the enemy had realised that PQ 17 meant business and that feeling did us good.' It was with considerable shock, therefore, that in the evening a series of 'most immediate' signals was received from the Admiralty. The first, at 21.11, read 'Cruiser force to withdraw to the westward at high speed'. Twelve minutes later, at 21.23, came the second signal, 'Owing to threat from surface ships, convoy is to disperse and proceed to Russian ports'. And finally, at 21.36 came, 'Convoy is to scatter', this last message indicating that the attack by surface ships was imminent. When the signals were passed to Commodore John Dowding in the *River Afton* he was incredulous and asked for them to be repeated. Captain Charlton later wrote: 'This order bewildered me as it seemed absolutely fatal for thirty odd ships to proceed independently without protection through the Barents Sea'. His sentiments were echoed by all those in the convoy who had previous experience of this dangerous road to Russia.

The responsibility for the seemingly nonsensical decision taken on the future of PQ 17 lay in London with the First Sea Lord,

Admiral Sir Dudley Pound. The Admiral was not one to run away from a fight, having commanded with distinction the battleship *Colossus* at the Battle of Jutland, but the attack in force on PQ 17 by the Luftwaffe caused him a great deal of concern. He was convinced – and not without good reason – that this was the preliminary to an attack on the convoy by the German big guns, known to be in Altenfjord and possibly already at sea. Dudley Pound feared that the combined fighting power of the *Tirpitz*, *Scheer*, *Lützow* and *Hipper*, backed up by aircraft and U-boats, might not only wipe out the merchant ships altogether and Admiral Hamilton's cruisers as well, but might even endanger the big ships of Admiral Tovey's distant covering force. This was an attitude very foreign to the usual thinking of the Royal Navy and Churchill was later to comment: 'Admiral Pound would probably not have sent such vehement orders if only our own warships had been concerned. But the idea that our first large joint Anglo/American operation under British command should involve the destruction of two United States cruisers as well as our own may well have disturbed the poise with which he was accustomed to deal with these heart-shaking decisions.' The Prime Minister, as usual, was probably right.

The day might yet have been saved, had not PQ 17's destroyer escort also been withdrawn. There is some difference of opinion as to how this came about. One reason put forward was the confusion that existed following the order for the convoy to scatter. A more likely explanation given was that Commander Broome, believing a fleet action between Hamilton's cruisers and the German capital ships to be imminent, decided that his destroyers would be better employed using their torpedoes to good effect in any such action. In retrospect, it might be said that no one seems to have given too much thought to what would happen to the unprotected merchantmen when the German aircraft and U-boats got amongst them in earnest.

The outcome of Sir Dudley Pound's fatal order was that the men in the merchant ships, none of whom with the exception of those on the bridge of the *River Afton*, really knew what was going on, had the unnerving experience of seeing their escorting cruisers and destroyers suddenly go through a 180 degree turn and sweep past the convoy heading west at twenty-five knots.

PQ 17, with orders to scatter to the four winds, was left with a handful of corvettes, minesweepers and trawlers, not one of which was armed with more than a couple of 4-inch guns, to run with them and pick up the pieces as they fell.

History shows, with cruel irony, that the German Naval Staff's fear of a major confrontation was even greater than that of the Admiralty. All eyes were on Tovey's big ships, and particularly the aircraft carrier, which were thought to be much closer than they actually were. In consequence, Admiral Raeder waited for Hitler's permission before sailing his big ships with their destroyer screen. This came late on the morning of 5th and Schniewind sailed at noon. By this time he had been advised by his air reconnaissance that the Allied cruisers and destroyers had withdrawn to the west and PQ 17 had scattered.

As soon as Schniewind's ships cleared Altenfjord, they were sighted, firstly by a Russian, and then by a British submarine, which were keeping watch off the entrance to the fjord. Radio signals from the British submarine reporting the sighting were picked up by a German station and relayed to Schniewind. This caused the German admiral to hesitate, for with his sailing betrayed to the enemy he was more than ever mindful of the sixty Albacore torpedo bombers carried by HMS *Victorious*, but he pressed on to the north-east in search of the convoy. However, a decision was now to be taken at the highest level. Hitler, still smarting from the loss of the mighty *Bismarck* in the Atlantic a little over a year before, largely brought about by carrier-borne aircraft, was in a state of funk. Ten hours after weighing anchor, Schniewind was ordered to bring his ships back to Altenfjord. The official reason given for the withdrawal of this powerful fleet was that Schniewind's destroyers were running short of fuel. It is questionable whether Hitler's big ships would have had much success in hunting down the ships of PQ 17, which had all scattered, but they were saved from one threat by the vacillations of Germany's leaders. The attentions of the other predators, hunting above and below the Barents Sea, they would be unable to escape.

After receiving the order to scatter, and watching in horror as the greater part of the convoy's escort force disappeared over the horizon, Captain John Wharton, Rear Commodore, in the *Empire Byron*, decided salvation for his ship lay to the north in the ice. His intentions were to put as many miles as possible between his ship and the German airfields and once inside the ice edge, hopefully safe from the U-boats, to sail east before making a dash for the White Sea and Archangel. He estimated he had 700 miles to steam before reaching safe waters. The *Empire Byron*, a wartime replacement ship built in a north-east coast shipyard was, like all her class, woefully underpowered and the best Wharton could expect from her was ten knots. It promised to be a long three days.

By midnight that night, the ships of PQ 17 had fanned out in all directions and were well scattered around the horizon. Wharton still had one or two other ships in sight to the north and south, but by and large he had a clear field, which after spending eight days in close company with thirty other ships in poor visibility was a great relief. There was only one outstanding problem in the form of a German reconnaissance aircraft to be seen circling at a respectful distance. Wharton was heartened when, at 02.00 on the 5th, this plane flew away and was not replaced by another. The weather was fine with a smooth sea, light airs and excellent visibility. Only two other ships were still in sight, one on the starboard bow and the other astern and overtaking. At 07.45 Wharton, who had not left the bridge for thirty-six hours, decided it would be safe for him to go below to freshen up. Leaving Chief Officer William Prance in charge, with eight lookouts posted in various parts of the ship, he left the bridge.

Neither Prance nor any of the *Empire Byron*'s lookouts saw the track of the torpedo as it came streaking in on the port side half an hour after Captain Wharton left the bridge. The torpedo struck the ship in her No.4 hold, just forward of the mainmast. The 750lbs of high explosive packed into the warhead blew a jagged hole in the British ship's side, the blast sending beams, hatchboards, tarpaulins and cargo high in the air. The *Empire Byron*'s DEMS gunners were housed in accommodation built into her No.4 tween deck, and some, like Captain Wharton, were below taking a well-earned break when the torpedo hit. Six of them died when cases of aircraft stowed in the deck broke adrift and smashed them against the ship's side.

Captain John Wharton arrived on the bridge wiping away the

last flecks of shaving soap with a towel to find his ship rapidly sinking by the stern. His first action was to ring the engine room telegraph to stop but there was no reply to his order. Seconds later, a breathless chief engineer reached the bridge to report all the steam spindles to the main engine, including those of the emergency shut-off valve on the boat deck, were broken. There was no immediate means of stopping the engine. The *Empire Byron* was condemned to sink while going full speed ahead.

The *Empire Byron* had on board a complement of seventy-two, which included eighteen DEMS gunners – six of whom were now dead – a team of three naval signallers led by Lieutenant Eakins RNVR, and four passengers. Three of the latter were Russian merchant seamen returning home after losing their ship and the fourth was Captain Rimmington, a British army officer whose mission was to have been to instruct the Russians in the tanks the ship was carrying. This was a mission now at an end and Rimmington would have to take his chance with the others in the boats. The *Empire Byron* carried four lifeboats, two full-sized boats abaft the funnel and two smaller boats abreast the bridge. The sea was calm and the ship upright, but when Wharton gave the order to abandon ship, she was still going ahead at seven knots, fast enough to make launching boats difficult. Under the careful supervision of Wharton and his deck officers, the two large boats took to the water successfully and cast off. When it came to lowering the smaller and lighter bridge boats, disaster struck. The starboard boat was launched with a crew of three, but before they could cast off, the boat was slammed against the ship's side and capsized. The three crew jumped clear and swam to one of the boats standing off. The other bridge boat was immediately dragged under and swamped. One of the boat's crew, Third Radio Officer Richard Phillips, was thrown into the water and later died from shock and exposure.

By this time, the *Empire Byron*'s main deck was awash, all her boats were gone and nine men, Captain Wharton, Chief Officer Prance, the Third Officer, First and Second Radio Officers, the Gunlayer, Leading Seaman T.J. Evans and two Maritime AA Regiment gunners, were still on board. The only means of survival for these men lay in the *Empire Byron*'s wooden life-rafts, stowed on chutes on the main deck. Wharton led the way to the raft furthest aft on the port side, where the sea was lapping over the ship's side rail. The slip of the launching gear was already under water but it was a simple matter to kick this loose, then the raft, with eight men clinging to it, floated easily off the ship. Wharton swam after it and clambered aboard.

They had left the ship only just in time. The *Empire Byron* was slowly slipping beneath the waves, only her bridge house and foredeck being still above water by the time they had paddled 100 yards or so. Wharton, wet through after his short swim and feeling the grip of the cold, watched in horror as the unseen enemy put another two torpedoes into his sinking ship. When the smoke and debris cleared, the *Empire Byron* had gone from sight.

What the future held for the nine men clinging to the unprotected raft did not bear contemplation. When the first torpedo struck, Wharton had instructed the radio-room to send out an SOS, but as the ship's main receiver had been smashed, it was not known whether anyone was listening. The two ships then in the vicinity, the British steamer *Earlston*, three miles off on the port bow and the American *Peter Kerr*, only half a mile astern, had given no sign. The *Earlston* carried on as though she had seen or heard nothing, while the *Peter Kerr* reversed her course and steamed off in the opposite direction. So much for the fellowship of the sea, Wharton thought, as he looked around the grim, forbidding face of the sea, which had suddenly become a very lonely place.

Hope was restored when, fifteen minutes later, the Second Officer's boat closed the raft and took the nine men off. Two other boats were in the vicinity – the port jolly boat had been salvaged – and Wharton learned that apart from the six gunners killed when the first torpedo struck, the only other casualty was Third Radio Officer Phillips. Wharton called the other boats in, but as they rowed towards each other the conning tower of a submarine emerged from the sea about a mile away. *Kapitänleutnant* Heinz Bielfeld had brought *U-703* to the surface to investigate the survivors of her morning's work.

Bearing in mind the U-boat's nasty habit of making prisoners of masters and chief engineers of ships that had sunk, Wharton quickly slipped off his uniform jacket with its tell-tale four gold bands and stuffed it out of sight in the boat's locker. When the

U-boat then approached his lifeboat, he was suitably anonymous. The submarine motored to within about ten yards of the boat and an officer, young, very blonde and speaking perfect English, climbed down onto the casing and ordered them alongside. This they did so warily, eyeing the sailor leaning over the conning tower rail covering them with a sub-machine gun. There were three other men in the conning tower, Wharton noted, all dressed in clean khaki uniform. The man he took to be the commander, looked to be in his mid-forties, clean shaven and with a very dark complexion.

Wharton had briefed his men on what was likely to happen, and when the question came, 'Where is the Captain?', there was complete silence. Then, realizing some answer must be given, Wharton spoke up, saying the Captain had last been seen on the bridge of the ship before she sank. To his great surprise, he was believed. But they were not to get off scot-free. The officer on the casing had spotted Captain Rimmington who, very foolishly, was still wearing his Army battledress, complete with badges of rank. Either gallantly, or naively, Rimmington offered himself up as a substitute for the *Empire Byron*'s master, and was ordered aboard the submarine and so into captivity. With that, the Germans went through a ridiculous charade of apologizing for sinking Wharton's ship and then handed over a small package of biscuits, a bottle of wine and a piece of German sausage. This generous gesture towards their victims was, of course, carefully photographed from the conning tower, no doubt to be used for propaganda purposes. Then *U-703* motored away.

When the submarine was out of sight, Wharton, whose lifeboat was equipped with an engine, rounded up the other boats and divided the survivors equally between the two larger boats. The jolly boat, which was damaged and waterlogged, was then cast adrift. From Chief Officer Prance, Wharton learned that Bielfeld had given him a course to steer for the land which he said was only ninety miles off. The course, S 50°E, appeared correct, but Wharton was of the opinion that land was more like 300 miles away.

At around 09.00, the two boats set off to the south-east under oars. There was virtually no wind, but sails were hoisted to provide a better target for any rescue ship that might be searching for them. The uncompensated magnetic compasses in the boats were not reliable, so they steered a rough course by the sun. Every two hours, the portable lifeboat transmitter was used to send out an SOS. Taking turns at the oars, they rowed steadily until 19.00, when Wharton called a halt and, starting his engine, took the other boat in tow for the night.

Using the engine sparingly, for there was little fuel on board, and taking advantage of occasional pockets of wind that filled the hanging sails, the two boats progressed slowly southwards. There was a good supply of food and water on board, supplemented by that taken from the abandoned jolly boat and raft, and even with the prospect of five days at sea – which is what Wharton antici-pated – it was unlikely that the survivors would suffer from hunger or thirst. However, as a precaution against the unknown, he set the rations per man at two biscuits spread with pemmican three times a day, washed down by two ounces of water morning and evening. With the occasional Horlicks tablet and square of chocolate, this was a reasonable fare under the circumstances, but every man, without exception, would have forgone it all for a hot drink. It was not particularly cold, the temperature never falling below about 40°F, but most of the survivors had had a thorough wetting in abandoning ship, and to sit huddled in an open boat was a miserable experience. On the other hand, this gave them an incentive to take the oars and there was never any lack of volunteers.

A lone aircraft, believed to be German, was sighted on the morning of the 7th and later that day they saw an unidentified merchant ship, on fire and apparently abandoned, probably another lone runner from PQ 17 caught by the bombers. It was debated whether to try to board this ship, but the consensus of opinion was that they were better off where they were. This proved to be the case, although they were to spend another three wretched days in the boats before rescue came. It was noon on the 10th when Wharton's insistence on keeping the sails set at all times paid dividends. The scraps of red canvas were sighted from the crow's nest of the corvette *Dianella*, which happened to be passing on her way in to Archangel. When taken aboard the corvette, at 13.20 on the 10th, the *Empire Byron*'s survivors had been over five days in their boats and had covered a distance of

250 miles towards the land. They were landed in Archangel six days later, most of them none the worse for having spent five and a half days sitting shoulder to shoulder in an open boat, other than badly swollen feet and the craving for a hot meal and a long sleep.

John Wharton singled out some of his men for praise:

> I would like to recommend Leading Seaman, Acting Gunlayer T.J. Evans. While the crew were abandoning ships he displayed initiative and energy in rescuing the gunners from their accommodation and did in fact haul two men to safety, and it was entirely due to his efforts that these men were saved.

> Chief Officer Prance did splendid work in getting the boats away and it was due to his leadership and organisation that No.3 and 4 boats were successfully lowered.

> I would like to recommend Third Wireless Officer R. Phillips who was making his first voyage. He carried the portable set to the lifeboat and although ordered by the Second Officer would not get into the boat, but returned to the bridge to see if his services were required by me. He lost his life while trying to get away in the port bridge boat.

> The Carpenter, F. Cooper, launched the rafts and remained with me until the end, having to swim off when the ship sank. He remained cool throughout assisting others to escape from the sinking ship and was with me until the last possible moment.

> (It is recorded that Frederick Cooper pulled young Richard Phillips from the water and held him in his arms when he died.)

It was a bone of contention with the *Empire Byron*'s survivors that the two ships in sight when she was torpedoed on the morning of 5 July had done nothing to help them. The American ship *Peter Kerr*, then only half a mile astern, turned round and ran away, while the British ship *Earlston* just carried on as though nothing had happened. It is inconceivable that the *Peter Kerr*, being so close, was not aware of the torpedoing, but her reaction is not on record. The *Earlston*, on the other hand, certainly knew what had transpired. The first inclination of her master, Captain H.J. Stanwick, was to drop back to pick up survivors but,

131

knowing that at least one U-boat was lurking under the surface, he felt his first duty was to his own men and for this Stanwick can be forgiven. The 7195-ton *Earlston*, owned by Chapman & Willan of Newcastle, was a very vulnerable ship. In her holds, along with the field guns, lorries and crated Hurricanes, she carried several hundred tons of naval ammunition, while her decks were covered with drums of high octane fuel and toluol, the latter being the chief constituent of TNT. The *Earlston* was a floating bomb, primed and ready to explode.

Shutting his ears to the rumble of explosions astern, Stanwick urged his engineers to squeeze a few extra revolutions out of the ship's already hard-pushed engine. This they did, but the *Earlston* was another box-like wartime replacement and the improvement in her speed was negligible. The sinking *Empire Byron* dropped astern and as the morning wore on they ran into patchy fog, which gave them some cover, but at around 14.30, two submarines were sighted astern. The U-boats – and Stanwick assumed them to be U-boats – were on the surface, running trimmed down with their casings submerged, and overtaking. The 4-inch gun on the *Earlston*'s stern was manned and Stanwick gave the order to open fire. The gun barked enthusiastically but after only four rounds had been fired two ship's lifeboats, with survivors on board, suddenly drifted out of a fog bank into the line of fire. Stanwick ordered the gun to cease fire.

It is hard to judge who was the most surprised, Stanwick, the U-boats or the men in the lifeboats who, it transpired, were from the American steamer *Honomu*, sunk by Max-Martin Teichert's *U-456* only a few minutes earlier. The *Earlston* was in the middle of a killing ground and Stanwick decided it was time to get out. The four shells fired by the *Earlston*'s 4-inch, if achieving nothing else, had caused the U-boats to submerge and Stanwick now took the opportunity to make a wide alteration to starboard. It was his intention to abandon the attempt to reach Archangel and head for the Kola Inlet, then some 350 miles to the south.

Luck was with the Newcastle ship. The visibility was deteriorating further, already down to one mile, and it seemed that her large alteration of course must have fooled the U-boats, for they did not reappear. Unfortunately, half an hour later, as the *Earlston* appeared to be making good her escape, the drone of aircraft engines announced the arrival of yet another threat. Five torpedo-carrying planes, probably Heinkel 115s, appeared out of the mist on the starboard bow, flying very low over the water and converging on the ship. Stanwick took the only action possible, altering wide to port to bring his 4-inch to bear. The men manning the gun were cool and deliberate, their second shell bursting close in front of the leading plane, causing it to swerve violently. The Heinkel recovered quickly and returned to the attack, levelling off at fifty feet, but the German pilot was obviously shaken for he released his torpedo when just under a mile off the ship. This gave Stanwick ample time to alter course to comb its track. The torpedo passed harmlessly down the starboard side of the *Earlston*, but not more than fifty feet clear. Having witnessed their leader's abortive attack, the other Heinkels gave up and flew off in search of other targets.

Elated with the success of his tactics, Stanwick brought the *Earlston* back on her southerly course and with the visibility still falling he began to feel more confident of escape. It was not to be. Another half an hour passed and his hopes were dashed by the sound of yet more aircraft engines. Minutes later, a flight of seven Stuka dive-bombers appeared on the port bow, flying at about 300 feet. As the first gull-winged plane peeled off and began its screaming dive on the ship, with the exception of the low-angle 4-inch, all the *Earlston*'s guns opened fire. This constituted a considerable barrage, for she carried four 20-mm Oerlikons, one twin 0.5-inch Browning, two twin Marlins, two single Hotchkiss, one single Lewis and two multiple rocket launchers, known as 'pig troughs'. The eager German pilot was given no opportunity to dodge; he was simply blown out of the sky before he had a chance to release his bombs.

The loss of their leader did not deter the other Stukas. They now attacked the *Earlston* from all sides, dropping their bombs in sticks of four. Stanwick threw his ship from side to side under full helm, his gunners fought back, and it seemed that the *Earlston* might just survive. Then a stick of four bombs fell within a few feet of her bows and she staggered as though running into a brick wall. The next Stuka to attack did not miss; its stick of bombs scored a direct hit on the *Earlston*'s engine room creating chaos. The blast fractured steam pipes, unseated pumps and smashed open the main injections, which had the effect of opening up the hull to the sea. The engine room was filled with scalding steam, water poured in and the engine stopped.

The Chief Engineer's report to the bridge could not have been worse. Both engine room and stokehold were flooded, the water rising unchecked, and there was no hope of restarting the main engine or any pumps. Stanwick now had to consider the possibility of abandoning ship. The matter was decided for him when three U-boats were seen on the surface ahead. Still unwilling to give up, Stanwick tried to turn the *Earlston* to bring her 4-inch to bear, but she had lost too much way and would not answer the helm. Reluctantly, he gave the order to abandon ship, telling his men they would return if the ship was not sunk.

The evacuation was carried out in copy-book style, all fifty-five crew and five passengers getting away in two lifeboats and a jolly boat in the space of fifteen minutes. The three boats pulled clear of the ship and were in the process of transferring men from boat to boat to even up the numbers when the end came very suddenly for the *Earlston*. One of the U-boats – later established as *U-334*, commanded by *Kapitänleutnant* Hilmar Siemon – fired a torpedo into the ship at point blank range and at the same time a Stuka scored a direct hit with a stick of bombs. The torpedo struck in No.4 hold, thereby completing the destruction of the after part of the ship, but it was the bombs that dealt the fatal blow. All four exploded in No.2 hold, which was packed with ammunition. The *Earlston* went up in a sheet of flame and sank within minutes. She had lasted less than nineteen hours from being given the order to scatter.

Second Officer David Evans, who was in charge of the *Earlston*'s starboard lifeboat, later described the events that followed:

> Directly the ship had disappeared a submarine steamed towards us and signalled for us to unship our oars whilst he came alongside. The Captain of the U-boat asked for the Master and ordered him to go on board. We had burned all our papers and notes about the attack before the submarine came alongside, so that there was no evidence for the Germans to get hold of. The Captain spoke good English with a slight German accent and intonation, but it was

good English, quite grammatical. His words were, 'I want the Captain to come on board'. I heard the Master ask the U-boat Captain to tow the boats nearer to the land, but he replied, 'I am sorry, I cannot'. He then called out, 'Look out for your boat', started up his engines and steamed off on the surface with our Master as prisoner on board. He remained on the surface for quite half an hour after leaving us.

I closed the Chief Officer's boat and asked what he intended to do, and he suggested the three boats should try to keep together and make for Murmansk. I agreed, and we set sail, but there was only a light wind so we got out the oars and rowed, steering a southerly course. There were 7 men in the jolly boat, 33 in my lifeboat, and 19 in the Mate's boat. The weather became hazy and by 2300 on the 5th we had lost contact with the other two boats. My boat continued on a southerly course, rowing most of the time, until 0300 on the 6th when we sighted the jolly boat. We closed it and found it had been abandoned, all the stores and water having been removed, so I presumed the 7 men had transferred into the Mate's boat. We continued on a southerly course until 0800 when we sighted the Mate's boat about 2 miles ahead, a little on our port bow. We drew alongside at 1100, compared notes and checked compasses, and agreed that if we again became separated we would both try to make Murmansk. The boats remained together until 1800 on the 6th, when foggy weather again set in and the boats again became separated, not to meet again.

David Evans calculated his boat was roughly 270 miles north of the Kola Inlet, a challenging voyage for an open boat in the Barents Sea. The wind was light and variable, hardly enough to take the creases out of the sails and if it stayed so they were in for a very long haul. Bearing this in mind, Evans made his preparations carefully, dividing up the thirty-three men in the boat, including himself, into three watches, one watch to row while the other two rested. The arrangement worked well for a day and a half, the heavy boat crawling across the surface of the calm sea at a slow, measured pace. However, the wonder of discovering they were still alive and stood a good chance of reaching the land soon wore off. By the morning of the 8th, there were rumblings from some of the men, who complained they were too exhausted and too thirsty to carry on rowing. Evans suspected the latter problem might have been brought on by the generous tots of whisky handed out by Captain Stanwick during the action with the German planes and U-boats. Very necessary at the time, perhaps, but dehydration was the result.

The situation took a turn for the worse when it was discovered that one of the galvanized steel fresh water tanks had burst a seam and ten gallons of the boat's total supply of thirty-five gallons of water had been lost. The weather was the culprit, the temperature being down below freezing during the night hours, and as water expands on freezing, a full tank is likely to burst. There were other forms of liquid in the boat, a case of rum and a case of brandy some well-meaning person had put aboard, but it would be dangerous to make free use of this. As a compromise, in the coldest part of the night, Evans issued a drink made up of two teaspoonsful of rum mixed with a little condensed milk and water. This was palatable but not thirst provoking. As to provisions, the boat was well stocked with condensed milk, corned beef, ship's biscuits, Horlicks tablets, chocolate and, what was meant to be the mainstay of a survivor's diet, an ample supply of tinned pemmican. This was a paste of fried meat extract, originally produced for Captain Scott's ill-fated expedition to the South Pole in 1911. Pemmican is highly nutritious, but as Scott's men found out, particularly unappetizing. Most of those in Evans' boat were unable to stomach it, so he set their rations at two ounces of water and two biscuits every two hours, with corned beef twice a day, supplemented by Horlicks tablets, chocolate and condensed milk. Under the circumstances, this should have been ample to hold hunger and thirst at bay, but after a while some of them lost their appetite for the nourishing food and preferred to exist on a diet of chocolate and condensed milk, washed down with a few sips of water.

It soon became clear to Evans that the water would not last, however sparingly he issued it. The exertion of rowing was making the men thirstier than ever, so during the morning the oars were abandoned and lashed outboard to give more room in the overcrowded boat. From then on they would rely on what wind came along, which at that time was very little.

The cold and wet – freezing spray was coming over the bows at times despite the calm sea – were beginning to take their toll. The majority of survivors were wearing warm clothes and thick

Arctic underwear, but some of the firemen, those on watch when the ship was attacked, had on only thin denim dungarees. There were ample rubber survival suits in the boat, but these were uncomfortable to wear, causing excessive perspiration. Fortunately, some of the sailors had spare woollen jerseys and they shared them with the firemen. That solved one problem but there was another, the curse of the lifeboat inhabitant known as 'immersion foot'. This painful swelling is brought on by the cold and prolonged immersion in the water always lying in the bottom of the boat. The recommended treatment for immersion foot is to keep the feet warm and dry, an obvious impossibility in the conditions prevailing. A rummage in the boat's lockers produced a can of whale oil, which was used to massage the feet of the worst affected, with good results.

The boat had been drifting aimlessly for some hours but their fortunes changed around noon, when the wind freshened from the north, and with both sails set, they began to make progress towards the land. Early that afternoon, they were surprised to be overtaken by two other lifeboats, one under power and towing the second. These turned out to be from another PQ 17 casualty, the British ship *Bolton Castle*, sunk within minutes of the *Earlston* by German dive bombers.

Chapter Eleven

Lancashire Shipping's 5203-ton *Bolton Castle*, commanded by Captain J. Pascoe, was in the thick of the fight for PQ 17 right from the start, surviving two separate attacks by torpedo-carrying Heinkels. When, on the night of the 4th, the convoy was ordered to scatter, Pascoe also elected to seek the cover of the ice edge. The British ship reached the southern limit of the ice at 11.00 on the 5th and later in the day she was joined by two other fugitives from PQ 17, the Dutch steamer *Paulus Potter* and the US-flag *Washington*. Pascoe and Captain Sissingh of the *Paulus Potter* were old friends, their ships having loaded at adjacent berths in Glasgow, while the master of the *Washington*, which was armed with only two light-calibre machine guns, was glad to join up with any ship able to give him some protection. The *Bolton Castle* certainly fitted that bill. She was armed with a 4-inch, a quick-firing Bofors, four Oerlikons, two twin Hotchkiss, two single Hotchkiss, two 'pig troughs' and an assortment of PAC and FAM rockets, all manned by an expert team of twenty-one DEMS gunners.

The three ships continued in company, making good a speed of ten and three-quarter knots, and skirting the ice edge as it trended first to the east, then to the north-east. The weather was exceptionally fine, with good visibility, a smooth sea and light airs blowing. The conditions were ideal for the ships but, at the same time, it was perfect flying weather for the German reconnaissance planes, one of which found the three ships just after noon on the 5th. Adopting the usual tactics, the plane circled out of reach of the ships' guns for a while, then banked and flew away again. The merchantmen hurried on to the eastwards, their guns manned, lookouts alert. They knew the enemy would be back.

True to form, an hour later, at 15.30, a single Ju88 arrived overhead and, with uncanny perception, made for the weakest ship, attacking the *Washington* with a stick of three bombs. Fortunately, the German pilot's aim was wide, due largely to the reception given him by the *Bolton Castle*'s guns, her Bofors coming very near to shooting his plane out of the sky. One scare was enough and the Ju88 flew off without attempting another attack.

The reprieve for the ships was short-lived. The Germans returned again at 17.45, a Blohm & Voss 138 appeared in the south-east, leading a flight of six Ju88s flying at about 7000 feet. As they approached, the bombers split up, three of them singling out the *Bolton Castle*, two coming in from astern, the third from ahead. It was a tactic designed to confuse the British ship's gunners and to some extent it did just that. All guns concentrated on the two aircraft attacking from astern, which were perceived to be the main threat. Faced with such a heavy barrage, the planes sheered away without dropping their bombs, but while all attention was focused astern, the other Ju88, coming in from the east, began its bombing run unopposed.

On the bridge of the *Bolton Castle*, Captain Pascoe had a clear view of the three bombs leaving the underside of the Ju88 and made a bold alteration of course away from them. His avoiding action was only partly successful, two of the bombs scoring a near miss in the water to port, but the third was right on target, smashing its way into the *Bolton Castle*'s No.2 hold. It could not have landed in a worse spot, for stowed in this hold were 300 tons of cordite. The hold exploded like an erupting volcano, hurling clouds of flame, smoke and debris hundreds of feet into the air. The ship stopped dead and immediately began to settle by the head. Miraculously, there were no casualties but, fearing his ship had not long to go, Pascoe ordered the lifeboats into the water. When everyone had been accounted for and the confidential papers and books dumped over the side in their weighted box, he passed the word to abandon ship.

The *Bolton Castle* carried four lifeboats, two of which were small jolly boats. One of the latter had been smashed by the bomb blast, the other was swamped when the falls ran away during lowering, leaving only the two large boats for her complement of seventy men. As a result, both boats were seriously overcrowded. Captain Pascoe's boat, which was equipped with an engine, had thirty-three men on board, while Chief Officer Keeting's boat, with no engine and therefore more room, had thirty-seven. The water was lapping within a few inches of the gunwales of both, but so long as the sea remained calm they were seaworthy.

The boats cleared the ship in the nick of time, for at 17.57, just twelve minutes after she had been hit, the *Bolton Castle* lifted her stern high and slid under bow first. When she had gone, Pascoe motored around searching the debris spreading over the sea for anything that might be of use and he was delighted to come across ten five-gallon cans of petrol, part of the ship's deck cargo. This was treasure indeed, sufficient for the motor boat with the other boat in tow, to make the land under her own power. The petrol was divided up between the two boats, taking up precious leg-room, but there were no complaints.

The *Washington* and the *Paulus Potter* had also come under attack by the Ju88s. The 5564-ton *Washington*, commanded by Captain Richter, her decks loaded with tanks and truck chassis and 500 tons of TNT in her holds, was first to be hit. She fought back bravely with her two puny machine guns but bombs fell all around her, until one well-placed stick exploded within a few feet of her starboard side. Her hull was blasted open, the sea poured in and she began to list heavily. A second stick of bombs destroyed her steering gear and tracer fired by the attacking planes set her deck cargo on fire. As it was only a matter of time before the fire reached the explosives stowed below decks, Captain Richter decided it was time to leave. The boats were lowered and the crew of the American ship began their long row to the shore.

The *Paulus Potter* was next, crippled by a series of near-misses. Her steering gear was knocked out, her rudder damaged, a main steam pipe was fractured, filling the engine room with scalding steam, and her stokehold watertight bulkhead was cracked. The ship was not sinking but, rather than lie helpless waiting for the next wave of German bombers to arrive, Captain Sissingh decided to abandon ship. There was a difference of opinion between Sissingh and his chief engineer, Jan Kluwen, who believed he would be safer staying with the ship, but the others, including fifteen Russian seamen, passengers in the *Paulus Potter*, left the ship in her four lifeboats. As they were pulling away from the ship, the Ju88s came back and the bombs fell again. The ship was not hit but this renewal of the attack was sufficient for Chief Engineer Kluwen to change his mind. He took to a raft and narrowly missed being killed when a bomb fell very close to it. He was picked up by one of the boats a few minutes later, very wet, and a chastened man.

When the German bombers had gone away and it became clear that the *Paulus Potter* was in no immediate danger of sinking, Sissingh allowed Chief Officer van der Mey and two seamen to reboard to collect dry clothing and blankets. Van der Mey also brought back a sextant and a few bottles of rum.

The forlorn little flotilla of lifeboats now came together to discuss their various plans of action and, as they lay drifting, a bizarre incident occurred which serves to illustrate the effect the trauma of this disastrous voyage had had on the survivors, British, American and Dutch. The American steamer *Olopana*, commanded by Captain Mervyn Stone, which had somehow managed to escape the attentions of the German bombers, arrived on the scene. Stone was prepared to pick up all the survivors, but to a man they refused his help on the grounds that they had had quite enough of being a target for the U-boats and bombers, and preferred to take their chances in the boats, however long and uncomfortable their voyage might be. Captain Stone distributed loaves of bread and cigarettes among the boats before going on his way. As it transpired, those in the boats made a wise choice. The *Olopana* was torpedoed by *U-255* three days later and sank with the loss of six of her crew.

The *Washington*'s boats went their own way, but Pascoe and Sissingh stayed together to discuss further their predicament. Pascoe proposed that they keep company and attempt to reach the Kola Inlet, some 470 miles to the south. Sissingh did not agree, opting to head for the island of Novaya Zemlya, 370 miles to the east. Pascoe warned Sissingh that although he might have a shorter distance to sail, he would be close to the ice edge and in freezing conditions for much of the time, whereas going south the

141

weather would become progressively warmer. Furthermore, the British master cautioned, Novaya Zemlya was largely uninhabited and that, assuming Sissingh reached the island, he would be landing on a deserted coast with no help at hand. But there was no meeting of minds and eventually the boats went their separate ways, Pascoe to the south and Sissingh to the east.

There was no appreciable wind, but with Chief Officer Keeting's boat in tow, Pascoe was averaging a speed of about three knots. The weather was not unpleasant, cold and crisp, with the temperature hovering around freezing. However, the men in both boats had plenty of warm clothing and they had ample food and water so their prospects of survival were good and likely to increase with the weather becoming warmer as they moved south. On the morning of the 8th, the wind freshened from the north and the sails were hoisted to conserve petrol. Soon afterwards, a small boat was sighted ahead, possibly a fishing vessel. Pascoe approached cautiously, lighting a smoke flare. This was answered by a similar flare from the other boat, indicating it was a ship's lifeboat. It was, in fact, the *Earlston*'s boat with Second Officer David Evans at the helm. When the boats drew together, dead reckoning positions were exchanged and compasses compared. Evans asked Pascoe if he would take his boat in tow, but Pascoe, concerned that his petrol was running low, declined to do so.

It was with some misgivings that Evans watched the *Bolton Castle*'s boats motor towards the horizon, leaving him to crawl along in their wake, but he did not blame Pascoe for looking after his own men first. As the wind had now freshened enough to fill the sails, he was content to carry on alone. The *Earlston*'s men had the last laugh, however, for an hour later they sailed past the *Bolton Castle*'s boats which were stopped and drifting, their engine having broken down.

During the next twenty-four hours, the *Earlston*'s boat, her sails drawing well, made good speed running before the fresh northerly breeze, but the weather and the overcrowding in this unprotected boat – they were packed like sardines – was beginning to take its toll on the occupants. Evans was suffering from stomach cramps and most of the others, despite regular massaging with the whale oil, had painfully swollen feet. On the 10th, the fresh breeze that had served them so well became a near-gale and the deep-loaded boat laboured in the rising seas. Soon the bottom of the boat was awash with freezing water which the hand pump was unable to keep in check. To add to the misery of the survivors Evans, uncertain as to how much longer it would be before they reached land, was obliged to cut the water ration to two ounces per man every six hours, hardly sufficient to slake their growing thirst.

The next forty-eight hours passed as in a bad dream, few now caring whether they lived or died. Then, at 07.00 on the 12th, seven days after they had taken to the boat, land was sighted ahead. Now there was no lack of willing volunteers to man the oars and the boat surged ahead, eager to meet the land. But there was one more obstacle for these wretched men to overcome. Second Officer Evans wrote in his report to the Admiralty:

There was a reef outside to be negotiated, but some Russian soldiers saw our boat approaching and came out to guide us through to the beach. We had to sail close hauled through the reef, all hands who were able took an oar, and we finally reached the beach safely. The Russians, in broken English, asked for the Commanding Officer to come ashore, so I went, being able to walk fairly well. They asked, in broken English, if I could speak Russian. I said 'No', then they asked me if anyone in the boat could do so. Mr Watson (one of the *Earlston*'s passengers) could speak Russian fluently so he came ashore and acted as an interpreter. The Russians asked why we had landed at that place, and I explained that we had landed there quite by chance, certainly not by choice. We told them we had been 7 days in the boat, and when they understood at last that we were survivors they went down to the boat and carried the men who could not walk up the beach and along to an underground shelter like a large barn, which they called 'Stalin Hall'. We spent about an hour there, they lighted the stove, making it as hot as 'Hades', and gave us pickles, tea and bread and butter to eat. Meanwhile, they had sent for lorries, which soon arrived and took us all to the base hospital on the Peninsular. They would not tell us where we had landed, and it was not until we left in the hospital ship for Archangel that they informed us it was the Rabachi Peninsular (fifty miles west of Kola Inlet).

On reaching the base hospital, those of us who could walk were taken away for a bath, whilst the others were put to bed and given an injection to make them sleep. After the bath we were given some

143

fish and coffee, and put to bed about 02.00 on the 13th. We were called again at 06.00 and taken on board a Russian hospital ship, a small converted coaster, but very well fitted out, which took us to Polyarno, where we arrived at 20.30 on the 13th. We were all put to bed, the Russian doctor came round and examined those who said their feet were painful. He asked if mine were, and when I said no, he passed on. The food was very poor. Two days later the doctor came again and asked me if I could walk. I said 'Yes', so he said I could leave the hospital. He looked at my feet to see if they were swollen, but they were all right. Some of the others could not walk for three weeks.

Evans and his men were then sent to a Russian military rest camp at Vaenga, sixteen miles from Murmansk, where they received excellent treatment and a great deal of sympathy from the Russians. The food was not exactly to their liking, consisting mainly of very tough roast yak with boiled barley, but there was plenty of bread, butter, fruit and sugar. They stayed at the camp until 21 July, when they were transferred to Archangel by train and, with other survivors, accommodated in the Intourist Hotel. Second Officer Evans, the *Earlston*'s chief engineer and eighteen ratings were returned to the United Kingdom, arriving on 26 September.

Evans later commented on the action in which his ship was sunk:

I was Gunnery Officer for the ship prior to the Lieutenant RNVR being appointed so I carried on these duties during the voyage, acting as his understudy in case of necessity. I consider our weapons were very good and all the gunners were very satisfactory. The .5 Browning jammed a lot and had to be stripped several times. The Oerlikons were excellent, also the 4-inch. I think the enemy was completely mystified by the pig trough, and did not know what to expect from it. We also fired the FAMs, and found them very satis-factory. We fired our pig trough and FAMs when the plane was brought down, but so much stuff was being fired that it was diffi-cult to tell what actually caused the plane to crash.

Evans singled out for praise some of those who helped him through the long ordeal in the lifeboat:

The apprentice, A.B. Watt, and I had during the first four days kept watch at the tiller. Watt behaved splendidly in the boat, he was of great assistance to me during these four days, and during one spell, when I slept for 8 hours in the bottom of the boat, he did not wake me but took over complete charge on his own. He was perfectly trustworthy and capable of attending to the sailing of the boat on his own initiative. During the period when I was ill, three of the ABs, Holman, Hooper and Folwell, took over the tiller and steered. Holman was a very fine leader and behaved magnificently; he set watches for the others and, being a Newfoundland fisherman, he could handle the boat well, he was always cheerful and a really fine character. He also kept a keen eye on the other two, who were not so experienced in boat sailing.

There was an unhappy ending for the others who survived the sinking of the *Earlston*. Captain Stanwick, taken prisoner aboard *U-334*, not surprisingly, spent the rest of the war in a German prisoner of war camp. The Chief Officer's lifeboat reached the land but had the misfortune to come ashore behind the German lines, near the North Cape. All twenty-seven men on board were also made prisoners of war.

Having watched the *Earlston*'s lifeboat sail past him on the morning of the 8th, and still being unable to restart his engine, Captain Pascoe decided to abandon the tow and take advantage of the freshening northerly wind. Both boats set off under sail, steering a south-easterly course, Pascoe being anxious not to strike the coast to the west of the Kola Inlet, where he believed there was little habitation. They kept together until, on the 10th, they ran into the same gale in which the *Earlston*'s boat was labouring, and soon became separated. At this point, like Evans, Pascoe concluded it would be wise to reduce the water ration in his boat as a precaution against a long voyage. Several of his men were by now suffering from immersion foot and one or two appeared to have frostbite.

Later that day, they sighted two other lifeboats sailing well to the westward, who turned out to be from an American ship and on the 11th they came across an abandoned boat from the Panama-flag *El Capitan*, from which they salvaged some water and cigarettes. The American ship, name unknown, and the *El Capitan* were two more victims of the attacks on the dispersed

PQ 17. In all, twenty-one ships had now gone down, and the Barents Sea to the north of the Kola Inlet was littered with ship's lifeboats making for the shore.

On the morning of the 13th, Pascoe calculated they must be very near to the land although, having no sextant or chart and with a suspect compass, he knew his dead reckoning might be well in error. But his judgement was vindicated when that afternoon a large motor launch was seen heading their way. This proved to be a Russian patrol boat and the survivors were soon on board, their ordeal over. The Russian crew gave them a warm reception, which included a slice of sausage and a large glass of vodka. Through one of his Russian passengers Pascoe learned that they had been picked up 120 miles to the east of the Kola Inlet. Next day they were landed at the Russian naval base of Polyarno. There Pascoe was given the good news that Chief Officer Keetings' boat had been picked up on the morning of the 13th, close inshore and only fifty miles east of Kola. All on board were safe.

With some regrettable exceptions, Captain Pascoe had high praise for his boats' crew:

Most of the men were very good and they did all they could to help, but the Arab firemen refused to do anything and just lay in the bottom of the boat waiting to die, but they did not die. It was obvious that the health of those who did move about working was very much better than those who just sat all the time. When we were within about 20 miles of the coast I called for everyone to take the oars and kept the boat close hauled, but still these Arab firemen refused to help. I punished them by reducing their ration of water, a terrible punishment for thirsty men after nearly 9 days in a boat.

Second Officer Jackson was with me and I should specially like to mention his outstanding work. He is an excellent man in a boat, he thoroughly understands motor engines and was of great assistance throughout, being able to run the engine and get more out of it than the engineers who were with us. Mr Jackson has already been awarded the MBE for his fine work in the *Muncaster Castle*. (Jackson was in the *Muncaster Castle* when she was sunk in the Atlantic by *U-68* on 30 March 1942, only a few weeks before he joined the *Bolton Castle*).

I should also like to mention the Chief Steward, W. Arnott, whose assistance and work in the boat was invaluable. He has already been bombed during a previous voyage to North Russia, and it takes a lot more courage to make this journey a second time when one fully knows what to expect from air and submarine attack.

Pascoe had praise for his gunners, too:

Leading Seaman Noakes was very keen and good at his job, being in charge of the 4-inch gun and the Oerlikons. On one occasion an Oerlikon jammed badly but he quickly cleared it and had it working again. He is an excellent all-round man, and a man I should certainly like to have with me again. When the ship was under heavy fire he kept perfect control of his gun's crew and was outstanding during all attacks.

Sergeant Moir, in charge of the Bofors gun was outstanding and the crew of his gun were all excellent. They stuck it through all attacks, also during fire from our own ships, mostly Americans, who often fired at random at anything they could see, irrespective of any ships being in their line of fire.

Captain Sissingh and the men of the *Paulus Potter* had a sorry tale to tell. After declining to take the advice of Captain Pascoe to go south into warmer waters, Sissingh had taken his boats along the ice edge, steering an easterly course for Novaya Zemlya, eventually making a landing on the island's west coast after a long and difficult journey. The bitter cold of the ice edge cost the survivors dear, Sissingh and ten of his men suffering the agonies of frostbite. It was not until 24 July that they finally reached Archangel, where in hospital Captain Sissingh and the ten others had toes, and in some cases feet and part of their legs amputated. Included in these were three Britishers who sailed in the *Paulus Potter*, W. Macdonald, fireman; seventeen-year-old galley boy J. Newman and sixteen-year-old mess boy P.F. Brind. They had all paid a heavy price for taking the northern route. As to the ship they had – prematurely as it seems – abandoned, she suffered perhaps a greater humiliation.

Left to fend for herself, the *Paulus Potter* was not sunk by the Luftwaffe's bombers, as Sissingh had anticipated. Low in the water but still buoyant, she had drifted eastwards along the ice edge for some ninety miles until, on 13 July, she was sighted by *U-255*. Commanded by *Kapitänleutnant* Reinhart Reche, *U-255* had already run to ground and sunk two American ships, the *John Witherspoon* and *Alcoa Ranger,* and when Reche saw the *Paulus Potter* apparently slow-steaming among the ice floes, it seemed he had found the ideal target for his last remaining torpedo. Reche submerged and cautiously moved in closer and, as he studied the ship through his periscope, it occurred to him that there was something strange about her. There was no sign of life on board, not even a movement on the bridge. Then, as he edged in closer still, he saw the lifeboat davits were empty and rope ladders hung over the side. The ship had apparently been abandoned, yet she was upright and showed no sign of damage. Still suspicious, Reche spent another three hours observing the *Paulus Potter* before he was satisfied that she was indeed abandoned. Then he surfaced and sent away a boarding party led by one of his engineer officers, Ewald Müller, to examine the state of the ship. A plan was already forming in Reche's mind for sending this ship and her valuable cargo back to a Norwegian port with a prize crew on board.

Müller reported back that the *Paulus Potter*'s engine room was flooded right up to the cylinder tops and that there was no possibility of getting the ship under way again. Disappointed, but not surprised, Reche sent over his senior watch officer, *Oberleutnant* Hugo Deiring, to search the ship thoroughly. To his amazement, Deiring found he was aboard a twentieth century *Marie Celeste*. It was as though the *Paulus Potter*'s crew had suddenly disappeared into thin air. Everything was in place, neat and ready for use. The tables in the officers' saloon were set and even the current chart which would have been in use was still laid out on the chartroom table. But, Deiring's most valuable discovery was the *Paulus Potter*'s complete set of Admiralty code and signal books, sailing instructions for PQ 17 and the routes to be followed through the minefields around Iceland and in the approaches to Archangel. All were stowed in their perforated and weighted steel box ready to be thrown overboard, but had obviously been forgotten in the rush to abandon ship. Deiring lost no time in carrying his priceless find back to *U-255*, but first he held a small ceremony of lowering the Dutch flag, still flying from the *Paulus Potter*'s stern.

When his men had returned, bringing with them the box and a choice selection of provisions looted from the Dutch ship's storerooms, Reche then used his last torpedo on her. The *Paulus Potter* broke in two and sank within two minutes, taking her valuable cargo with her down into the cold depths of the Barents Sea.

Chapter Twelve

The rescue ship *Zaafaran* was at work picking up survivors from the British ship *Navarino*, victim of the torpedo bombers, when the order came through for PQ 17 to scatter. With thirty of the *Navarino*'s crew on board – the rest had been picked up by the *Rathlin* – Captain Charles McGowan then stopped to pluck another eight men from the water who had jumped overboard from the Russian tanker *Azerbaidjan* when she was torpedoed. The situation McGowan now found himself in was that although the *Zaafaran*'s work as rescue ship to PQ 17 had only just begun, it must now be ended. Reluctant though he was to run away, with the other ships fanning out in all directions, McGowan knew he could not play nursemaid to them all. The *Zaafaran* being a 15-knot ship, he decided to make directly for Archangel.

The morning of the 5th was fine and crystal clear, the sea smooth, barely ruffled by the light breeze. Perfect weather. The *Zaafaran* was on a course of 120° and making a smart fifteen plus knots as she pulled steadily away from the other ships, one or two of which were just visible about twelve miles to the north. McGowan was confident he had enough speed to outpace the U-boats, but the German planes were another matter. He could only hope to put the maximum distance between himself and the Luftwaffe's airfields in Norway in the shortest possible time. This he was not allowed to do, for with the morning only a few hours old a Blohm & Voss 138 appeared and settled down to shadow the *Zaafaran*. By mid-morning, the circling flying boat had called in a flight of six Ju88s.

They came in at 5000 feet, in line astern, to drop their bombs one after another and, while his guns filled the sky with tracer and shell bursts, McGowan found himself engaged in a macabre game of cat and mouse, desperately trying to judge where each stick of bombs would fall and altering course at the last minute. His tactics worked for, apart from one tense moment when a bomb fell within 100 yards of the beam and deluged the bridge with icy water, the *Zaafaran* came through unscathed. When they ran out of bombs and had failed to as much as dent this elusive little ship, the Ju88s flew away, their crews no doubt seething with frustration. McGowan then stood down his gunners, called on his engineers to coax the last possible revolution out of their machinery and resumed course to the south-east.

Another four hours passed, in which the *Zaafaran*, vibrating enthusiastically to the beat of her racing engine, moved another sixty miles closer to Archangel – and still the sky remained reassuringly empty of enemy planes. Then the spell was broken when, at 15.20, a lone Ju88 was sighted approaching from the south-east at about 2000 feet. *Zaafaran*'s twenty DEMS gunners were back at their guns and immediately opened fire, the quick-firing Bofors and Oerlikons, backed up by the twin .5 calibre Vickers and an assortment of light machine guns, throwing such a concentrated hail of lead at the plane that it veered sharply away and flew off. At first, it seemed that their attacker must have cold feet, but the Ju88 climbed steeply, levelling off at about 8000 feet. Then it came in to attack again, diving to around 5000 feet as it approached the *Zaafaran* on her starboard side. The guns opened up again, but this time the bomber ignored the flak and held steady, releasing a stick of three bombs as it roared in. It was a perfect bracket. The first bomb fell fifty feet short, the second scored a direct hit in way of the engine room and the third fell only ten feet clear of the port side of the ship. The Ju88 zoomed away followed by the angry shells and bullets of the rescue ship's gunners.

The *Zaafaran* was mortally hit, the second German bomb blowing a large hole in the ship's side below the waterline and destroying the watertight bulkhead between the engine room and the after hold. The sea poured in, flooding the engine spaces and the hold within minutes. The ship took a heavy list to starboard and settled heavily by the stern.

151

All indications were that the *Zaafaran* would go down very quickly and McGowan decided to abandon ship without delay. However, the decision taken, he soon discovered that he had a problem with numbers. Including the survivors from the *Navarino* and the *Azerbaidjan*, the *Zaafaran* had on board a total of ninety-eight persons, of whom three were injured. Being equipped for rescue, her lifeboats, of which she had four, would have accommodated this number without effort. Unfortunately, the direct hit had blown one of the starboard boats away and the near miss had reduced its opposite number on the port side to matchwood. That left McGowan with one full-sized boat – luckily the motor boat – and a jolly boat to take nearly 100 men, an obvious impossibility. The six wooden rafts and eight buoyancy floats carried would have to be brought into use.

As a matter of habit, Charles McGowan's first thought was for the men he had rescued earlier. The majority of the *Navarino* survivors, plus the three injured men, were put in the motor boat, while the balance of the rescued were crammed into the jolly boat, along with three of his own crew. Only when the two boats were safely in the water did McGowan and the remainder of his men take to the rafts and floats. Thanks to the discipline and training of the *Zaafaran*'s crew, the complete evacuation of the ship was carried out in seven minutes and then only just in time. One minute after the last raft cleared the ship, she went down, obligingly sliding beneath the waves smoothly and barely disturbing the surrounding water or creating any suction to threaten the boats and rafts. To the very last, the *Zaafaran* looked after those who had put their trust in her.

It was fortunate for Charles McGowan and his crew, cold and wet, clinging to their tossing rafts, that help was near at hand. One of the ships earlier seen on the horizon to the north turned out to be the *Zaafaran*'s sister ship *Zamelek*, commanded by Captain Owen Morris. The *Zamelek*'s radio-room had picked up McGowan's SOS and Morris immediately came to his rescue, arriving two hours later. With the exception of one man, a DEMS gunner who was washed off one of the rafts and drowned, all the survivors from the *Zaafaran*, *Navarino* and *Azerbaidjan* were picked up by the *Zamelek*. Morris then rejoined the other ships he had been sailing in company with, the anti-aircraft ship

Palomares and the corvettes *Lotus* and *Poppy*. The four ships then set off in company for the Matochkin Strait, the narrow passage dividing the north and south islands of Novaya Zemlya where they hoped to find temporary shelter before making a dash for Archangel. They reached the strait late on the 6th, to find several other fugitives from PQ 17 already at anchor.

In summing up the behaviour of his crew during the *Zaafaran*'s final hours, Captain McGowan was unstinting in his praise:

During the whole of these attacks, all the crew behaved magnificently, fighting the guns continuously without the slightest sign of fear. I would specially like to mention the three gunners – D. Cooper P/JX/178/916. Sergeant J. Smith 1638202 and Gunlayer Acting AB C.R. Weaver DJX/249/581. These men definitely accounted for at least one enemy plane each, they fought their guns magnificently, and with outstanding gallantry throughout all the attacks. Bo'sun Patrick Willock was outstanding and set a fine example both during the action and in getting the crew away in the boats and rafts. He is a very powerful type of man and his great strength was of utmost value. He is a very fine leader of men. Chief Engineer W. Millar was outstanding, and with his staff he rendered valuable assistance in getting away survivors, remaining until the end. After the rescue ship *Zamelek*, which picked up survivors, was damaged by a near miss from a bomb, he rendered valuable assistance to that ship's Engineer in repairing the damage, thus enabling the vessel to reach harbour. R. Mariner was the Station Quartermaster; he always took the wheel during all attacks, and was very cool and calm, and of great assistance. The Donkeyman, T. Penny, manned the Oerlikon gun on the after end of the boat deck for three days, and also kept his watch. Although he did not actually claim to have shot down any planes, he fought his gun all the time and undoubtedly did much to keep the planes at a great height. Chief Officer G.C. Longfield was always in the thick of the fight, assisting and directing the guns' crews, and set a fine example. He supervised the lowering of the boats and rafts and remained until the end. I would also like to pay tribute to the Galley Boy (name unknown) who was just celebrating his 16th birthday. He was in a vessel which was torpedoed a short time before in PQ 15, and on arriving home on leave, his mother asked him why he had come home. He told her he had been torpedoed and had come home on a month's leave. 'A month's leave!' retorted his mother, 'I have no food for you here', so he immediately volunteered for sea again and was sent to my ship. While on the rafts, the men on his raft were joking and telling him there were too many men on the raft and that he had better swim to another less crowded one. They told him that he did not really need his lifejacket, so, taking this off, the boy swam with a heaving line to another raft and secured the line, thus enabling the rafts to be pulled together.

Captain H.W. Charlton, commanding the Commodore's ship the *River Afton*, was completely taken aback when the order came through for PQ 17 to scatter. Most of the other ships' masters were bemused, but willing to carry out the order without questioning it, but Charlton was aware, through Commodore Dowding, of the unprecedented strength of the convoy's escort, including the very formidable presence of ships of the Home Fleet. He found it difficult to understand the need to run away. He was, however, like the others obliged to carry out orders, and so set course to the north-east, seeking the protection of the ice edge.

There was no rest for Charlton that night for, within hours of leaving the others, the *River Afton* ran into dense fog, which was harbouring numerous small icebergs, none big enough to sink a ship but liable to cause serious damage if hit. He remained on the bridge throughout the night, peering into the fog, straining his ears to catch the sound of another engine or a fog signal, and making last-minute alterations of course to avoid the glistening white bergs that came gliding silently out of the murk. To his great relief, the fog cleared at 05.00 on the 5th and he then altered course to due east, leaving the bergs and growlers behind him and to the north. Seeking shelter in the ice had lost its appeal for Captain Charlton.

During the course of the day, the *River Afton*'s radio-room listened in to the plaintive calls for help from ships under attack by U-boats and aircraft, but there was nothing Charlton could do for them. By noon, four other ships were in sight, two of which were American, all making their best speed to the east. Very soon, they were joined by a lone Ju88, which began to circle some two miles off. Confronted by four relatively heavily-armed merchant ships in company, it was unlikely that the lone Ju88 would attack

154

but, unfortunately, the two American ships panicked and broke radio silence to transmit a string of frantic messages reporting they were being shadowed by a suspicious aircraft. With every U-boat and German surface ship within listening range probably tuning in their direction-finding sets to take bearings of the signals, Charlton decided it was high time to leave the area. Now nothing would be lost by making a dash directly for the Matochkin Strait, taking advantage of the cover of any fog banks found on the way.

As commodore ship, the *River Afton* was fitted with a new innovation for merchant ships known as an Acoustic Wireless Ear (AWE). This was a sensitive sound detector specifically designed to pick up the noise of aircraft engines from a distance. It was not an instrument Charlton had any great faith in, but when, during the course of that afternoon, the alarm on the AWE began to ring persistently, he was obliged to take notice. There were no aircraft in sight, nor could he hear the sound of distant guns, indicating the ships he had left behind were under attack. As the alarm continued to ring, it occurred to Charlton that he might have a U-boat on his tail, the diesel engines of which were triggering the alarm. He cautioned his men, particularly those on the guns, to be on the alert. They responded, but the stress of the past days under attack was beginning to take its toll. They were desperately tired. But all was quiet for the rest of the afternoon and into the evening, with the *River Afton* steaming at eight knots in calm seas and the visibility frequently down to 800 yards in fog. There was nothing in sight, but the AWE alarm continued to ring sporadically. Charlton tried to convince himself that the machine was malfunctioning but he could not shake off the growing suspicion that he was being shadowed by a U-boat.

Charlton's suspicions were well-founded, for since early that afternoon *Kapitänleutnant* Heinz Bielfeld in *U-703* had been following closely on the *River Afton*'s heels, on the surface but trimmed well down, so that in the foggy conditions the U-boat was invisible to the steamer's lookouts. At 20.05, when in approximate position 76°N 43°E, some 200 miles from the Matochkin Strait, Bielfeld overtook the *River Afton* and manoeuvred into a favourable position to attack.

Bielfeld's torpedoes ran true, their tracks unseen by the

155

lookouts on the British ship. Two of the fan of three torpedoes missed, but the third caught the *River Afton* squarely in her engine room, her most vulnerable spot.

The *River Afton* was an early 'engine-aft' vessel, with her bridge located amidships and in isolation from the main accommodation. When the torpedo struck, Captain Charlton was in the chartroom and heard only a muffled explosion, but when the ship staggered as though pushed by a giant hand, he knew that the thing he had been dreading throughout the day had at last happened.

Charlton rushed out into the wing of the bridge, his worst fears confirmed when he looked aft and saw devastation and confusion. The 4-inch gun mounted on the poop had been blown away, the port after lifeboat – the *River Afton* carried two boats aft – was smashed and hanging in two separate pieces in its davits and the after deck was a smoking shambles. Amongst the smoke and debris men were milling round the remaining lifeboat in a blind panic and, although no order had yet been given to abandon ship, were attempting to lower the boat.

Charlton snatched up a megaphone and hailed the panicking men – they were a mixed crowd of sailors and firemen – ordering them to hold fast. His voice went unheard. Although it was obvious that the ship still had considerable way on her, the fully loaded boat was on its way down to the water. These were doomed men, for Heinz Bielfeld, who had crossed astern of the ship, had not finished with her. As the lifeboat touched the water, a second torpedo slammed into the hull only a few feet away. The effect was catastrophic, the lifeboat and all on board being blown to pieces. Those on the deck above lowering the boat were cut down by a hail of flying debris and splinters. Only one man was left alive and he was badly injured.

The *River Afton*, her hull breached on both sides by the torpedoes and her engine spaces flooded, was finished, and at 20.12 Captain Charlton, realizing the hopelessness of the situation, gave the order to abandon ship. He described what happened next:

The officers lowered my small dinghy amidships and I collected my briefcase and made my way to it. The ship was now settling slowly by the stern. I found several of the officers already in the dinghy alongside, with some of the crew and, getting into the boat found there were 13 people already in her. The ship still had about two knots weigh and the fore part of the boat was being dragged under, so the painter was cut. The boat then fouled the wreckage of the port motor lifeboat, throwing all the occupants into the water.

The 2nd and 3rd Officers managed to catch hold of the lifelines hanging from the boat deck and regained the ship. The Chief Officer, who had his duffel coat on was floating but unable to swim owing to the water collecting in the sleeves and hood of his coat. I heard him shouting for help, but owing to the weight of my case on my back and the extremely cold water it was all I could do to keep myself afloat and struggle to the upturned boat. AB Hanford attempted to rescue the Chief Officer but he too got into difficulties and had to abandon the rescue in order to save himself. Several members of the crew got away on 4 rafts, and some of the men from the dinghy managed to swim to these rafts. At 2220, a third torpedo struck the ship, this explosion caused a terrific flash and it probably penetrated No.3 hold where the explosives were stowed. There was a violent explosion on the starboard side amidships, clouds of smoke and debris blotted out the ship from view, when it cleared I saw the ship had broken in two, and a second or so later she disappeared.

Charlton had no time to mourn the passing of his ship, for his own life was in the balance. As he trod water to keep himself afloat, he was joined by Lieutenant Cook, a Royal Navy Sea Transport officer, passenger in the *River Afton*. The two men climbed onto the keel of the upturned dinghy and attempted to right it. With a concerted heave they succeeded in rolling the boat over, but instead of righting itself it went over bottom-up again. They persisted, rocking and heaving, until eventually they had the boat right way up, floating but completely waterlogged, the gunwales being a foot below the surface. Drastic action was now called for or the boat would sink altogether and exhausted though they were by now, Charlton and Cook climbed into the bows of the boat and stood upright. This had the effect of lifting the stern out of the water and spilling some of the water out of it. Charlton then emptied his briefcase, scattering to the winds the ship's papers he had tried so hard to save and used the empty case as a bailer. It was a long heartbreaking job, but with Charlton using his case and Cook his cupped hands, they finally succeeded in lowering the water level in the boat until the gunwales were above water again. Then, sitting on the thwarts with their legs immersed in freezing water, they rowed the boat back to the sea of wreckage left by the *River Afton*, looking for survivors. They found only one man in the water, Able Seaman Thompson, a signaller with Commodore Dowding's staff. They pulled him aboard, wet and shivering with the cold, but so grateful for his deliverance. Further along, they came across the starboard lifeboat, floating keel-up, which Charlton was determined to right, but first they needed more men. They rowed on, finding rafts drifting among the debris, two men on one raft, Commodore Dowding and three of his staff on another, then the two remaining rafts, which were crowded with survivors. Among them was Able Seaman Marsh, who reported sighting the periscopes of two submarines after the ship was torpedoed. One of these U-boats surfaced alongside the raft Marsh and a number of other survivors were clinging to and took him on board for questioning. All he disclosed Marsh said, was the name of the ship, after which he was given a bottle of water and some bread and returned to the raft. The U-boat then took photographs of the survivors on the raft, gave them a course and distance to Novaya Zemlya and then motored off. The token gift of food and water was gratefully accepted, but as Novaya Zemlya lay 200 miles away, the course to steer was only a gesture – a sop to Bielfeld's conscience perhaps. Even given a favourable wind and with its scrap of sail set, the progress of the heavy, box-like raft towards the land would be so slow that none of the survivors would live to see it.

Charlton brought all four rafts together and told their occupants to rig the canvas screens to cut down the wind, but with hands frozen numb and despair creeping over them, the task was beyond them. Two men had already died on one of the rafts and Charlton took time to say a half-forgotten prayer over them before committing their bodies to the deep. He then set about bullying and cajoling those left on the rafts to paddle towards the capsized lifeboat, which he considered their only hope of salvation.

Righting the heavy, waterlogged boat proved to be a hopeless task, even with every man Charlton was able to persuade into the water heaving and pushing. The boat would not roll. But as they abandoned the attempt, a fresh hope was borne. A ship was sighted close by and the spirits of the cold and bedraggled men soared. A tin of smoke flares was produced from one of the raft lockers and these were burned one after another. But the ship steamed past, giving no indication of having seen them.

For the pathetic band of survivors, some huddled on the rafts, others in the waterlogged jolly boat and a few balanced astride the upturned boat, this was a bitter blow, and they settled down to await whatever end was in store for them. Another hour passed and they drifted aimlessly, without hope, and then the ship came back – and this time they were seen. Their rescuer was the British corvette *Lotus*, which had been picking up survivors from the American ship *Pan Kraft*, sunk by aircraft earlier in the day, and was then on her way back to the Matochkin Strait. By midnight, *Lotus* had on board all thirty-four men who had survived from the *River Afton*'s total complement of fifty-eight. The corvette reached the strait at 18.00 on the 6th.

In a report written to the Admiralty in October 1942, Captain Charlton paid tribute to his crew:

I would like to bring to your notice several members of my crew; first the Chief Steward, P. Gray, who remained behind after the ship was abandoned although he heard the order, attending to the injured members of the crew. He also assisted in rescuing the Second Engineer from the engine room and put him on a stretcher and onto the raft. Whilst doing this the third torpedo struck the ship and the Chief Steward went down with the ship but was able to swim to a raft.

The 2nd Cook, A. Waller, also stayed behind and assisted to rescue the 2nd Engineer from the engine room after he had heard the order to abandon ship. After assisting the 2nd Engineer to a raft, he went around the ship distributing life jackets to the numerous members of the crew who had lost theirs. When the 3rd torpedo struck the ship I am afraid A. Waller was killed by falling debris and went down with the ship.

The Chief Engineer, Edward Miller, also behaved magnificently, first in leading the rescue party to the 2nd Engineer who was trapped in the engine room, in spite of knowing that the order had been given to abandon ship. Although injured in the legs, he carried

159

on with the rescue work showing great bravery and finally only just managed to get away from the ship on a raft.

The 2nd Engineer, J.W. Wood, had already been on three trips to Russia with me and volunteered for this trip. This time he was not so fortunate and was trapped in the engine room when two torpedoes struck one from either side. Although badly injured in the leg and spine, with the aid of the Rescue Party he was hauled up and put onto a raft and was blown into the sea when the 3rd torpedo struck the ship. He managed to cling onto a hatch and was pulled back onto a raft where he died from his injuries and exposure. I should like to pay very special tribute to this gallant officer, whose bravery and cheerful example during all his trips to Russia was outstanding.

The Senior Wireless Operator, G. Garston, behaved with outstanding cool courage and succeeded in getting his messages away, and in spite of the order to abandon ship he remained until he was satisfied that his message had got through. This man showed remarkable coolness and was of great help in assisting in getting everybody out of the ship and finally managing to get away on a raft.

When the *Lotus* arrived at the anchorage she found it contained the remnants of Convoy PQ 17. The merchantmen did not amount to much: the British ships *Ocean Freedom* and *Empire Tide*, three Americans, the *Benjamin Harrison*, *Samuel Chase* and *Hoosier*, the Panamanian *El Capitan*, and the rescue ship *Zamalek*. The little ships of the Navy were better represented, with the minesweepers *Britomart*, *Halcyon* and *Salamander*, the trawlers *Lord Middleton*, *Lord Austin* and *Northern Gem*, the corvette *La Malouine*, and the anti-aircraft ships *Palomares* and *Pozarica*. Many of these escorts were running short of fuel and ammunition, while the merchant ships were a battered looking collection, their sides scoured by the ice they had tried to find cover in, their upperworks pockmarked by bomb splinters. The 6978-ton *Empire Tide*, commanded by Captain Harvey, had on board survivors from three other ships she had picked up on her way to Novaya Zemlya.

The *River Afton*'s survivors were transferred to the two AA ships, and at 17.00 on the 7th, with the *Ocean Freedom* in the lead, this rump of a convoy set sail for Archangel. The plan was

160

to steam south, hugging the west coast of Novaya Zemlya until the southern end of the south island was reached, to then cut across the open water to strike the coast of the Russian mainland near Kolguyev Island and westwards to the White Sea. It was a risky enterprise but the best they could do under the circumstances.

Luck was with the makeshift convoy, for it found cover from the enemy in thick fog soon after clearing the Matochkin Strait. But with seventeen ships steaming in close company in fog, there was a price to pay. Speed was reduced to a safe minimum, but even with fog buoys in use and the ships sounding their whistles at intervals, the days and nights were plagued by hair-raising near-collisions. Progress to the south was painfully slow and the strain on the bridge watchkeepers was enormous. Their burden was doubled when, on the afternoon of the 8th, they ran into heavy pack ice. Inevitably, the ships became scattered and it was not until the morning of the 9th, when the fog lifted, that they were able to reform. And then, of course, with clear skies and good visibility, the enemy found them again. They appeared at 21.00, a flight of fifteen Ju88s flying high up. *Palomares* and *Pozarica* immediately put up a sustained barrage which, combined with the gunfire of the other ships, deterred the planes from coming lower. They dropped their bombs at random as they passed overhead and all went wide. The convoy steamed on unharmed.

There was a short respite, then at 23.00 a second wave of fifteen Ju88s came in and this time, in spite of equally heavy AA fire, the attack was more determined although again the bombs were dropped from high level and most were wasted. The only casualty was the *Hoosier*, damaged by a near miss with three bombs and abandoned by her crew. This seemed to satisfy the enemy's appetite, for the planes flew away and for the next three hours the convoy was left in peace. The *Hoosier*, her steering gear out of action, was sunk by HMS *Poppy*.

The drone of high-flying aircraft was heard again at 02.00 on the 10th, and another flight of Ju88s was soon overhead. This was the start of an all out attack on the ships which lasted for the next five hours, wave after wave of bombers coming in, queuing up to unload their bombs on this battered collection of ships, which was now only forty miles or so from the Russian mainland. Once again, it was largely the very effective and concentrated fire put up by *Palomares* and *Pozarica* that saved the day. Most of the large number of bombs dropped were ineffective, but one cluster fell within twenty feet of the *El Capitan* crippling the Panamanian. She was abandoned and when the bombers had left she was sunk by gunfire.

The ships reached Cape Kanin and the entrance to the White Sea later that morning but, although now in Soviet waters, they were still not free of the attentions of the Luftwaffe. The final attack in this brutal game of hit and run came at 10.00, when the bombs came down again and the *Samuel Chase* was damaged, but still able to proceed under her own steam. What was left of the convoy, now down to three merchant ships, greatly outnumbered by their escorts, reached an anchorage off the North Dvina river at noon on 11 July.

Thirteen

PQ 17's vice commodore ship, the 5082-ton *Hartlebury*, owned by J.&C. Harrison of London and commanded by Captain George Stephenson, was another veteran of the Russian run. Her first Arctic voyage had been with Convoy PQ 2, sailing from Scapa Flow in October 1941 with Stephenson in command and largely the same crew. After spending a month in Archangel, she returned with QP 3, and was back again with PQ 11 in February 1942. This time her destination was Murmansk, where she passed a month under fire before heading home with QP 9. Returning north again in May, she lay swinging to an anchor in Hvalfjord for twenty-seven days. When the order came to join PQ 17, Stephenson and his men were so bored that running the German gauntlet again seemed like a welcome relief. Little did they realize what awaited them out on the high seas.

When, on that fateful evening of 4 July 1942, PQ 17 was ordered to scatter, Captain Stephenson was as taken aback as anyone in the convoy but, being by now well experienced in these waters, he had no hesitation in deciding on a plan of action. He took his ship to the north-east until reaching the edge of the ice barrier and then steered eastwards, taking cover in any available fog bank each time he heard the sound of aircraft approaching. The tactic worked for the rest of that day but in the early hours of the 5th the *Hartlebury* was sighted by a Blohm & Voss 138 making a sweep over the area. Stephenson's gunners gave the plane a hot reception and it decided to go elsewhere.

Now that he had been discovered, Stephenson left the ice edge and made a beeline for Novaya Zemlya, seeking cover in the fog

163

banks as he had done before. This run-and-hide tactic was again successful. Steaming south-eastwards at eleven and a quarter knots, the *Hartlebury* made a landfall off Novaya Zemlya's west coast, near Admiralty Inlet, at around noon on the 6th. She then steered southwards, maintaining a distance of three miles off the coast, until late in the afternoon, when Stephenson set a south-south-westerly course for Kolguyev Island, near the entrance to the White Sea. The weather in the vicinity of Novaya Zemlya was fine with a moderate north-easterly wind, a moderately rough sea, scattered high cloud and good visibility. The sky and visibility worried Stephenson, for they offered ideal conditions for German bombers. But it was not from the sky that the attack came.

Kapitänleutnant Günter La Baume, at the periscope of *U-355*, had been watching the *Hartlebury* for some time and ten minutes after she altered course away from the coast of Novaya Zemlya he pounced.

Stephenson was in the *Hartlebury*'s wheelhouse when La Baume's torpedo hit directly under him on the starboard side. The shock of the explosion threw him against the bulkhead, his head sang and the stench of burning cordite filled his nostrils. He rushed out into the wing of the bridge and was immediately knocked unconscious as debris thrown up by the explosion fell back on the bridge. The debris was followed by a deluge of water, which brought him round again.

When he came to, Stephenson found himself buried under pieces of plastic armour that had once protected the Oerlikon gun platform. He was bleeding from a cut in the head but was otherwise unharmed. He dug himself out and as he got to his feet La Baume's second torpedo found its mark in the *Hartlebury*'s engine room. It exploded immediately below the starboard lifeboat, which some of the crew, realizing the urgency of the situation, were already lowering to the water. The blast reduced the boat to matchwood.

The third torpedo struck a minute later and this was the final blow for the *Hartlebury*. She was hit in her No.5 hold, in which was stowed the usual large consignment of ammunition for the Red Army. There was a violent explosion, black smoke billowed out of the hold and the smell of burning cordite was stronger than ever. Stephenson watched in horror as his ship broke into three pieces, the deck opening up before and abaft the bridge. The mainmast came crashing down and the remaining lifeboat, which was in the process of being lowered, was left hanging by one fall. All the lights had failed and most of the midships accommodation had collapsed. Over all chaos reigned. Not knowing how many of his crew were still alive, George Stephenson gave the order to abandon ship. When he hurled himself over the side, the bridge deck was only five feet above the water. At 16.46, six minutes after La Baume's first torpedo struck, the *Hartlebury* disappeared from view beneath the waves.

Accompanied by one of his deck crew, who had joined him in the water, Stephenson swam to the port lifeboat which, having been swamped when it hit the water, was floating on its buoyancy tanks. One man had already reached the waterlogged boat and they joined him. A frantic search for bailers or buckets with which to bail out the boat revealed nothing, so the three men, glad to be alive, sat in the boat up to their waists in freezing water. Other survivors appeared and dragged themselves over the gunwales and soon there were seventeen in the boat. Looking around, Stephenson saw two life-rafts nearby crowded with men; the remains of his crew. Then the cause of their miserable predicament put in an appearance. Stephenson later reported:

> After the ship sank the submarine surfaced. It was a large submarine and had U-13 painted in black on the side of the conning tower, round the U-13 was a black horseshoe. The conning tower was small, and there was a 3' gun well forward of it. The submarine closed my waterlogged boat and asked if the Master was a survivor. I told him no, he then went over to a raft and the men on it thought I had been lost with the ship and told the commander of the submarine so. The Commander spoke to the Chief Officer and asked if he was a Bolshevik, and on learning that he was not he said, 'What the hell are you going to Russia for?' The Chief Officer told him that 38 ships had been sunk from the convoy, he was given the course and distance to Nova Zembla and also a bottle of wine and another of gin and 5 loaves of black bread. The submarine had a machine gun trained on the crew during the conversation and was taking cine-photographs of the men on the rafts as they were receiving the food, etc. The commander

of the submarine had a red beard and was about 5ft 10in tall. He spoke English fluently and was dressed in an ordinary peak cap and a coat similar to our duffel coats. After about 5 minutes conversation the submarine submerged and went off.

Dense fog came down shortly afterwards, separating the survivors. Stephenson attempted to rally the men in his boat and they began to bail with their cupped hands. It was a thankless task, for as fast as they emptied water from the boat, the waves lopping over the gunwales filled it again. The temperature of the water was only a degree or so above freezing and they soon gave up.

Four men died during the first five hours, succumbing to the cold and the terrible melancholy that overcame them. Stephenson could do nothing for them while they were alive and when they were dead could only offer a brief prayer as he tipped their stiffening bodies over the side. Soon after the last man was buried, at 21.40 by Stephenson's watch which still functioned, the weather moderated and the fog lifted. A bucket was then found, the boat's hand pump was brought into use, and slowly, very slowly, the water level in the boat was lowered. By morning, it was down to the bottom boards, but now only Captain Stephenson and three others were alive.

When the horrors of the night were over and the last man was buried, Stephenson turned his mind to survival. He issued a meal of biscuits spread with pemmican and washed down with a generous tot of brandy, which put new life into them all. The boat's mainsail was hoisted and course set south-eastwards for Novaya Zemlya, which was estimated to be only sixteen miles away. Later in the morning, they picked up nine other men from a drifting raft, bringing the total complement of the boat up to thirteen, all of whom, although they had been through a harrowing ordeal, were in good spirits and reasonable condition. Nature was at work ensuring the survival of the fittest.

The wind was light and the boat was barely moving, but in the right direction. It was twelve hours later, at 22.00 on 8 July, before they finally made the land, coming shore in Pormorski Bay, at the southern end of Novaya Zemlya, a place which Stephenson knew to be completely uninhabited. On landing, the survivors rigged a shelter with the boat's sails and lit a fire, on which they made a hot pemmican soup laced with a few bird's eggs they had found. They dried their clothes and, continuing with a diet of hot soup, rested for two days, by which time they had regained a great deal of their strength and were ready to attempt to escape from this desolate shore. The opportunity came later that morning when the fog cleared and they sighted a merchant ship close inshore and apparently stopped. Without waiting to signal, the men launched their boat and piled into it, hoisting the sail.

The ship was further off than they had thought and with the wind light and fitful it was late afternoon before the boat was alongside. A ladder was lowered from the deck and Stephenson and his men boarded the US-flag *Winston Salem*, also from PQ 17 which, in attempting to make Archangel, had run hard and fast on a shoal. The crew of the American ship welcomed them aboard, to join seven other survivors from the *Hartlebury*, whose raft had drifted towards the ship quite by chance.

The twenty *Hartlebury* men, all that remained of her crew of fifty-nine, were on board the *Winston Salem* until 16 July, when they and the ship's crew were taken off by a Russian survey ship. They were then transferred to the *Empire Tide* and finally reached Archangel on the 25th.

The sad tale of Convoy PQ 17 came to its painful conclusion on 28 July 1942 with the arrival in Archangel of the *Winston Salem* which had been refloated and brought south. Of the thirty-nine ships that sailed from Hvalfjord on 27 June, twenty-four had been lost and with them 153 men. The unfortunate ships had taken to the bottom with them 3,350 motor vehicles, 430 tanks, 210 aircraft and 99,316 tons of other military supplies. The Luftwaffe flew 202 sorties against the convoy, sinking eight ships for the loss of five aircraft, while the U-boats sank sixteen ships without loss to themselves. It was a cheap victory for Germany, a crushing defeat for the Allies.

Viewed in retrospect, the battle for Convoy PQ 17 was a classic example of both sides being unwilling to commit their capital ships to a major action. Hitler was traumatized by the sinking of the *Bismarck* and feared more than anything the humiliation of losing the *Tirpitz* as well. On the other side of the North Sea, the First Sea Lord, Admiral Sir Dudley Pound, had equally not recovered from the destruction by the guns of the *Bismarck* of

Britain's biggest warship, the battlecruiser *Hood*. However, big ships apart, while the withdrawal of Rear Admiral Hamilton's cruiser force may have somehow been justified, to pull out the destroyers of PQ 17's close escort and then order the convoy to scatter was a catastrophic mistake. The close escort, consisting of six destroyers, four corvettes, three fleet minesweepers, four anti-submarine trawlers, two anti-aircraft ships and two submarines, was very substantial. If the merchant ships had stayed together with this escort around them, then PQ 17 could conceivably have fought its way through the massed aircraft and U-boats without heavy losses. It was not to be and, as a result of the shambles in which PQ 17 ended up, the reputation of the Royal Navy was damaged for decades to come and a severe strain was put on Anglo-American relations.

A communique issued by the German High Command on 7 July gives the other side of the story:

> Since July 2nd a great combined operation of air and naval forces directed against the enemy convoys destined for the Soviet Union has been carried out between the North Cape and Spitzbergen, 300–400 nautical miles from the Norwegian coast. In the White Sea German aircraft and submarines attacked an Anglo-American convoy, most of which was wiped out. The convoy was composed of thirty-eight merchant ships and was carrying planes, tanks, munitions and food. Destined for Archangel, it was strongly protected by heavy naval forces, destroyers and corvettes. In close cooperation with the navy, the air force sank an American cruiser and nineteen merchant ships with a gross tonnage of 122,000 tons; while the submarines sank nine ships of 70,000 tons, i.e. twenty-eight units altogether and 192,000 tons. Battle continues against the remains of the convoy, now completely dispersed. A considerable number of American sailors have been picked up and made prisoner by rescue planes.

To close the regrettable saga of PQ 17, it is worth quoting in its entirety the report on the action written for the US Navy Department by Lieutenant John E. Sexton, USNR, officer commanding the Armed Guard unit aboard the merchantman *Samuel Chase*.

Rounding the northwestern tip of Iceland the convoy, which was steaming in two columns, ran into heavy fog and also occasional ice floes. On Sunday June 28, the S/S *Richard Bland* sent out a message saying she was aground on the rocks. We later learned that the S/S *Exford* damaged her bow in the ice and had to return to Iceland so that when the convoy formed up on June 29, we were 38 ships including three rescue vessels, nine columns abreast with four ships to a column and two rescue ships making a fifth column. The original convoy number of the *Samuel Chase* was 93 (third ship in the 9th column) but we took position 91, formerly the station of the *Richard Bland*. This placed us first ship in the starboard column of the convoy. We sailed without incident until Thursday July 2 when the first German reconnaissance planes were sighted at approximately 1100. Our position was about 200 miles due west of Bear Island. The planes were Heinkel 115 torpedo reconnaissance and a Blohm & Voss reconnaissance. The Heinkels darted at the convoy on the flanks and drew fire but no attack was launched. During the entire day of June 2 (sic) the escorts seemed particularly busy with submarines and twice on the starboard side of the convoy following the explosion of depth charges black water was seen to erupt. Later in the day our ship ran through an enormous oil slick and to all appearances these signs pointed to the destruction of three submarines, but there was no official information. The Blohm & Voss plane remained with the convoy until 0300 July 3, where we ran into heavy fog. During the day the weather cleared and a task force of four cruisers and two destroyers appeared on the port bow of the convoy. This included three British cruisers and the USS *Wichita* and two British destroyers. They moved across the convoy and were soon on the starboard bow of the convoy where they remained until they left us. The reconnaissance plane picked us up again at 1940 July 3, but we again ran into fog and lost it. The fog lifted at 0140 July 4 and the reconnaissance plane picked us up immediately. The sea was smooth and there was no wind and a light fog was still present. A Heinkel 115 appeared and was seen in the rear of the convoy. The fog became thicker reducing visibility to 1000 yards and the Heinkel was lost. At 0345 she appeared out of the fog on the starboard flank of the convoy and released a torpedo which passed between the *Samuel Chase* and the S/S *Carlton* (#92) and struck the S/S *Christopher Newport* amidships. The plane was not heard until she was seen. All machine guns on the *Samuel Chase* opened fire and the range was so short that all guns hit but no effective damage was seen and the plane was lost in the fog. The *Christopher Newport* was #81 and was slightly behind station and received the torpedo at what appeared to be the engineroom on the starboard side. The starboard lifeboats were gone and there was much damage to the bridge but at no time while she was in sight did she appear to be settling. The port lifeboats were put over and it was later learned that the crew was taken aboard the rescue ship *Zamelek*. Possibly she was sunk by gunfire but I cannot say this to be a fact. The fog again set in at 0700 but lifted in the afternoon. At 1700 the Blohm & Voss appeared and at 1800 six Heinkel 115s and a Junkers 88 appeared. They made two complete swings from the starboard flank of the convoy to the port flank but never closed in. The ceiling was low, there was no fog on the water, and the sea was smooth. The JU 88 flew over the convoy hidden by the ceiling and when fired upon released her bombs which did no damage. At 1900 the six Heinkels and the JU 88 disappeared. At approximately 1915 more than 25 Focke Wulf planes appeared on the starboard quarter of the convoy flying very low and made straight for us. They flew within 75 feet of the water and attacked the convoy from the rear and starboard side, releasing torpedoes, then banked, and left the scene immediately. From the *Samuel Chase* not more than 5 planes were seen to fly through the convoy, the majority banked away within 1000 yards.

Four ships were hit and fell astern of the convoy. One was identified as the *William Hooper*, the rest we could not identify. However, two of these four rejoined the convoy, two were left astern, and again I cannot say positively that these were sunk by gunfire. The *William Hooper* settled slightly at the stern but did not seem to be sinking. Three planes were seen to fall in the water, the crew from one plane being picked up and placed aboard a former USS "four-stacker" destroyer. The attack was over at 1930. At 2136 the convoy was ordered by the commodore to scatter and proceed to the port of destination (Prior to this all ships in the convoy were told that their port of destination was Archangel). The dead reckoning position of the *Samuel Chase* at 2136 July 4 was 76-12N 30-00E. The cruiser-destroyer task force was evident during the entire attack but was approximately six miles away on our starboard bow. All the destroyers escorting the convoy headed south. The cruisers headed west. When these two forces joined, the entire force headed west and was soon lost to sight. When last seen, this force consisted of four cruisers and at least 7 destroyers included in this was the USS *Wainwright* and *Rowan*.

The ships were to scatter according to the plan in Mersigs. The Blohm & Voss remained over the convoy the entire time we were scattering and was with us until approximately 0300 July 5. The two anti-aircraft ships (which joined the convoy three days out of Hvalfjord) and the corvettes, sloops and trawlers scattered with the merchant ships. All hands were on watch from this time on. The ship was steering 105° true, heading for Nova Zemlya.

On July 5 at 0500 a black dot was seen dead astern which by 0645 was identified as a German submarine. She was steaming on the surface and crossed to our starboard quarter and began to over-haul us on the starboard side. Then she disappeared from sight at 0800. A ship which we presumed to be the *Daniel Morgan* was hull down on the horizon behind the submarine. She was seen to turn and head north. At 0830, dead reckoning position 75-44N 37-00E, the Captain ordered engines full astern and told all hands to get into the lifeboats. All boats were away from the ship by 0845 and they gathered and laid 600 yards from her. At 1100 the Captain and the Chief Officer and the Engineers went aboard and got up steam, and at 1200 the boats were called back to the ship. At 1220 the ship was under way steering 075° true at 12 knots, and immediately we picked up speed the submarine reappeared dead astern. No attack was made on the ship while the boats were in the water.

The visibility was excellent, no wind, smooth sea, no clouds. The submarine again hauled to our starboard side and could be seen from the crow's nest to be paralleling our course, running on the surface. About 1400 a JU 88 bomber was seen dead astern flying high and headed north-west. At that instant a fog bank appeared and we entered it and commenced zig-zagging. The fog was in patches and for the next six hours we ran from fog patch to fog patch, with brilliant clear weather between, or ran through low hanging fog with a clear sky overhead. At one point in the fog a plane was heard passing our port side quite close. Machine gunners were instructed not to fire, least we reveal our position, and the plane was heard no more. At 2330 July 5 we sighted one of the AA ships accompanied by two corvettes. Evidently he had picked up a TDF transmission, as the first thing he told us was to maintain silence. He then informed us that he was heading for any bay on the coast of Nova Zemlya at his utmost speed, as the *Tirptiz*, *Admiral Hipper* and six destroyers were steering a course 060° from North Cape at 22 knots. A few minutes later he told us he was heading for Matochin (sic) Strait and advised us to do the same. To our question, 'Can we accompany you?', he replied, 'My course is 150° my speed is 14 knots'. As our best speed was a fraction over 12 knots he pulled ahead and was lost to sight in the early hours of July 6. We were steering 75° true when we met him but on his information we came to course 150° true and followed him. Our dead reckoning position when we changed course was 76-13N 46-05E. During the afternoon of July 5 we listened in on 500 KC and heard numerous distress calls, often two ships at the same time. We listened for just a short time, and then shut down, lest we give away our position, but while we were receiving the following ships were heard from:-

BCR6 – *Earlston* (BR) submarine attack 76-35N 33-41E.

No call letters – 2 submarines attacking ship 75-04N 37-50E.

No call letters – ship torpedoed 75-05N 38-02E.

WSPO – attacked by seven planes 74-43N 34-20E.

SS *Washington* – dive bombed 76-40N 33-41E.

SS *Daniel Morgan* – aircraft attack 75-49N 43-00E.

SS *Pan Kraft* – aircraft attack 76-50N 38-00E.

We laid down the course line of the German fleet on the chart and crossed this line at 0500 July 6. At 1315 July 6 we made a landfall on Nova Zemlya due west of Matochin (sic) Strait. At the same time we sighted three ships headed south along the coast. They proved to be the SS *Hoosier*, *El Capitan* and *Empire Tide*. We flashed to them our information on the German fleet. The *Hoosier* and *El Capitan* followed us but the *Empire Tide* continued south. At this point a ship was sighted heading north. She proved to be the *Benjamim Harrison*, and she too headed in after us. At 1600 a Blohm & Voss plane was sighted heading north. The *Empire Tide* made no attempt to follow us in. She was seen to head west and tried to hoist her balloon which broke away. Then she headed south and disappeared. A Free French-British corvette came out and led us into Matochin (sic) Strait. There we found the two AA ships and 8 sloops, trawlers and corvettes. Our course was plotted first for heading south along the coast, heading south-west passing Kolgeuv thence to Cape Kanin and Iokanski. On July 8 the course was changed to take us east and south of Kolgeuv, thence to Cape Kanin. The run south along the coast was made in heavy fog and the *Benjamin Harrison* was lost. Whether she was torpedoed or ran aground we do not know. At 1600 July 8 we encountered

173

heavy ice. We were steering approximately due south at this point. We worked our way through and ran clear at 2100. However, at 2350 we again ran into very heavy ice, and by steering NW we succeeded in breaking clear. At 0400 July 9 when we came out we joined with the *Ocean Freedom*, two sloops and a trawler and headed west skirting the ice field. At 1430 we headed approximately SW and maintained that course until 2330 when we came to a SSW heading for Iokanski.

At 0300 July 10, we heard gunfire ahead in the distance and saw heavy smoke. The mirage effect was very extreme all during the day of July 10 so that we could not see real outlines of ships. We later learned that this was the attack on the *Hoosier* and *El Capitan* in which both ships were lost, all hands being saved. At 1100 July 10 we sighted a Russian reconnaissance plane and almost immediately afterwards we sighted German planes. There were not more than six over us and seemed to be JU 88s. They dive-bombed us at first pulling out quite high and not coming close with the bombs. However, as the attack proceeded and they felt out the AA fire, they came in closer and their bombing was more accurate. At this point we were still with the *Ocean Freedom* two sloops and a trawler. We received not less than six near-misses all within 60 yards of the ship. The effect of this was to snap off all our steam lines, stop the engine and cut off the auxiliaries so that the ship lay dead in the water. The compass was knocked from the binnacle and damaged, and light damage done inside the ship. We received no direct hits and at 1145 the attack was over. The *Ocean Freedom* pulled ahead and the British sloop J-42 took us in tow and soon we had steam on the steering engine. By 1500 we had effected enough repairs to proceed under our own power. At this point two more sloops joined us as escort. At 1535 we were again attacked by dive bombers but the protective fire was better, the planes were kept higher, and no further damage was sustained, the attack ending at 1615. During the attack at noon two planes were seen to fall into the sea and one was seen on the horizon fighting a fire. At 1800 we sighted ships ahead. From 1900 we had Russian planes over the convoy. At 0130 July 11, we joined up with the ships, which consisted of the two AA ships, *Ocean Freedom*, *Zamalek* and sloops/corvettes, and were led into the White Sea by a Russian pilot boat which had met us in the forenoon of July 10. At 1130 we anchored at the entrance to Archangel channel and a Russian pilot came on board and we proceeded to Molotovsk. We anchored outside to await high water and at 1900 the Captain and

174

51 officers and men from the S/S *Hoosier*, including Ensign Blackwell and nine enlisted men, were transferred to the *Samuel Chase*. On Sunday July 12 we came alongside the dock at Molotovsk.

No casualties were sustained aboard and the gun crew and also the majority of the civilian crew must be complemented on their splendid behaviour.

Chapter Fourteen

On 27 June 1942, as PQ 17 was leaving the inhospitable waters of Hvalfjord, its opposite number, QP 13, was forming up in the Barents Sea ready to return to the west. In accordance with Admiralty practice, the two convoys were routed to pass midway between the North Cape and Iceland, thus enabling ships of the Home Fleet to give cover to both at once.

Twenty-three ships sailed from Murmansk and twelve from Archangel, meeting at a prearranged rendezvous ninety miles east-north-east of the Kola Inlet on the 28th. They were the usual mixture, eight British, sixteen American, four Panama-flag, seven Russian and one Dutch, but all with a common goal; they were bound to the west to load more cargo for the hard-pressed Soviets. Some of the ships carried small cargoes on the return trip, the British ship *Chulmleigh*, as a typical example, with 927 tons of pit props, 357 tons pine tar, 256 tons liquorice root, 83 tons white arsenic, 77 tons gum spirit turpentine, 48 tons potassium chloride, 41 tons gum resin and 65 tons sundries. The *Chulmleigh* also had on board five passengers, Distressed British Seamen, as the bureaucrats of the Board of Trade labelled returning survivors. They were part of a contingent of 150 DBSs with the convoy from the thousands of shipless Allied merchant seamen now kicking their heels in Russian ports.

The Murmansk section of QP 13 was under escort by the destroyers *Inglefield*, *Achates* and *Volunteer*, the corvettes *Hyderabad* and *Roselys* (Free French), the fleet minesweepers *Niger* and *Hussar*, the trawlers *Lady Madeline* and *St. Elstan* and the submarine *Trident*. The Royal Navy ships also carried passengers, 400 distributed among them, survivors from the cruiser *Edinburgh* sunk on 2 May. The Navy men had also been a long time waiting for a passage home.

The twelve merchantmen from Archangel were accompanied by the destroyers *Intrepid* and *Garland* (Polish), the corvettes *Honeysuckle* and *Starwort*, the fleet minesweepers *Bramble*, *Hazard*, *Leda* and *Seagull*, the AA ship *Alynbank* and the Russian destroyers *Grozni*, *Gremyaschi* and *Kuibyshev*. Having delivered their charges safely to the rendezvous point, the four British minesweepers and the Russians returned to Archangel.

QP 13, now consisting of thirty-five merchant ships, formed up into nine columns abreast, with the four corvettes and two remaining minesweepers in close attendance, *Inglefield* scouting ahead, the other four destroyers guarding the flanks, the two trawlers bringing up the rear and the submarine *Trident*, hanging well back, on the lookout for shadowing U-boats. The *Alynbank* was in the middle of the convoy, where her massed anti-aircraft guns would be most effective. The convoy commodore, Commodore N.H. Gale, RNR, was in the 7167-ton *Empire Selwyn*, lead ship of Column 5.

The convoy was complete and under way at eight knots by 16.00 on the 28th. The weather was fair, with light winds, smooth sea and a thin mist reducing the visibility to about one and a half miles; ideal conditions, in fact, to enable a convoy to hold together and yet slip past unseen by enemy eyes. This, it was hoped, would be just another 'milk run'. The Germans, not un-expectedly, were largely ignoring the westbound convoys, reserving their strength to attack the outward bound ships carrying the cargoes to Russia.

There was the customary false alarm later on this first day at sea, when the *Alynbank* reported aircraft engines heard, possibly caused by an over-enthusiastic operator manning the sound detector. No aircraft appeared. Next day, the convoy lost its cover when fine, clear weather set in, but the skies remained empty of enemy aircraft and no U-boats were seen or detected. At noon, course was altered to the north-west to pass to the north of Bear Island.

At 08.00 on the 30th, QP 13 had reached its most vulnerable position with regard to attack from the air, being then only

170 miles north of the North Cape. The weather had changed again, being overcast with mist patches, offering good cover for the enemy and he was not long in coming. At 16.37, a lone aircraft was sighted approaching from the south, flying high. The plane made no attempt to close the convoy, but circled out of gun range for over an hour. During this time it sent out homing signals on 680 metres, consisting of a series of 'A's sent every fifteen minutes. Ships in the convoy listening in knew what must inevitably follow. Consequently, when a few hours after the spotter plane had flown away dense fog enveloped the ships, a great surge of relief swept through the convoy. These were men who had received their baptism of fire from the Lufwaffe on the voyage east and the memories of this were still fresh in their minds.

QP 13 passed some fifty miles to the north of Bear Island in the early hours of 1 July, thus reaching the furthest point north on their route to the west. The fog had lifted again by this time, but there was a great deal of drifting ice around. Course was altered to the south-west and the night passed without undue incident as the ships weaved and bumped their way through the ice towards warmer waters.

Next morning in overcast weather with mist patches, the enemy returned, this time in the form of a brace of the all too familiar Blohm & Voss 138s circling low down on the horizon. They were still there at noon, when a pall of black smoke was seen in the sky to the north and word went round the convoy that the eastbound convoy PQ 17 was passing on its way to Archangel. Both QP 13's shadowing planes then flew off in the direction of the smoke and soon their homing transmissions were heard winging out across the ether. PQ 17, which was by then surrounded by U-boats, came under attack by Heinkel 115 torpedo bombers later that day.

PQ 17's nightmare, then only just beginning, proved to be QP 13's salvation. The enemy had found a more worthy prey and, in the feeding frenzy that followed, the thirty-five westbound ships sailed on unmolested. The next day passed without incident and at 14.00 on the 4th, when the decision was being made to throw PQ 17 to the wolves, QP 13 then 140 miles to the north-east of Iceland, split into two sections. The sixteen ships bound for British ports peeled off and, led by the *Empire Selwyn* and accompanied by the major part of the escort force, set course for Loch Ewe, 700 miles to the south. One ship lost its way in fog and turned back for Iceland but the others arrived safely in the Scottish loch on the morning of the 8th. For some of them, the hard road to Russia would soon begin all over again.

The remaining nineteen ships, all bound for ports in the USA via Iceland, formed up into five columns and, with Captain John Hiss in the 5172-ton *American Robin* acting as convoy commodore, continued on a south-westerly course. Their escort consisted of the fleet minesweeper *Niger*, commanded by Commander Anthony Cubison RN, Senior Officer escort, the other minesweeper HMS *Hussar*, the Free French corvette *Roselys* and the anti-submarine trawlers *Lady Madeline* and *St. Elstan*. The five ships of the escort force mounted between them only seven 4-inch guns, but they were all well equipped with Asdic and depth charges. In these waters, where few U-boats ventured, they were considered adequate protection.

When the two sections of QP 13 went their separate ways, the weather was as it had been for forty-eight hours past, overcast, with light winds and mist and fog patches. As a result, no sun or star sights had been obtained for at least two days. All calculations were being made using dead reckoning, that is using an assumed course and speed – calculated guesswork, in other words. For the UK-bound ships this would not present a problem; they had plenty of open water to cross, and time to fix their position accurately before closing the land. Those making for Hvalfjord would need to exercise extreme caution. When off the north-west corner of Iceland, the North Cape, they would have to find their way through a ten-mile-wide channel between the coast and an extensive minefield laid in the Denmark Strait to prevent German surface raiders breaking out into the Atlantic. No one in the merchant ships was aware of the existence of this minefield and Commander Cubison had not seen fit to enlighten them.

As the convoy approached the north coast of Iceland early on the morning of the 5th, the barometer was falling rapidly and the cloud was lowering. By 06.00, it was blowing a full gale from the north-east, the cloud was down to mast-top height and,

179

in the driving rain, the visibility was less than one mile. This was not the kind of weather in which to be attempting to make a landfall on an unfamiliar coast having had no accurate fix for two and a half days but, confident in his navigation, Cubison pressed on.

The day went by and there was no improvement in the weather, no glimpse of the sun and, relying on compass and log, the convoy crept nearer to the coast. At 19.00, Commander Cubison signalled the *American Robin*, advising Captain Hiss to form the ships into two columns for the approach to the North Cape. Hiss, still unaware of the minefield, conformed. Cubison now took *Niger* on ahead, hoping to make a landfall, with *Hussar* following about a mile behind to maintain visual contact with the leading ships of the convoy. At 20.00, Cubison signalled his estimated position by DR and soundings as 66° 45' N 22° 22' W, which would put him fifteen miles due north of the North Cape. He advised Hiss to bring his ships around onto a course of 222° (true) which, if his calculations were right, would take them into the swept channel and clear of Straumness, the north-western tip of Iceland. Hiss complied.

After continuing on this south-westerly course for an hour, a lookout on the *Niger* reported land three points abaft the minesweepers' port beam. Peering through the mist and driving rain, Cubison identified this as the North Cape, distance about one mile. If it was indeed the North Cape, the Commander realized that his calculations must be very badly in error and that he was leading the convoy straight onto the land. He immediately signalled, through *Hussar*, to the *American Robin*, for an emergency alternation to starboard, onto a course of 270°. Captain Hiss led the nineteen merchantmen round onto the new heading.

Minutes later, in a temporary clearance of the mist and rain, Cubison found to his horror that what he had thought was the North Cape was in fact the face of a large iceberg. Steering due west, the *Niger* was leading the convoy directly into the minefield.

A signal was flashed to Hiss to make an emergency turn to the south and while this was being acknowledged *Niger* hit a mine. There was a massive explosion accompanied by a sheet of flame and the 815-ton minesweeper was blown apart. She sank at once, setting the sea around her alight with burning oil.

The *Niger* took with her Commander Anthony Cubison, most

of his crew of eighty and thirty-nine passengers; men who had survived the sinking of HMS *Edinburgh* and thought they were making a safe passage home. When the minesweeper had gone, with a last muffled explosion as her boilers burst underwater, there was silence. Then the merchant ships following in her wake, unaware of what was happening, were thrown into a state of complete confusion. Ensign J.C. Guibert, Armed Guard Commander in the 6120-ton Lykes Line Ship *Hybert*, described the scene:

> July 5 1942 at 2113 (GMT) a ship about two ships ahead was seen sinking by the stern. Gun crew went to battle stations. Ships ahead were firing their 4-inch 50 calibre guns and machine guns. Visibility was about 700 yards. Seas were commencing to get heavy. This reporting officer sighted nothing but shell splashes on the starboard side, convoy in two columns, the s.s. *Hybert* in the starboard column. . . .

In omitting to inform the convoy of the existence of the minefield Commander Cubison had committed a grave error. When the *Niger* blew up, the merchant ships, quite understandably, assumed they were under attack by U-boats or surface ships which were unseen in the mist and added to the confusion by opening fire in all directions. Some of their shells set off other mines, which in turn increased the intensity of the gunfire, so that, in the half-light, the mist and the rain, the scene resembled a full-scale battle, a battle with no tangible enemy. In the midst of all this, the *Hybert* hit a mine. Ensign Guibert reported:

> At 2115 there was an explosion in the stern on the port side. Throwing debris, water and hatch covers fifty feet up in the air. Several members of the gun crew were blown from the gun platform to the deck below while others were blown one or two feet up and landed on the gun platform. When the smoke cleared the port pill box was missing. The ship started sinking by the stern and listed to port. The Captain ordered all hands to abandon ship. At 2119 there was a second explosion about the No.2 hatch. Four lifeboats were lowered and all hands were saved. There were slight injuries to the gun crew. Five members of the gun crew were picked up by a British trawler at about 2230. The remaining members of

181

the gun crew were picked up by a Free French corvette. The gun crew was taken to the Naval operating base in Iceland. The officers at the NOB gave out the official report that we had run into a British minefield. This reporting officer saw nothing but one of his reliable men reported sighting a submarine from his lifeboat. The British trawler *Lady Madeline*, that this reporting officer was picked up by, abandoned a lifeboat half full of men because a torpedo was seen coming at them. They had several contacts and dropped depth charges.

The mining of the *Hybert* – or the sinking by a U-boat as it was then believed – increased the chaos and ships, their guns blasting away at shadows, were scattering in all directions. Inevitably, for they were now in the middle of the minefield, others came to grief. Next to go were the *Heffron* and the *Massmar*, who blundered into the sensitive horns of mines packed with 500lb of TNT tethered just below the surface. Both ships blew up and sank in less than two minutes, leaving over 100 men fighting for their lives in the wreckage-strewn icy water. Close on the heels of these two unfortunates came the 7191-ton Liberty ship *John Randolph*. She hit a mine head-on and her bows were blown off, but her watertight collision bulkhead held and she remained afloat.

The confusion continued, ships' whistles blowing and rockets soaring skywards adding to the panic. And in the midst of all this the Russian ship *Rodina* met her end. Altering course to avoid another ship running across her bows, the 4000-ton cargo ship slewed sideways into a mine which hit her amidships on the starboard side. The violent explosion blew a huge hole in her hull and, as the sea rushed in she leaned heavily to starboard, still turning under full helm. Within minutes she was gone, rolling over and plunging into the depths, leaving another mess of wreckage, in which a handful of survivors struggled to stay afloat. Among those on board the *Rodina* were the wives and children of Soviet diplomats stationed in London. They did not live to be reunited with their husbands and fathers again.

Immediately astern of the *Rodina* was the 6115-ton Panama-flag, US-manned *Exterminator*. She met an equally quick end when she made a bold alteration of course to avoid the sinking

Russian. She blundered onto a mine which blew the bottom out of her. Seconds later, she broke her back and the bow and stern went down separately, leaving those of her crew who survived fighting for their lives in the water.

Disregarding the danger to themselves, the corvette *Roselys*, commanded by Lieutenant de Vaisseau Bergeret, and the trawlers *Lady Madeline* and *St. Elstan*, entered the minefield and spent the next six and a half hours searching for survivors. Between them, they picked up 211 men, some of whom, having been in the water for some hours, later died of exposure. Given the extreme circumstances prevailing, the danger of mines, the rough seas, poor visibility and the temperature of the water, this was a truly remarkable feat of rescue by a very brave band of men.

HMS *Hussar* meanwhile, having plucked from the sea the few who survived the sinking of the *Niger*, had obtained an accurate fix with shore bearings and was able to lead the surviving merchant ships to safety. The remains of the convoy reached Reykjavik on 7 July.

An inquiry into the QP 13 affair, conducted by the Flag Officer Iceland, Rear-Admiral Dalrymple-Hamilton, concluded as might be expected, that the main cause of the disaster had been poor navigation by HMS *Niger*, which in its turn was due to the poor weather preventing sights being obtained during the last three days before making the land. The Admiral commented, again as might be expected, on the failure of Commander Cubison to advise Captain Hiss, acting commodore, of the existence of the minefield. But then, Cubison was dead and unable to answer for his actions. Had he been able to do so, he could not have excused the failure to warn Hiss of the danger of mines. As far as the so-called poor navigation was concerned, like any other seaman of his day, having only very basic navigational equipment, Cubison had taken an unavoidable risk. Unfortunately, his judgement proved to be in error.

The loss of the American ships in QP 13 to British mines and while under British escort, was a huge embarrassment to the Admiralty, but it was completely overshadowed by the debacle of PQ 17, and went largely unnoticed. PQ 17, on the other hand, created something akin to blind panic in Whitehall. It led to a proposal to suspend convoys to north Russia until the winter darkness offered some cover from attack. Churchill did not agree. Under pressure from Stalin to keep the ships coming, he suggested forcing the convoys through using the big ships of the Home Fleet, heavily supported by cruisers and destroyers, and covered by aircraft from several aircraft carriers. This 'death or glory' attitude was all very well, but at that time the Royal Navy was heavily engaged in getting relief convoys through to the Mediterranean island of Malta, which was then on the point of surrendering. The United States Navy was equally committed in the Pacific. Churchill was forced to bow to the Admirals. He telegraphed Stalin on 17 July:

> My naval advisers tell me that if they had the handling of the German surface, submarine and air forces, in present circumstances, they would guarantee the complete destruction of any convoy to North Russia. They have not been able so far to hold out any hopes that convoys attempting to make the passage in perpetual daylight would fare better than PQ 17. It is therefore with the greatest regret that we have reached the conclusion that to attempt to run the next convoy, PQ 18, would bring no benefit to you and would only involve dead loss to a common cause.

Stalin replied with what Churchill described as a 'rough and surly answer' on 23 July:

> I received your message of July 17. Two conclusions could be drawn from it. First, the British Government refuses to continue the sending of war materials to the Soviet Union via the Northern route. Second, in spite of the agreed communique concerning the urgent task of creating a second front in 1942 the British Government postpones this matter until 1943.
>
> (2) Our naval experts consider the reasons put forward by the British naval experts to justify the cessation of convoys to the northern ports of the USSR wholly unconvincing. They are of the opinion that with goodwill and readiness to fulfil the contracted obligations these convoys could be regularly undertaken and heavy losses could be inflicted on the enemy. Our experts find it also difficult to understand and to explain the order given by the Admiralty that the escorting vessels of the PQ 17

should return, whereas the cargo boats should disperse and try to reach the Soviet ports one by one without any protection at all. Of course I do not think that regular convoys to the Soviet northern ports could be effected without risk or losses. In any case, I never expected the British Government would stop dispatch of war materials to us just at the very moment when the Soviet Union in view of the serious situation on the Soviet-German front requires these materials more than ever.

Churchill commented on this reply:

These contentions were not well founded. So far from breaking 'contracted obligations' to deliver the war supplies at Soviet ports, it had been particularly stipulated at the time of making the agreement that the Russians were to be responsible for conveying them to Russia. All that we did beyond this was a goodwill effort.

The Russians did make some of their merchant ships available for bringing the cargoes in, but the Soviet Navy which at the time was a substantial force, did little to help with the protection of the convoys beyond sending out two or three destroyers at the last minute to escort them into Russian waters.

Being obliged, mainly by political pressure, to sail PQ 18 early in September, Admiral Sir Dudley Pound was uneasy being of the opinion that there was a huge element of risk involved. There would still be some sixteen hours of daylight in the Barents Sea in September and the Germans, flushed with their success against PQ 17, could well decide to bring their big ships out. Consequently, Dudley Pound planned to give the convoy a three-part escort, consisting of a close escort of destroyers, corvettes and minesweepers, a 'fighting escort' of destroyers led by a cruiser and also a cruiser cover force. Ships of the Home Fleet, as usual, would give distant cover for PQ 18 and the returning convoy QP 14, which would contain many of the ships that survived PQ 17.

The main section of PQ 18 sailed from Loch Ewe on 2 September. Other ships joined off Iceland to make up a convoy forty-four strong, comprising fifteen British, twenty American, three Panamanian and six Russian ships. In their bottoms this cosmopolitan fleet carried one and a half million tons of cargo, namely 4400 vehicles, 835 tanks, 566 aircraft, 11,000 tons of explosives, 9541 tons of fuel oil and 157,000 tons of general military supplies. The ships rendezvoused off Iceland on 8 September and, when clear of the coast, formed up in ten columns abreast. The Convoy Commodore was in Lambert Brothers *Temple Arch*, the vice commodore was the Swansea ship *Dan-y-Bryn*, and the rear commodore the MOWT's *Empire Snow*. There were four fleet tankers with the convoy, the *Atheltemplar*, *Black Ranger*, *Grey Ranger* and *Oligarch*, the CAM ship *Empire Morn*, the rescue ship *Copeland* and three motor minesweepers for delivery to the Russian Northern Fleet, which would also act as rescue ships.

The close escort for PQ 18 consisted of the destroyers *Achates* and *Malcolm*, the corvettes *Bergamot*, *Bluebell*, *Bryony* and *Camelia*, the fleet minesweepers *Gleaner* and *Sharpshooter*, the anti-aircraft ships *Alynbank* and *Ulster Queen*, the trawlers *Cape Argona*, *Cape Mariato*, *Daneman* and *St. Kenan* and the submarines *P-614* and *P-615*. In support of the close escort was the aircraft carrier *Avenger*, a new breed of carrier, an ex-merchant ship with a flight deck built on and carrying fifteen Hurricanes and Swordfish. The *Avenger*, a rather vulnerable ship, was herself guarded by the destroyers *Wheatland* and *Wilton*. Dudley Pound's 'fighting escort', which would operate independently of the other escorts, was led by the Dido-class cruiser *Scylla*, in which Admiral Burnett flew his flag, and was composed of the destroyers *Ashanti*, *Eskimo*, *Faulknor*, *Fury*, *Impulsive*, *Intrepid*, *Marne*, *Martin*, *Meteor*, *Milne*, *Offa*, *Onslaught*, *Onslow*, *Opportune*, *Somali* and *Tartar*. This powerful force had spent the summer in training as a unit and was easily capable of fending off any attack by German destroyers.

The third element of PQ 18's impressive escort was a cruiser covering force made up of the three 8-inch cruisers *Norfolk*, *Suffolk* and *London* which would also operate independently. On call in Spitzbergen, where they were engaged on a relief operation, were the heavy cruiser *Cumberland*, the light cruiser *Sheffield* and nine destroyers. Ships of the Home Fleet, the battleships *Duke of York* and *Anson*, the light cruiser *Jamaica*, and the destroyers *Bramham*, *Keppel*, *Mackay* and *Montrose*, were to act as distant cover. In addition, and this was a very new innovation, two squadrons of Hampden torpedo bombers had been flown to a Russian airfield to be held in readiness should the *Tirpitz* or any other big German surface units threaten the convoy.

PQ 18 looked invulnerable, but the German challenge was immediate. The huge armada was spotted by long-range Focke-Wulfs soon after clearing Iceland and twelve U-boats were sailed from Norway to lie in wait, while ninety-one torpedo bombers and 133 high level and dive bombers were stood to at Banak and Bardufos ready to attack when the convoy was within range. Due to the unprecedented size of PQ 18's escort force and the presence of an aircraft carrier, action by German surface ships was ruled out by Admiral Raeder.

First blood went to the Royal Navy when, on 12 September, the destroyer *Faulknor*, scouting ahead of the convoy, detected and sank *U-88*, commanded by *Kapitänleutnant* Heino Bohmann. This was a blow struck for PQ 17, for Bohmann had sent two of its ships to the bottom. The U-boats had their revenge next day, when three of their number, *U-405* (*Korvettenkapitän* Rolf-Heinrich Hopmann), *U-408* (*Kapitänleutnant* Reinhard von Hymen) and *U-589* (*Kapitänleutnant* Hans-Joachim Horrer) made a joint attack on PQ 18. Hopmann and von Hymen wasted their torpedoes but Horrer, who had his sights on the high-sided *Avenger*, redressed the balance. Firing a spread of torpedoes, he missed the carrier, but sank two merchant ships on the far side of it, the Russian-flag *Stalingrad* and the American *Oliver Ellsworth*.

Avenger's aircraft chased off the Focke-Wulfs shadowing the convoy, but a flight of Ju88s arrived on the 13th and made an attempt to bomb from high level. Their effort was in vain. Later in the day, when wave after wave of torpedo bombers came in from the south, it was a different story. It seems the convoy was caught unawares, *Avenger* being slow to get her Hurricanes in the air, and the ships in the outer columns to starboard failed to open fire until the enemy planes were on them. Six ships, the US-flag *Macbeth*, *Oregonian* and *Wacosta*, the Panamanian *Africander*, the Russian *Sukhona* and the British *Empire Stevenson*, all paid for their tardiness. Thirty thousand tons of shipping and an equal amount of cargo ended up on the bottom and just five German aircraft were shot down.

Next day the attack came from beneath the sea again. Around dawn, Karl Brandenburg in *U-457* broke through the cordon of escorts and torpedoed the 8992-ton British tanker *Atheltemplar*, the rear ship of Column 4. The tanker stayed afloat and did not catch fire, but it was later found necessary to dispatch her with gunfire. There were further attacks by torpedo bombers during the day and in one attack the 5049-ton *Mary Luckenbach* was hit. The American ship was carrying 1000 tons of explosives and when the smoke cleared there was nothing left of her but scraps of wreckage on the water. As a small recompense for her loss, she took her German attacker with her, the plane being blown out of the sky as it flew over its victim. Twenty other enemy aircraft were shot down during the attack and HMS *Onslow*, operating with a Swordfish from *Avenger*, sank *U-589*.

The torpedo bombers were back again next day but were driven off without loss on either side. On the 16th, it was the turn of the U-boats once more and they had a similar lack of success. By this time, Russian-based Catalinas were giving air cover, and with their cooperation the destroyer *Impulsive* sank *U-457* as she tried to attack the convoy.

The 17th passed without incident, but on the 18th when PQ 18 was approaching the entrance to the White Sea and nearing the end of its voyage, the bombers made a last desperate bid, severely damaging the American steamer *Kentucky*, which subsequently ran ashore. The convoy reached Archangel next day having, in spite of the very heavy escort force, lost thirteen ships. The westbound convoy QP 14, twenty ships, ten of which had come out with PQ 17, had also come under attack by the U-boats. Four ships were lost.

The savaging of these two convoys despite the lengths the Admiralty had gone to in their protection, was the deciding factor for Allied convoys to north Russia in 1942. Preparations were then under way for the Anglo-American invasion of North Africa, Operation 'Torch' and, with large convoys crossing the Atlantic with troops and equipment for the landings, escorts were at a premium. The convoys to north Russia were suspended for the rest of the year but, in order that the Russians would not feel entirely deserted, it was decided to sail a series of selected ships independently and unescorted from Iceland to Murmansk. Operation 'FB' which was mounted between 29 October and 2 November, involved thirteen ships, namely the British-flag *Briarwood*, *Daldorch*, *Chulmleigh*, *Empire Galliard*, *Empire Gilbert*, *Empire Scott* and *Empire Sky*, the American *John H.B. Latrobe*, *William Clark*, *Hugh Williamson*, *Richard H. Alvey* and *John Walker* and the Russian ship *Dekabrist*. These ships were all well-armed and capable of a good turn of speed and, given favourable weather, it was hoped they would slip through to Russia unnoticed. They were to be given some measure of protection by seven anti-submarine trawlers stationed at strategic points along the route, while Catalinas of RAF Coastal Command were to patrol overhead.

Operation 'FB' got off to a bad start. The weather was so atrocious at the time that three ships, the *Briarwood*, *Daldorch* and *John H.B. Latrobe*, were forced to return to Iceland and were not to sail again. They were the lucky ones. The unusual presence of British Catalinas in the air alerted the Germans to the possibility that something was afoot, with the result that U-boats and aircraft were sent to investigate. The *Empire Gilbert*, *Empire Sky* and *William Clark* were sunk by U-boats and the *Dekabrist* fell to the Ju88s. The *Chulmleigh*, attempting to sneak through by the furthest possible route to the north, ran onto rocks off Spitzbergen in a blizzard and was also lost. Some of her crew of fifty-eight managed to reach the shore, but in the end starvation and exposure killed all but nine of them.

The five remaining ships reached Murmansk safely, but it could not be said that Operation 'FB' was a success.

Chapter Fifteen

The supply of arms to Soviet Russia by the northern sea route was carried out against the most fearful odds and ranks as one of the greatest feats of courage and endurance in the history of war at sea. The merchant ships, underpowered and slow to manoeuvre, their decks piled high with aircraft and vehicles, their Plimsoll Lines often submerged – a necessary concession to war – faced so many enemies along the way. Their naval escorts were permanently overstretched and very often outgunned.

The paramount threat on the voyage came from the bombers and torpedo bombers of the Luftwaffe, flying from airfields so close that they were able to attack, return to base, rearm and be back over the convoy before it had progressed more than a score or so miles on its way. There was, in the main, a complete lack of air support for the convoys. They were sailing outside the range of British air bases and the Russians showed a marked reluctance to provide air cover, except on rare occasions. The ships were left to rely solely on their own guns to fight off the Ju88s, the Stukas, the Heinkels, the Messerschmitts and anything else the Germans could put into the air. Anti-aircraft fire has always been a poor substitute for fighters overhead and the ships suffered accordingly.

When the bombers were unable to get through, in darkness or thick weather, their work was continued by the U-boats, who always seemed to have ample warning of the approach of a convoy. Whether setting up an ambush or picking off stragglers and those crippled by the bombers, they exacted a steady toll. And then, lying just below the horizon like an unsheathed sword, was the ever-present threat of Admiral Raeder's big ships. They were, without exception, fast, modern, extremely powerful warships capable of decimating a convoy without even venturing within range of its escort's guns. This they could have easily done on many occasions, if only Hitler had been prepared to give his Admirals free rein.

One of the inevitable and accepted perils of seafaring, in war or peace, is the constant battle that must be waged against the elements. This is never more present than in Arctic waters, which are an environment of extremes. It is a place of violent and unpredictable gales and of calms that breed the dense and long-lasting fogs, in which lie in wait for the unwary navigator, the silent denizens of this frigid region, the icebergs, the growlers, the ice floes and the pack ice. Add to this forty-plus ships steaming blind in close proximity to each other and you have a recipe for multiple disasters. In winter, when the sun rarely rose above the horizon, the misery of the convoys was compounded by driving rain, stinging sleet and swirling snow, with the mercury in the thermometer sometimes plunging to immeasurable depths. Summer brought a modicum of relief; the gales were less frequent, the temperature at more acceptable levels, but the fog was always there, with an increased number of icebergs drifting south into the sea lanes. At the same time, the hours of daylight matched the long darkness of winter, the ships being exposed up to twenty-four hours a day to the watching eyes of the enemy.

And what waited at the end of this long and perilous voyage for those who survived? Even in a world three years into total war, Communist Russia was a desperately bleak place, and the two northern ports available to the ships, Murmansk and Archangel, were as uninviting as ports come. The escort vessels at least had the advantage of being able to refuel and return to sea – albeit for another hard slog home – but the merchant ships faced a long incarceration. Both ports were ill-equipped for cargo handling, inefficiently run and stifled by bureaucracy. British naval officers stationed in Murmansk and Archangel did their utmost to move things along, but they were frustrated at every turn.

Murmansk, the all-year-round ice-free port which handled the bulk of the cargoes, lay no more than seventy miles from the nearest German airfield at Petsamo, on the Soviet-Norwegian border – only twenty minutes flying time at the most for a loaded bomber. Low-lying hills to the west of the port gave excellent cover for the incoming planes and they were all too often overhead, and dropping their bombs, before any warning was sounded. The end result was that ships' guns had to be manned at all times, day and night, which put an intolerable strain on their crews. There was no hiding place in Murmansk and for the German pilots, skimming over the tops of the hills and swooping down unannounced on the crowded harbour, it must have been like shooting ducks in a barrel. The port was ringed with Russian anti-aircraft batteries, which put up a spirited defence, but much of the time the gunners found themselves firing at planes disappearing at high speed after having dropped their bombs. There were a few Russian fighters in the air at times, but they appeared to be hopelessly outclassed. Their pilots had little combat experience, they were not equipped with voice radio and had to resort to waggling their wings First World War style to communicate with each other.

George Evans, a Canadian merchant seaman serving in the Dutch ship *Pieter de Hoogh*, which arrived with PQ 14, described the chaos of Murmansk:

> They were coming over bombing and dropping a lot of mines in the harbour and we had to get out pretty quick. They bombed the hell out of it. When we were alongside the bow of the ship got bombed but there wasn't much damage done to it. We had to pull away because the piers were on fire. When we were out in the harbour you'd see the whole dock ablaze and – BOOM! – all the black smoke, and everything going up in flames, the cargoes we had discharged had been blown up. The Russians used to haul in a load of timber and rebuild them again after the bombing for the ships to come alongside and discharge. Oh yeah, a daily routine. They used to load cargoes into trains to take down to Leningrad and then the train to come back with a load of timber from Leningrad or around that area to rebuild the docks.

For the Allied merchant seamen, the Russian run was unlike any other trade. On a wartime voyage to the United States, Africa, or even India and the East, there was always the prospect of bright lights at the end, bars, restaurants, cinemas, dances with friendly girls. In port was a time to relax and forget the war for a short while. Not so when sailing to Russia. At the end of the voyage, having survived the best efforts of the weather and the enemy, the war was still there. One American ship, the 5432-ton *Yaka*, came out with PQ 14 and returned with QP 13, after spending ten weeks in Murmansk, during which time she endured no fewer than 156 air raids. On the rare occasions when some crew members were able to get ashore, there was little on offer for them except the vodka bottle, assuming they could lay their hands on it. There was an insurmountable language barrier, and although these men were risking their lives for Soviet Russia, the country wanted very little to do with them. At one point relations became so bad that Churchill had occasion to telegraph Stalin:

I must ask your help in remedying the conditions under which our Service personnel and seamen at present find themselves in North Russia.

a. No one may land from one of HM ships or from a British merchant ship except by a Soviet boat and in the presence of a Soviet official and after examination of documents on each occasion.

b. No one from a British warship is allowed to proceed alongside a British merchantman without the Soviet authorities being informed beforehand. This even applies to the British Admiral in charge.

c. British officers and men are required to obtain special passes before they can go from ship to shore or between two British shore stations. These passes are often much delayed, with the consequent dislocation of the work in hand.

d. No stores, luggage, or mail for this operational force may be landed except in the presence of a Soviet official, and numerous formalities are required for all stores and mail.

e. Private Service mail is subject to censorship, although for an operational force of this kind censorship should, in our view, be left in the hands of the British Service authorities.

In other words, the Russians were loathe to tolerate the British in their midst, and did everything in their power to make them feel uncomfortable.

The stifling bureaucracy imposed by the Soviet authorities probably did more to delay the delivery of the cargoes they claimed they so urgently needed than all the efforts of their German enemy. Two months in port to discharge a cargo that under normal conditions would be landed in as many weeks was common. Three American merchantmen were recorded as having spent eight months in port for one cargo.

If conditions in Murmansk were bad for the Allied seamen, they were infinitely worse for the local Russian population. George Evans, of the *Pieter de Hoogh*, observed:

> You could see the railroads with all the cars loaded up with ammunition, tanks guns and planes and it would be mostly women loading them. They were White Russians who refused to fight for Russia during the war. You'd see a soldier with a machine gun guarding them. When we were discharging they'd be hungry and you'd give them a slice of peanut butter or jam bread and the guard would come and take it away from her. They tried to keep us away from the civilian population as much as possible. They wouldn't let us go out with any girls there or associate with us. If they were caught with foreigners they were taken and sent to Siberia or somewhere. Or they say they were crazy or something like that and they'd end up in the asylum. Any excuse in the book.

George Evans' thoughts on the treatment of Russian civilians by their own authorities may have appeared to be far fetched at the time, but history has proved them to be true. Certainly, no Allied seaman was allowed contact with ordinary Russians except under the most strict supervision. The only ones who made any contact on a personal basis were some of the survivors from ships sunk. They had nothing but praise for the Russians, whom they saw as doing their utmost under very difficult circumstances. Captain Charlton, of the *River Afton*, wrote:

> During my stay in Russia the Russians treated us as best they could, the food was not very good, but we had the best that was available.

Our principal diet was porridge and raw fish. We were housed in the local hotels, hospitals and schools.

But the shortcomings were many. Captain Charles McGowan, of the *Zaafran*, wrote:

Surgeon Lieutenant McBain, RNVR did magnificent work during his stay in Archangel, where he found the medical arrangements in absolute chaos. Through his zeal, untiring energy and devotion to duty, he was able to restore order in the shortest possible time. He sorted out the various illnesses of the numerous survivors, and put them into separate hospitals as far as was possible and kept records of treatment of every sick survivor. When it is realised that there were some 1,287 survivors, of whom some 270 were suffering from frostbite and exposure, the magnitude of this officer's work can be understood.

If anything, as far as the British merchant seamen were concerned, their own authorities came in for the severest criticism. Of them, Captain George Stephenson, of the *Hartlebury*, wrote:

There was a NAAFI canteen at Archangel for the use of Naval personnel only and this caused a certain amount of justified ill feeling amongst the merchant seamen. During our stay at Archangel there were two British destroyers anchored outside all the time but apparently they were not allowed to take us back to the UK, although all the American survivors were taken away by American naval vessels soon after landing. We were anchored in Hvalfjord for 27 days during which there were several entertainments provided by HMS *Renown*. HMS *Renown* sent her liberty boats round to all the American ships but the British vessels were apparently not included. The only chance my crew had of a little entertainment was when the Marine Band gave a performance on board the s.s. *River Afton* and then we were only notified about it at the last minute when only three of my men were able to attend.

Captain Stephenson added a footnote:

My crew behaved magnificently through this terrible ordeal. It is impossible for me to single out any man as being outstanding. They were all magnificent and I could not wish for a finer crew.

Captain Charlton, of the *River Afton*, illustrated how the ingenuity of the British merchant seaman came to their aid while in Archangel waiting for a ship home:

> We managed to secure a small amount of tobacco but we had no paper to make cigarettes, the Chief Officer was using his wife's letters while I resorted to toilet paper. There was a NAAFI canteen there but it was for Naval personnel only, but luckily for us one night the canteen was blitzed and the stores had to be moved. We were called in to assist in the moving and by a strange coincidence about 30,000 cigarettes disappeared during the transfer.

The merchant seamen were in an ambiguous position, being neither Armed Services nor true civilians. Even though they were at war, they were still regarded as being part of a commercial enterprise. They were expected to deliver the cargoes and maintain their ships as they had done in peacetime and yet they were required to man their guns, and die if necessary, to get their ship through. Inevitably, their casualty rate was far higher than that of any of the Services, yet they were accorded none of the privileges enjoyed by those who manned the escort ships and bases ashore. Their total allegiance was demanded at all times, yet their employment was terminated at the end of each voyage and, if their ship was sunk, their pay was stopped the minute they went over the side into a lifeboat or into the sea. On the demanding and dangerous run to north Russia there were some who refused to sail – went missing before the ship left port – but they were few and who would blame these men, anyway? They were faced with the prospect of running the gauntlet of shells, bombs and torpedoes, of being blown apart, burned to death or drowned. Should they survive, they so often went through the agonies of frostbite, perhaps to end up having limbs amputated in some Russian hospital that resembled a Dickensian workhouse, where even the anaesthetic was rationed.

Now the convoys to north Russia are old history, it is fair to question whether they were worth the huge sacrifices they demanded. This highly complex and hazardous operation lasted from August 1941 until May 1945 and resulted in the loss of

105 merchant ships and twenty-three escort vessels, including two light cruisers and claimed the lives of nearly 3000 Allied seamen. The main burden of organizing and escorting the convoys fell on Britain and in the early years a great deal of the arms and equipment sent was diverted from her forces, which were then heavily engaged in the Western Desert and the Far East. General Alan Brooke, Chief of the Imperial General Staff, expressed his opinion on the subject after the war:

> When we consider, that a fair proportion of tanks for Russia were destined to be sunk in transit by submarine action and that the Russian maintenance of mechanical vehicles was poor, it is doubtful whether the tanks sent there achieved much. . . . We kept on supplying tanks and aeroplanes that could ill be spared and in doing so suffered the heaviest losses in shipping conveying this equipment to Arctic Russia. We received nothing in return except abuse for handling convoys inefficiently.

There is now little doubt that the Russian convoys were motivated more by politics than strategy. Churchill and Roosevelt were well aware that if Stalin was not placated, he might well make a separate peace with Hitler. It was essential for its successful outcome that Soviet Russia be kept in the war, even if it did mean a heavy loss of ships and men and a constant drain on resources needed elsewhere. No one could be expected to foresee the eventual result, a generation-long Cold War, with the Soviet Union committed to the downfall of those who helped her frustrate Hitler's ambitions.

Epilogue

It is winter now in Loch Ewe, and as I write, sixty years after PQ 13 sailed for Iceland and Murmansk, there is snow on the hills and a keening wind sends tiny white horses galloping across the iron-grey waters of the loch. It is said that at one time, so many ships lay at anchor in the loch it was possible to cross over them from shore to shore without getting your feet wet. But now only a handful of wintering yachts tug at their cables and a few small fishing boats put-put their way out to sea. In the lee of the eastern shore, captive salmon breed and fatten in fish farms that feed the hotels of England, while sheep graze among the abandoned oil tanks that long ago held millions of gallons of fuel for the anchored fleet of ships.

Close by the jetty at Aultbea, where liberty boats once queued to come alongside, the 'Jam Jar' Inn is now the three-star Aultbea Hotel, with en-suite rooms and an up-market restaurant. Fine Caithness crystal has replaced the jam jars, there are fresh croissants for breakfast and fancy hors d'oeuvres at dinner. The bar still serves good beer, although rare single-malt whiskies are more the vogue, but gone are the brave voices of the duffel-coated seamen raised in defiant song as they savoured their last pints before taking the road to Russia. Now, only the quiet murmurings of the well-heeled tourist and the loch fisherman are heard above the crackle of the logs in the open fire.

At the entrance to the loch over at Rubha nan Sasan, the tall headland that juts out into the Atlantic, the old gun emplacements are crumbling and overgrown. The guns are long gone and Nature is slowly, painstakingly, reclaiming that which is rightly hers. Nearby, the ghosts of the men who fell on that hellish road to Russia cluster around the simple stone memorial that commemorates their sacrifice. There is an eerie silence here and there is bitterness, for this memorial was not erected by a grateful nation but by their comrades who survived, the men of the Russian Convoy Club. They are old men now, those who came back, but they have not forgotten those they left behind in that cold Arctic sea.

It is far from certain now whether the cargoes carried to Russia at such enormous cost achieved anything, other than to assuage the consciences of the politicians of the West and still the hectoring of Joseph Stalin. Whatever was the motive and the end result, the job was well done, and it would have been some small recompense for the horrors they endured if a medal had been struck to honour the men who sailed in the ships. Yet it was not to be, and years of lobbying by the Russian Convoy Club had failed to stir the politicians. A Ministry of Defence spokesman recently tetchily proclaimed, 'These people have already been fully acknowledged. There are no plans to introduce new medals for these veterans.' And that is the final word from a government that showers honours on pop stars and sports personalities, most of whom, in the pursuit of their careers, do nothing but further their own ends.

In 1995, even the Russians, who at the time accepted everything that came their way and showed precious little gratitude, relented. Boris Yeltsin, not a man known for his compassion, decreed that the foreign veterans of the northern convoys be awarded the Jubilee Medal, instituted in honour of the fiftieth anniversary of victory in the Second World War. Each November, when they march past the Cenotaph in Whitehall, the men in the white berets wear that medal with pride. It is all they have to tell of their journey along the sea road to Russia.

Bibliography

Bekker, Cajus, *The German Navy 1939–1945*, Chancellor Press, 1997

Bryant, Arthur, *The Turn of the Tide*, Collins, 1957

Campbell, Vice Admiral Sir Ian and Macintyre, Captain Donald, *The Kola Run*, Frederick Muller, 1958

Churchill, Winston, *The Second World War, Vol 4*, Cassell, 1954

Elphick, Peter, *Lifeline – The Merchant Navy at War 1939–1945*, Chatham Publishing, 1999

Erickson, John, *The Road to Berlin*, Grafton Books, 1985

Gunson, Bill, *World War II German Aircraft*, Leisure Books, 1985

Hague, Arnold, *The Allied Convoy System 1939–1945*, Chatham Publishing, 2000

Heaton, P.M., *Reardon Smith*, P.M. Heaton, 1980

HMSO, *British Vessels Lost at Sea 1914–18 and 1939–45*, Patrick Stephens, 1988

Hope, Stanton, *Ocean Odyssey*, Eyre & Spottiswoode, 1944

Jane's Publishing Company, *Jane's Fighting Ships of World War II*, Random House, 2001

Kaplan, Philip & Currie, Jack, *Convoy – Merchant Sailors at War*, Aurum Press, 1998

Kemp, Paul, *Convoy – Drama in Arctic Waters*, Arms & Armour Press, 1993

Lund, Paul & Ludlam, Harry, *PQ 17 Convoy to Hell*, New English Library, 1978

Martienssen, Anthony, *Hitler and His Admirals*, Secker & Warburg, 1948

Mason, David, *U-boat – The Secret Menace*, Macdonald, 1968
McBrearty, Captain R.F., *Seafaring 1939–45 As I Saw It*, Pentland Press, 1995
Ministry of Information, *Merchantmen at War*, HMSO, 1944
Parker, Mike, *Running the Gauntlet*, Nimbus Publishing, 1994
Parker, R.A.C., *Struggle for Survival*, Oxford United Press, 1989
Pearce, Frank, *Sea War*, Robert Hale, 1990
Peillard, Léonce, *Sink the Tirpitz*, Granada, 1983
Rohwer, Jürgen, *Axis Submarine Successes 1939–1945*, Patrick Stephens, 1983
Roskill, S.W., *The War at Sea*, HMSO, 1954–61
Schofield, Vice Admiral B.B., *Arctic Convoys*, Macdonald & Janes, 1977
—— *The Russian Convoys*, Batsford, 1964
Slader, John, *The Fourth Service*, Robert Hale, 1994
Thomas, David, *Atlantic Star*, W.H. Allen, 1990
Woodman, Richard, *Arctic Convoys*, John Murray, 1994

Index

Rimmington, Captain, 127, 128
Richter, Captain, 140
Roosevelt, 11, 16, 110, 197
Ropner, Sir Robert, 31
Rowlands, Second Officer Evans, 39, 40, 55–61

Santos, Able Seaman, 36
Saunders, Captain L.S., 24, 26, 28–30, 35, 44–8, 99–103
Schendel, *Kapitänleutnant* Rudolf, 15
Schmundt, Admiral Hubert, 42
Schniewind, Admiral, 111, 117, 119, 125
Scott, Captain, 136
Seibecke, *Kapitänleutnant* Günter, 23
Sexton, Lieutenant John E., 168

Ships, Merchant
  Africander, 187
  Alcoa Ranger, 148
  American Robin, 179, 180
  Atheltemplar, 186, 188
  Azerbaidjan, 116, 122, 150, 152
  Ballot, 18, 32, 33, 36, 37, 39, 41, 56, 61–4, 95
  Bateau, 21, 42, 43, 66
  Beacon Hill, 80
  Benjamin Harrison, 160, 173
  Black Ranger, 186
  Bolton Castle, 137–40, 142, 146
  Braddovey, 92
  Briarwood, 189
  British Pride, 7
  Carlton, 118, 170
  Christopher Newport, 118, 170, 171
  Chulmleigh, 176, 189
  City of Omaha, 80
  Cold Harbor, 15
  Copeland, 186
  Daldorch, 189
  Daniel Morgan, 172, 173
  Dan-y-Bryn, 186

  Dekabrist, 189
  Dover Hill, 79
  Dunboynet, 16–18, 33, 39, 65, 95
  Earlston, 128, 131–4, 137, 142–5, 173
  Effingham, 18, 33, 39, 64–6, 89
  El Capitan, 145, 160, 162, 173, 174
  Eldena, 18, 42, 65, 95
  El Esterol, 18, 42, 65, 95
  El Occidente, 90
  El Oceano, 15
  Empire Byron, 113, 125–32
  Empire Cowper, 18, 42, 65, 82–8, 93, 95
  Empire Galliard, 189
  Empire Gilbert, 189
  Empire Lawrence, 107
  Empire Morn, 186
  Empire Ranger, 18, 28, 30, 42–6
  Empire Scott, 189
  Empire Selwyn, 177, 179
  Empire Sky, 189
  Empire Snow, 186
  Empire Starlight, 18, 31–3, 39, 65, 71–7, 79
  Empire Stevenson, 187
  Empire Tide, 160, 167, 173
  Exford, 114, 170
  Exterminator, 182
  Frances Scott Key, 80
  Gallant Fox, 18, 42, 65, 95
  Grey Ranger, 114, 186
  Harmatris, 1–9, 28
  Hartlebury, 113, 163–5, 167, 195
  Harpalion, 18, 28, 30, 42, 44, 65, 82–4, 88, 90–2, 94
  Heffron, 182
  Honomu, 132
  Hoosier, 160, 161, 173–5
  Hopemount, 79
  Hugh Williamson, 189
  Hybert, 181, 182
  Ijora, 21

206

Colossus, HMS, 124
Cumberland, HMS, 15, 112, 186
Daneman, HMS, 186
Dianella, HMS, 112, 130
Duke of York, HMS, 22, 99, 107,
    112, 186
Eclipse, HMS, 22, 24, 26–9, 35,
    36, 45, 49–51, 53, 66, 82, 107
Echo, HMS, 14, 22
Edinburgh, HMS, 14, 22, 96–9,
    103, 104, 177, 181
Escapade, HMS, 14, 22, 112
Eskimo, HMS, 23, 186
Faulknor, HMS, 23, 107, 112,
    186, 187
Foresight, HMS, 23, 95–8, 103,
    104
Forester, HMS, 95–8, 103, 104
Friedrich Ihn, (German), 21
Fury, HMS, 22, 24, 26–9, 44–6,
    48, 49, 51, 52, 82, 92–3, 107,
    112, 186
Garland, (Polish)
Gneisenau, (German), 13
Gossamer, HMS, 98
Gremyashchi, (Russian), 44, 65,
    96, 97, 177
Grozni, (Russian), 177
Halcyon, HMS, 112, 160
Hazard, HMS, 14, 177
Harrier, HMS, 3, 4, 7, 8, 52,
    64–6, 82, 98
Hermann Schoemann, (German),
    97
Honeysuckle, HMS, 107, 177
Hood, HMS, 168
Hussar, HMS, 64, 82, 176, 179,
    183
Hyderabad, HMS, 107, 176
Icarus, HMS, 23, 107
Impulsive, HMS, 186, 188
Inglefield, HMS, 23, 176
Intrepid, HMS, 107, 177, 186
Jamaica, HMS, 186
Kent, HMS, 22, 105, 107

Keppel, HMS, 112, 123, 186
King George V, HMS, 21, 22
Kuibyshev, (Russian), 177
Lady Madeline, HMS, 176, 179,
    182, 183
La Malouine, (Free French), 112,
    160
Lamerton, HMS, 18, 21, 24, 107
Leamington, HMS, 112
Ledbury, HMS,, 23, 107, 112
Liverpool, HMS, 82, 90, 105, 107
London, HMS, 107, 112, 114,
    186
Lord Austin, HMS, 112, 160
Lord Middleton, HMS, 95, 112,
    160
Lotus, HMS, 112, 153, 159, 160
Lützow, (German), 13, 106, 111,
    117, 119, 124
Mackay, HMS, 186
Malcolm, HMS, 186
Marne, HMS, 23, 82, 107, 112,
    186
Martin, HMS, 107, 186
Matebele, HMS, 3–8
Matchless, HMS, 98, 103, 104
Mayrant, USS, 107, 112
Meteor, HMS, 186
Middleton, HMS, 23, 107, 112
Milne, HMS, 186
Montrose, HMS, 186
Niger, HMS, 176, 179–81, 183
Nigeria, HMS, 105, 107, 112
Norfolk, HMS, 105, 107, 112,
    114, 186
Northern Gem, HMS, 112, 160
Offa, HMS, 112, 186
Onslaught, HMS, 112, 186
Onslow, HMS, 23, 107, 112, 186,
    188
Opportune, HMS, 186
Oribi, HMS, 44, 45, 49, 52, 65,
    82, 107
Oxlip, HMS, 95
P-614, HMS, 112, 186

P-615, HMS, 112, 186
Palomares, HMS, 112, 153, 160–2
Paynter, HMS, 21, 42, 45, 65, 82, 87, 88
Poppy, HMS, 112, 153, 161
Pozarica, HMS, 112, 160–2
Prinz Eugen, (German), 13, 104
Punjabi, HMS, 23, 82
Renown, HMS, 22, 195
Rhind, USS, 107, 112
Roselys, (Free French), 107, 176, 179, 183F
Rowan, USS, 197, 112, 114, 171
Sabre, HMS, 18
Saladin, HMS, 18
Salamander, HMS, 15, 112, 160
Saxifrage, HMS, 95
Scharnhorst, (German), 13
Scylla, HMS, 186
Seagull, HMS, 177
Seawolf, HMS, 107
Sharpshooter, HMS, 5, 186
Sheffield, HMS, 186
Shera, HMS, 21
Silja, HMS, 22, 32, 33, 35, 37, 39–41, 54, 64, 65
Snowflake, HMS, 95
Sokrushitelni, (Russian), 44, 49, 65, 96, 97
Somali, HMS, 3, 4, 7, 8, 98, 103, 104, 186
Speedwell, HMS, 3–6, 8, 64, 82
Speedy, HMS, 14, 15
Starwort, HMS, 107, 177
St Elstan, HMS, 176, 179, 183
St Kenan, HMS, 186
Suffolk, HMS, 186
Sulla, HMS, 21
Sumba, HMS, 22, 27, 28, 42, 45, 65
Tartar, HMS, 23, 34, 186
Tirpitz, (German), 13, 20, 22, 23, 42, 104, 106, 111, 117, 119, 122n, 124, 167, 172, 187
Trident, HMS, 107, 176

Trinidad, HMS, 3, 22, 24, 26–30, 32, 34–6, 43–54, 66, 82, 96–8, 100–4
Tuscaloosa, USS, 112, 114
Ulster Queen, HMS, 186
Victorious, HMS, 21–3, 34, 107, 112, 125
Volunteer, HMS, 107, 176
Wainwright, USS, 107, 114, 171
Washington, USS, 106, 107, 112, 122n, 173
Wasp, USS, 106
Wheatland, HMS, 107, 112, 186
Whetland, HMS, 23
Wichita, USS, 107, 112, 114, 122n, 170
Wilton, HMS, 112, 186
Z-24, (German), 42, 46, 49, 51, 53, 97, 98
Z-25, (German), 42, 46, 49, 51, 97, 98
Z-26, (German), 42, 44, 51, 53
Z-32, (German), 53

Short, William, 62
Siemon, Kapitänleutnant Hilmar, 134
Sissingh, Captain, 138, 140–2, 147
Slaughter, Galleyboy, 93
Sloan, Captain J., 77, 97
Smith, Sergeant J., 153
Sommerville, Admiral, 81
Stalin, Joseph, 11, 12, 106, 109, 183, 193, 197, 200
Stanwick, Captain H.J., 131–4, 136, 145
Stein, Captain C.H., 31, 39, 72–5
Stephenson, Captain George, 113, 163–6, 195
Stone, Captain Mervyn, 141
Stretlow, Kapitänleutnant Siegfried, 23, 64, 89
Stumpff, Generaloberst Hans-Jurgen, 34, 110
Stuy, Captain Hendrik, 79

209

Tatlow, Steward J.J., 88
Teichert, *Kapitänleutnant* Max-
    Martin, 23, 95–7, 132
Thomas, Captain, 31
Thomson, Able Seaman, 158
Tovey, Admiral Sir John, 112, 124,
    125

U-boats
  U-13, 165
  U-68, 146
  U-88, 97, 187
  U-104, 57
  U-134, 13, 15
  U-140, 57
  U-209, 23
  U-255, 141, 148
  U-334, 122, 134, 145
  U-355, 164
  U-376, 23, 55–7, 61
  U-405, 187
  U-408, 187
  U-435, 23, 64, 89, 90
  U-436, 23
  U-454, 3, 5, 6, 8, 13
  U-456, 23, 95–8, 132
  U-457, 188
  U-585, 13, 23, 52
  U-589, 23, 187, 188
  U-703, 128, 129, 155

Ulan Group, 13, 23, 55, 95
Ulhe, Fireman, 93
United States Maritime Commission
    (USMC), 16, 18, 28, 32, 33, 95

Van de Mey, Chief Officer, 141

Walford, Fourth Engineer, 76
Waller, Second Cook A., 159
Watson, Mr, 143
Watt, Apprentice A.B., 145
Weaver, Gunlayer Acting Able
    Seaman C.R., 153
Wharton, Captain John, 113,
    125–31
White, Steward, 93
Wigham, Captain J.H., 84–7, 93
Williams, Captain H.W., 84, 88,
    90–3
Williams, Lieutenant Commander
    T.E., 4
Willcock, Boatswain Patrick, 153
Winn, Lieutenant Commander (E)
    J.T., 8
Wood, Second Engineer J.W., 160

Yeltsin, Boris, 200

Zestörergruppe Arktis, 42, 45, 97

210